Armed Conflict

Armed Conflict
The Lessons of Modern Warfare

Brian Steed

Ballantine Books • New York

For Sheri
Her dedication, support, and faith have made all things possible.

355.0209
St32a

A Presidio Press Book
Published by The Ballantine Publishing Group

Copyright © 2002 by Brian Steed

Library of Congress Cataloging-in-Publication Data is available from the publisher upon request.

ISBN: 0-89141-803-2

Maps © Meridian Mapping, Philip Schwartzberg

Manufactured in the United States of America
First Edition: January 2003

Contents

Foreword

America's war on terrorism has drawn our attention to issues of national defense. Whether America succeeds or fails in defeating its enemies will depend in large measure on how well its armed forces first prepare for war, then adapt to unique, usually unforeseen conditions. In *Armed Conflict,* Brian Steed provides invaluable insight into the challenges of future ground combat. This is an important book that deserves the attention of military professionals as well as citizens interested in the national defense and the experience of soldiers and units in battle.

The American military is at a crossroads. Changes in the strategic environment and new technological capabilities have impelled a period of dramatic change that defense experts label a "revolution in military affairs." Visions of future combat are important because they influence doctrinal concepts of how armed forces intend to fight, material development and acquisition, training conditions, and leader development. Recently, soft concepts that define future war almost exclusively in terms of advanced technology, surveillance platforms, communications systems, and long-range bombing or missile strikes have gained wide acceptance despite evidence that close battle on land remains an enduring necessity. Brian Steed's analysis of five battles that occurred in the last half of the twentieth century helps define the nature of land combat and reveal limitations as well as possibilities associated with emerging technologies. As Prussian military philosopher Carl von Clausewitz observed, we cannot control war because the enemy "dictates to me as much as I dictate to him."

The five case studies highlight dangers associated with mirror imaging one's opponent and failing to consider countermeasures to one's own capabilities. As military operations in Afghanistan during Operation Enduring Freedom confirmed, enemies will attempt to avoid America's strengths and attack weaknesses. They will seek battle on their own terms to limit the effects of America's technological overmatch. Success or failure in land combat will depend on training before the fight and the leadership of sergeants and junior officers during the fight. Because the author reveals challenges that American combat leaders are likely to face, this book provides a starting point for preparing soldiers for battle.

Learning from history may be the only practical way to prepare for the intellectual challenges of combat. Before their first action all soldiers try to imagine what the experience will be like. Although conditions of battle vary widely, studying the nature of combat in breadth as well as depth can reveal trends and permit one to at least think clearly about the murky future. Steed does just that. He takes readers to a hilltop in Korea, a jungle clearing in Vietnam, the rocky landscape of the Falkland Islands, the featureless Iraqi desert, and the chaotic, crowded urban streets of Mogadishu. His battle studies are comprehensive and compelling.

The proposals and ideas advanced in the closing chapters deserve serious consideration. Each reader will judge whether the author's conclusions provide relevant answers to the problems of future land combat. The discussion that those conclusions generate, however, is certain to further our understanding of the challenges soldiers and leaders will face in future battle as well as what must be done to prepare for those challenges.

H. R. McMaster

Preface

On 11 September 2001 and during the days and weeks that followed the attacks on the Pentagon and New York City's World Trade Center, the president of the United States gave clear and direct focus to the U.S. military—be ready to fight the war on terrorism. Is the military ready for the task? This question applies most to the ground forces within the U.S. Department of Defense. Air and naval forces are critical in their ability to rapidly project power anywhere around the world, but it is the ground forces and their leaders who will have to eventually go in and get the terrorists after the other elements of national power "smoke them out." The training and proficiency of the U.S. military is the best in the world; however, that training has focused for a half century on defeating mechanized forces in open and restricted terrain. The terrorists and other future opponents of U.S. national objectives will not fight in these places, but will seek to draw American military power into the severely restricted jungles, forests, mountains, and complex terrain of the cities and urban sprawl of the world. They will also seek to fight the United States with nontraditional and atypical means.

The military dialogue today describes the nature of warfare as changing to a precision-directed adventure in which nations can be targeted into submission. This thinking has resulted in a technological shopping spree for the U.S. military that has placed it above all other nations in military technology. The supremacy is such that any armed conflict fought in the next twenty-five years will be across a technological gap or boundary. The United States and other industrialized nations have fought such conflicts before. Historical analysis of these past conflicts clearly demonstrates the flaws in the technological panacea approach.

There is always significant difficulty associated with determining the nature of future war. Despite this difficulty, it is critical that the definition of future war be the starting point for determining what ideological, doctrinal, technological, organizational, and personnel changes are necessary for U.S. military forces to remain relevant and prepared to meet the challenges to national security. This reasoning leads to the question that this book attempts to answer. What challenges will future ground commanders face in armed conflict and how does the United States prepare for them?

Historical analysis permits identification of certain trends in the nature of war. These trends are gathered from engagements across the last fifty years of the twentieth century. Initially, this book establishes a common foundation with a discussion of the changing context of warfare followed by a discussion of the trends associated with cross-technological tier conflict. These trends are further elaborated on by the use of five case studies or battle analyses. These trends carry forward to project the fundamental nature of future warfare. The battles and trends are:

- battle of Hill 219, Korean War: mass human wave attacks
- battle of LZ Albany, Vietnam War: use of intermixed forces to negate firepower advantages
- battle of Goose Green, Falkland Islands War: long deployment distances
- battle of 73 Easting, Operation Desert Storm: conventional engagement in unrestricted terrain
- battle of Mogadishu, Operation Restore Hope: use of urban /complex terrain

Following the case studies is a discussion of the military future, then the conclusions and recommendations produced by this study. The successes of World War II were a direct result of the improvements begun a decade or more before; the successes in Desert Storm were also a result of improvements begun decades earlier. The 11 September attack on U.S. citizens and property demonstrates that the time to act is now. The final recommendations are in direct contrast with technological solution—more gadgets, reduction of combat formations, focus on long-range precision fires, and less live maneuver training. The recommendations include the creation of a more flexible, less expensive force, as well as an increase in soldier training and better leader development. This book discusses the historical trends of combat operations and the realities of war—now and in the future; it also attempts to help military and civilian leaders prepare for and anticipate conflicts in the early part of the twenty-first century.

Acknowledgments

In 1996, I called my former squadron commander and asked his advice about a future master's degree program and what areas I should emphasize. After only a few moments of thought, Rob Soeldner put together a well-crafted reply that started me on a journey of discovery that continues today. His advice was to analyze the future of warfare as it relates to the elements of national power. Throughout my journey, the path that seemed so clear has meandered and changed course on many occasions, yet the heart of the work has remained constant. The results of that study are contained in the pages of this book and are really the synthesis of the support, advice, encouragement, and intellectual criticism of many. The faults and errors are mine alone.

It all begins with my parents, who instilled a love of reading and history that has created a passion for understanding why things are the way they are. This learning-focused environment has evolved through a group of outstanding mentors who have helped to shape my thoughts and channel energies toward a useful purpose. I owe special thanks to Douglas Lute, Clement Laniewski, Christopher Lucier, Thomas Pope, Thomas Aldrich, H. R. McMaster, and John Antal, who have provided encouragement, guidance, and assistance and created a climate that allowed for growth and development.

The metamorphosis of the book began in the graduate program of Vermont College of Norwich University, where the thoughts and ideas of people of varying backgrounds and very different philosophies helped shape the nature of the discussion. I am especially grateful to Verbena Pastor for her passion for free thinking and educated discourse and to Gina Booth for her efforts as a proofreader and editor.

During the research process, I had the tremendous opportunity to attend the U.S. Army's 1997 Army After Next Spring Wargame as an observer. This weeklong event afforded me the opportunity to discuss with a variety of technical experts and just plain brilliant people the future of warfare. I am grateful to all of them for their indulgence of my inexperience and constant questions.

Finally, I am extremely grateful for the support and assistance of the editors and staff of Presidio Press for bringing my synthesis of ideas to the public forum.

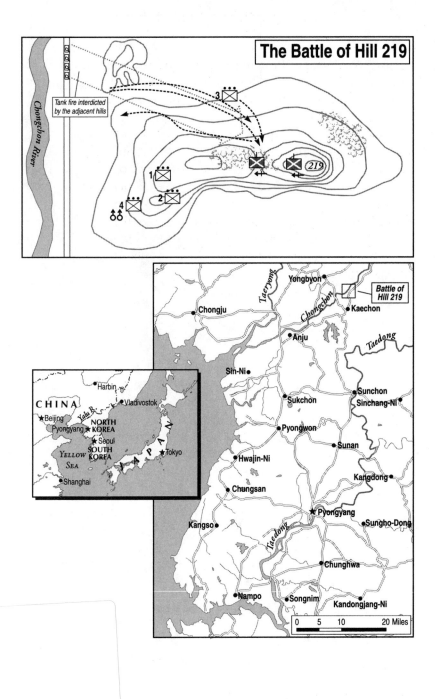

xiii

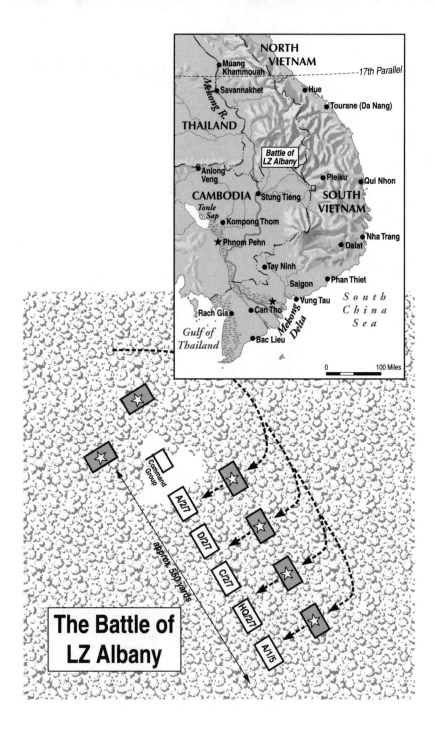

The Battle of
LZ Albany

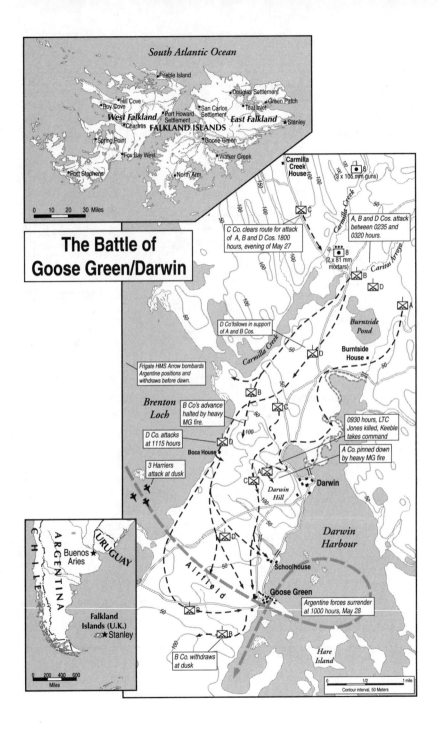

South Atlantic Ocean

Peeble Island

Hill Cove
Roy Cove
West Falkland
Chartres
Spring Point
Fox Bay West
Port Stephens

Douglas Settlement
Green Patch
Teal Inlet
San Carlos Settlement
Port Howard Settlement
East Falkland
FALKLAND ISLANDS
Stanley
Goose Green
Walker Creek
North Arm

0   10   20   30 Miles

The Battle of
Goose Green/Darwin

Carmilla Creek House

8
(3 x 105 mm guns)

C Co. clears route for attack of A, B and D Cos. 1800 hours, evening of May 27

A, B and D Cos. attack between 0235 and 0320 hours.

8
(2 x 81 mm mortars)

B

D

A

Burntside Pond

Burntside House

D Co. follows in support of A and B Cos.

Frigate HMS Arrow bombards Argentine positions and withdraws before dawn.

Brenton Loch

B Co's advance halted by heavy MG fire.

D Co. attacks at 1115 hours

Boca House

3 Harriers attack at dusk

0930 hours, LTC Jones killed, Keeble takes command

A Co. pinned down by heavy MG fire

Darwin Hill

Darwin

Darwin Harbour

Schoolhouse

Airfield

Goose Green

Argentine forces surrender at 1000 hours, May 28

B Co. withdraws at dusk

Hare Island

CHILE
ARGENTINA
URUGUAY
Buenos Aires
Falkland Islands (U.K.)
Stanley

0 200 400 600
Miles

0   1/2   1 mile
Contour interval, 50 Meters

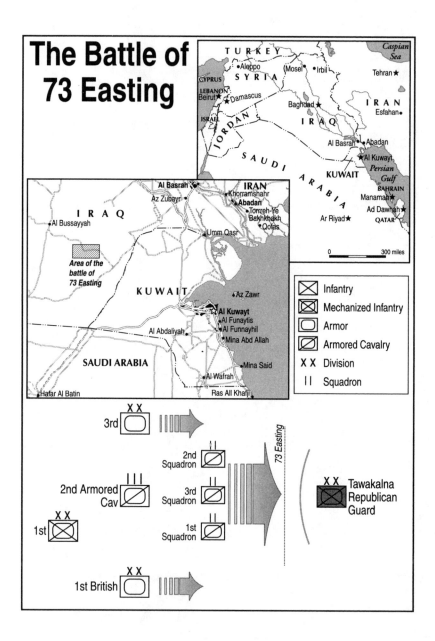

The Battle of 73 Easting

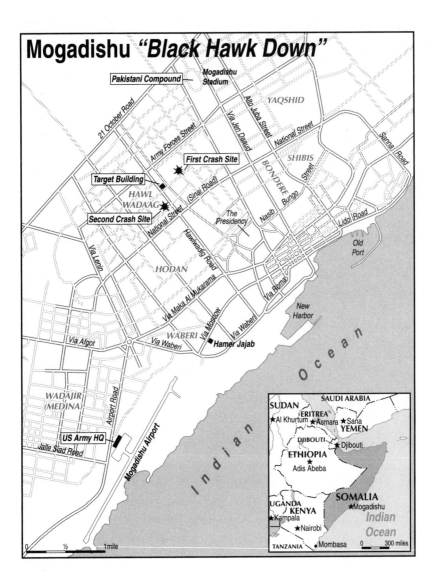

Mogadishu *"Black Hawk Down"*

Introduction

[O]bservers as far back as Thucydides have insisted that war can be perceived accurately only through the lens of history. To be useful, military theory must be grounded in the known realities of the past, not because the past repeats itself in specific ways, but rather because it reveals aspects of war which are timeless.
—Paul Van Riper and Maj. Gen. Robert H. Scales, Jr.

In the days following the horrific terrorist attacks on the World Trade Center and the Pentagon on 11 September 2001, President George W. Bush, Vice President Richard Cheney, Secretary of State Colin Powell, and Secretary of Defense Donald Rumsfeld all indicated that the United States of America was at war. For the previous twelve years, since the demise of the Union of Soviet Socialist Republics, the U.S. military had moved forward on a path of change and transformation without a focus on the threat. Now the president of the United States of America has provided focus.

This book discusses the future of ground military combat in general while also explaining how the war on terrorism fits in. Throughout the preparation of this book, I came to recognize some general thoughts among national security and military writers and professionals regarding the impact of emerging technologies on military operations. Despite the apparent focus on technology, each of these images carries a human face as well. These thoughts gave rise to numerous concepts, which I, in turn, recognized more as images than

1

specific statements. I describe these images in the following paragraphs:

- An armored knight being dragged from his mount in a crowded village square. The press of the mob and the lack of maneuver room force the weapons and armor of the knight to be as much a part of his fall as the grasping hands of the peasants.
- A person from the projects has won a Ferrari in a lottery. The fear of damage, vandalism, or theft forces the new owner to keep the vehicle secured within the confines of a well-protected garage. Occasionally the vehicle ventures forth, but only for a rare drive along the interstate.
- A moderate businessman from New York City in the summer of 1863 has hired a conscript to fill his position in the latest Civil War draft. A violent mob attacks and destroys the man's home, and his precious luxuries are scattered in the flames or among the looters in the New York draft riots.
- In popular science fiction, technologically advanced spaceships are destroyed with great regularity, then replaced with new versions of the vessels. Typically no mention is made of cost, because money is rarely addressed in the movies and books of this genre. Examples of this are the movies and television series based on the Star Trek theme. In the movie *Star Trek III*, the USS *Enterprise* is destroyed; the crew is presented with a replacement at the end of *Star Trek IV*.

Each of these images plays an important part in the underlying theme of this book.

The knight represents the dominance of the U.S. military in the unrestricted venues of the air, oceans, deserts, and plains of the world. Like the knights of old, the U.S. military can use its technology advantage and awesome machines to their full extent in open areas. However, also like the knights of old, these current warhorses are vulnerable in unfavorable terrain. The battle of Agincourt (1415 C.E.) along with the battles of Crécy (1346 C.E.) and

Courtrai (1302 C.E.) showed the weakness of cavalry in confined or marshy terrain and when faced with an entrenched and prepared infantry. The power demonstrated in Operation Desert Storm was not a vision of battles to come. It is, instead, analogous to the action of the proverbial mounted knight in unrestricted terrain. If the United States is drawn into the city either to rescue or assist an unpopular local leader or international policy, the Americans face the same possibility as the knight in our image or in the cases of Agincourt, Crécy, and Courtrai. This was demonstrated vividly in Mogadishu, Somalia.

The knight was pulled down not simply by the weight of his technology but by his lack of understanding of the revolting peasantry. Not to describe the world as peasantry, but this is a real concern to many Americans and many American foreign policy executors who often treat the rest of the world as the peasant class. Those who strike at the United States with terrorism do so much as the peasants used their strength of numbers to overwhelm their perceived unjust lords.

The Ferrari is an expression of the love affair of the American military with technology and gadgets. The pursuit of technology has given the United States some of the most powerful machines in history, but these machines are also complicated, expensive, and sensitive when engaged at close proximity. They also require a tremendous logistical burden to keep them supplied and mobile. The United States could afford to lose tens of thousands of tanks in combat in World War II. In Vietnam it could lose hundreds without much concern. In the early years of the twenty-first century, the U.S. Army will have only a little more than a thousand of the highest-technology tanks, each one costing nearly $6 million. How many can the United States afford to lose? An example of this is the 1999 American deployment of Apache helicopters to Albania, where they were never used. Whether the U.S. withheld them for training, logistical, or threat concerns is irrelevant; we had hundreds of millions of dollars invested in equipment positioned to fight but never brought into the conflict. Will America continue to protect these high-tech wonder vehicles for some future conflict against a "near-peer" competitor when American foreign policy needs their capabilities in the new war against terrorism? Is the United States protecting America's Ferrari, as it were, for infrequent road trips when it is really needed for the daily commute? The Ferrari image also conveys a lack of respect for the community in which the owner lived. His desire to protect his prized possession from the hands and eyes of his neighbors demonstrates arrogance that is often attributed to American policy and practice.

The businessman who suffers the anger of the draft riots is a warning to all who propose the use of surgical strikes by American technological wonder machines while allies provide the ground forces to do the dirty work. The expense of high-technology gadgets has risen, and the fear of casualties has become nearly paralyzing for American political and military leaders. This has caused the United States to look toward allies and coalition partners to perform the work of placing soldiers on the ground and in harm's way. In Bosnia and Kosovo, America hesitated to act, because any conflict there would have been complicated and rife with the difficulties of supporting soldiers placed on the ground—not the antiseptic fight that the American people had become familiar with during Operation Desert Storm. The United States struggled diplomatically to get other nations to provide the ground forces while it provided the high-tech, safe air, naval, and logistics support. The revolt of the world community was prevented by the implementation of the Dayton Peace Accords, which called for a substantial American ground force. However, unlike the fictitious rich gentleman, the United States must be wary of trying to hire replacements to put the nasty but still-important work on someone else's shoulders.

The replacement of the spaceship demonstrates some of the current predictions of future military force structure. The exploding expense of high-tech weaponry will force nations to build smaller militaries for the same money. Unlike the example of *Star Trek*, money is an issue. In 2020, ten M1A2 tanks will be irreplaceable within a reasonable time frame. The tank production facility will not be operating, and restarting the plant would bring the per unit cost to well over $10 million. If the loss of a few tanks could have this impact on the American military, what would be the impact of the loss of the current USS *Enterprise,* which has a price tag figured in billions of dollars? The U.S. leadership and the American people should not become too enamored with wonder weapons without first understanding the long-term costs in terms of money, maintenance, training, and morale associated with their operation and possible replacement.

The images just discussed provide the major concerns that create the need for the discussions to follow. These discussions rest on a foundation made up of the following premise. The basics of military success are encapsulated in five elements: identification, isolation, suppression, maneuver, and destruction.

- Identification is the ability to define and locate the opponent.
- Isolation is when the opponent is denied the ability to gain outside resources and assistance.
- Suppression is the process of denying the opponent the freedom of movement and ultimately maneuver.
- Maneuver is a combination of movement and firepower— either in a physical sense, a perceived sense, or in cyberspace— to achieve a position of advantage. Advantage means the placing of strength against an opponent's weakness. Once again this may be in reality or in the opponent's perceptions.
- Destruction is the end of the enemy resistance through either physical destruction of resources or destruction of the opponent's will.

To explain the relevance of this framework, the book discusses a variety of levels of strategy and a division of nations based on technology. This model is followed because that is the framework that the U.S. military and the American people understand best. Other aspects (cultural, economic, religious, etc.) that have an impact will be addressed briefly within this framework.

Research revealed the following three realities. First, the United States continues to be the only nation in the highest technological tier. Second, armed conflict continues as a means that nations use to accomplish their aims. An addendum to this is that nonnational entities use terrorism as a means to achieve their political, religious, or cultural aims, and the United States will respond to terrorism, in part, with military force. Finally, the aims of other nations and nonnational entities will, at times, run contrary to the interests of the United States; in other words, the United States will fight some form of armed conflict in the future.

Each of these premises and revelations is critical to the discussion of this book. When combined, they mean that any future conflict in which the U.S. military engages will be across technological tier boundaries. Again, this is not to say that technology is the driving factor in determining the outcome of a conflict; in fact, many of the historical case studies will demonstrate to the contrary. However, U.S. leaders must understand how to fight an opponent across this boundary to be successful.

There is always significant difficulty associated with determining the nature of future war, as is best illustrated by a vision of future warfare portrayed in 1959 and described following:

The Army's Combat Development Experimentation Center at Fort Ord, California, staged a showing of the "Soldier of Tomorrow" at this week's annual meeting of the Association of the United States Army in Washington, DC. The new battle garb, which may be available by 1965, is designed for a soldier who will traverse the nuclear battlefield either on an individual "flying platform" or as a member of a crew on a "flying car." When he leaves his vehicle, his individual "jump belt" will assist him in accomplishing his mission with minimum difficulty from small terrain obstacles such as streams, cliffs, etc. The jump belt will give him the ability to propel himself through the combat area at will. . . . He will be equipped with a face mask to guard against the thermal effects of a nuclear attack, as well as hand coverings such as gloves of molded plastic. . . . Further protection will be provided by explosive foxhole diggers, which he will carry slung across his back. In the event of impending nuclear attack, he need only emplace his explosive foxhole digger, ignite the fuze, and wait for the blast. The resultant hole in the ground will give him below-ground-level protection. . . . It is believed, however, that technology being applied by military-scientific teams will eventually produce a weapon extremely light in weight and of high velocity. This weapon, in conjunction with other types now under development, will make it unnecessary for the Soldier of Tomorrow to clash with the enemy in hand-to-hand and bayonet-to-bayonet type combat engagements.[1]

The "Soldier of Tomorrow" would endure numerous close-combat engagements in the jungles of Vietnam, the jungles and streets of Panama, the streets of Beirut, and the streets of numerous cities over the following four and a half decades. The thinking represented by this quote demonstrates that no prediction of the future of combat, however official, will be entirely correct. It also demonstrates the foolishness of believing that technology holds the key to addressing all the potential military challenges to a nation. This is also a reminder of the folly in predicting the end of war as we have known it and suggesting the ushering in of an entirely new phase of warfare. This book has no intent of doing so. Despite this difficulty, it is critical that the definition of future war must be the starting point for determining what technological, organizational, and doctrinal changes are necessary for U.S. military forces to remain relevant and prepared to meet challenges to national security. This reasoning leads to the question that this book attempts to answer: What challenges will future ground commanders face in armed conflict and how does the United States prepare for these challenges?

To answer this fundamental question, it is important to begin with an understanding that warfare has constantly undergone periods of transition and change. Military futurists and professionals who espouse the technological revolution believe in a progressive change in military operations from the current and recent wars of attrition to wars of disintegration.[2] There are others who espouse a type of warfare dominated by insurgency, cyberwar, and other techniques that target the internal aspects of an opponent rather than the external military.[3]

Disintegration in its purest sense is refuted by a simple numerical analysis of any potential threat. The most likely threats to U.S. interests will probably come from the developing world where large populations provide for large militaries or militias or widespread and smaller terrorist cells. Regardless of the organization or style, the willingness of developing nations or nonnational organizations to risk the lives of their citizens or members—as with the Chinese and North Vietnamese during the Korean and Vietnam Wars, respectively—will result in long wars of attrition. Not the attrition of France in World War I but the attrition of will and physical resources suffered by the U.S. military in Vietnam. In future wars, the commitment of a nation, rather than its technological level, will determine success. Many developing nations could afford the loss of a hundred soldiers for the loss of one American soldier and still be victorious in the end, as demonstrated in Korea, Vietnam, and Somalia. Furthermore, the loss of a terrorist or many terrorists so long as the losses inflict casualties, terror, and chaos is of nominal consequence in the minds of those nongovernment opponents.

The bombing campaign against Serbia in 1999 is an example of this philosophy. U.S. politicians and administration officials expected that a relatively limited campaign could effect sufficient pressure to cause the Serbian president to bow to the will of the United States and Western European allies. Instead, the campaign took more than three months. And the end came only after the economic infrastructure was targeted and the Russian support of Serbia was withdrawn. Though this war was significantly shorter than either the Korean or Vietnam War, the will of the people (or in this case a single person) or small group of leaders versus the power of machines was underestimated.

The numerical superiority of emerging nations and the national commitment of either nation are the fatal weaknesses of the current revolution in military affairs and the military technical revolution. These "revolutions" are based on the concept that technology, surgically applied, in dominating maneuver can allow for a rapid victory with limited loss of life. The revolutions ignore the understanding the other nations and nonnational entities have of the

American way of war and how to defeat the United States. Even a warlord in the poor and resource-deprived nation of Somalia understood how to defeat the Americans. These revolutions further refute the concept of attrition warfare, and they thrive on the idea of clean victory. This prediction has dangers, not the least of which is the misleading of the American people into a belief that wars in the future can remain relatively bloodless. Most recently, the Bush administration has changed its tone to be more open and forthright about the probability of casualties in the war on terrorism.

Even if the U.S. military has moved to a philosophy that departs from attrition-style warfare, to expect all potential adversaries to move similarly is unrealistic. This is an optimistic assumption, because the U.S. military has failed to truly adopt a maneuver mentality that avoids strength and seeks weakness. This discussion leads to an important question about the relationship between the United States and potential adversaries.

How does a technologically advanced nation deal with a people's army that so dramatically outnumbers its own army? This is a problem that has faced the U.S. military since before Lt. Col. George Armstrong Custer rode into the valley of the Little Bighorn River and lost a major portion of his command to a lower-technology, less-trained, larger force. It has occurred again and again: as Marines retreated from Chosin, as soldiers were ambushed en route to a clearing designated LZ Albany, as Soviet airborne soldiers were ambushed on the roads of Afghanistan, and as Soviet mechanized elements were humbled in the streets of the Chechen capital.

In each of these cases the more technologically advanced combatant failed to achieve one or more of the five elements. Lieutenant Colonel Custer, for example, failed to identify his opponent through effective reconnaissance or human intelligence. Further, he was unable to suppress the opponent once the engagement began, which allowed the Native Americans to reposition forces at will to fight each portion of his command separately as it approached. Finally, he was unable to ever move into a position that placed his strength against enemy weakness. All of this resulted in a failure to destroy his opponent or his opponent's will to fight. Although this is a relatively simple overview, it illustrates the challenge that the U.S. military faces with its opponents in the future. Chapters Three through Seven of this book discuss five battles that detail the clash between higher- and lower-technology nations. Each of these battles represents ways that a lower-tier force will seek to engage and defeat a higher-tier force.[4]

The national militaries of the world will evolve into four separate tiers. Those nonnational organizations will not fit into any single tier and, in many cases, will occupy tiers one and four simultaneously. These tiers were in effect for most of the last half of the twentieth century. Specifically, this is a construct of the Cold War and the creation of the superpowers. Prior to and throughout World War II, there was a series of roughly equivalent military powers. No one nation was so dominant as to be able to defeat a combination of other nations, and few could defeat another nation in direct conflict. This changed following the war and the economic devastation of most of the major European and Asian powers. The United States and the Soviet Union—by the development of massive nuclear weapons arsenals, long-range bombers, sophisticated naval forces, and large standing armies—became the technological military leaders. This condition continued until the collapse of the Soviet Union in 1989.

The following definitions clarify the tier divisions:

- The first tier is full information-age technology integration. Examples of this are digital communications and situational awareness in all armored vehicles and helicopters; UAV (unmanned aerial vehicle) and satellite downlinks at the battalion and brigade level; imagery and various tracking devices, to include JSTARS (joint surveillance and target acquisition radar system), AWACS (airborne warning and control system), and Aegis systems at the operational level; and all source information from national assets at the theater level. The only nation currently attempting to operate within this tier is the United States.
- The second tier is partial information-age technology integrated with industrial-age equipment and tactics. The informa-

tion-age component focuses on command, control, communications, computers, intelligence, security, and reconnaissance, but the majority of the combat power (tanks, infantry fighting vehicles, helicopters, et cetera) is an industrial-age force. Many of the nations in this tier will have their own satellite systems in place or will have national corporations with commercial satellite imagery capability. The nations in this tier make up the majority of the developed and industrialized world; Western Europe, Russia, China, Japan, and many other nations will seek to enter this tier. I feel that the majority of industrialized nations will not be able to upgrade their military and achieve a tier-one status and thereby fall into the second category. The two primary reasons for nations to be on the second tier are cost and presumed threat/global interests.

• The third tier is a mostly industrial-age force. This group consists of the nations that cannot afford to modernize at all and thereby must fight with an entirely industrial-age force. This is currently the largest group, but it will shrink as more nations move into the second tier. Mostly, these are developing nations or those whose national security is such that the expense is not deemed necessary. Many nations in Africa, South America, and Asia fit into this tier.

• The fourth tier is a terrorist or warlord/tribal clan force. These are nation-states that are so poverty-stricken or torn with internal strife that all they can muster are warlord militaries and terrorist actions. Several recent U.S. interventions have been in these sorts of nations—Lebanon, Somalia, Haiti, and Rwanda. Many nations will struggle to move from the fourth to the third tier, and many more will fall back from the third to the fourth as civil unrest, economic collapse, and political instability destroy the national organizations. Others will also enter this tier. These are nonnations, such as terrorist organizations, drug cartels, and information and physical pirates. At times this tier may in fact utilize some very high-technology tactics or techniques, but it does so for narrowly targeted or terrorist purposes.

Over time, almost all nations will acquire some information-age technology to improve their forces, but the percentages will be such that enough difference will remain to warrant four tiers. These groups are currently in effect, but the level of modernization and expense will further increase the separation between nations.

To fully answer the primary question posed by this book (What challenges will future ground commanders face in armed conflict and how does the United States prepare for them?), an understanding of strategy must be added to the understanding of technological division and the basic framework.

One of the most common understandings of strategy is through the ancient yet still popular game of chess. In this game each player moves pieces in a prescribed manner to checkmate the opponent. Checkmate results when one player's pieces are positioned skillfully enough that the opponent's king cannot move without being captured. At this point the player in checkmate has lost the game.

This process, involving sixteen pieces per side, can take days to accomplish, or it can be over in as few as three moves. For the game to be over in three moves requires that two situations exist simultaneously. First, one of the players must be totally ignorant of the consequences of his or her decisions. Second, the other player must be good enough to seize the opportunity presented. Typically these two situations do not coexist. Extraordinarily competent players do not usually play completely incompetent ones. However victory is achieved, and regardless of the quality of players, the plan and execution of the sequence required for victory can be termed *strategy*.

From game board to battlefield, strategy is a concept full of paradox. This is explained thoroughly in Edward Luttwak's *Strategy: The Logic of War and Peace*. Take the example of a normal person given a choice between two routes: One route is well maintained and well traveled; the second route is narrow, poorly maintained, and traverses difficult terrain through heavy vegetation. The obvious choice is the first route. In military conflict, this is not an obvious choice. The first route is certain to be expected by the enemy as the primary avenue of approach and will therefore receive significant defensive preparation. So, what appears to be the worst of two choices becomes, possibly, the best.

In the case of the Maginot line in World War II, the French built a string of prepared fortifications and trench systems along the Franco-German border to prevent invasion from that region. In preparation for the invasion of Belgium, the alternate route, the French deployed a significant number of divisions along the Belgian border. This was done to block the most obvious and expected avenues of approach of the German military. In between the Maginot line and the French defense of the Belgian border, the Ardennes region was, in comparison, lightly defended, because its terrain and vegetation made mechanized maneuver seem impossible. This is precisely the route the German advance took. The Maginot line was deemed impregnable, and the force arrayed closer to the English Channel was attacked to prevent repositioning. Then approximately 10 percent of the German force, containing the majority of the most mobile and best-equipped units, attacked along the least expected route to achieve a spectacular victory.[5] This counterintuitive logic—that the worst route is now possibly the best—is inherent in the difficulties of strategy at all of its levels.

United States Army doctrine reserves the term *strategy* for the highest level of conflict. Edward Luttwak, however, divides strategy into five separate levels that cover the entire spectrum of conflict, from the highest level of government interaction to the lowest engagement between two human beings. The levels are grand strategy, theater strategy, operational strategy, tactical strategy, and technical strategy.[6]

Grand strategy is the highest level and involves all the resources at a nation's disposal. Typically this level includes diplomatic, economic, and military power. Recently many scholars and strategists have included information as part of the power at the grand strategy level. The ability to coordinate all the assets of a nation requires significant purpose and foresight. This is typically why war efforts are confused and less effective in the initial stages of conflict. One of the best examples of a detailed grand strategy policy was that used against Iraq during the Gulf War. The U.S. administration was able to effectively isolate Iraq financially, politically, and finally militarily. The freezing of assets and the building of the international coalition against Iraq were as much a part of grand strategy as the military buildup.

Theater strategy, the second level of strategy, involves the combination of operations in the air, on the land, or on the sea. The various campaigns of different services and various platforms are combined into the theater strategy. This is at the highest level of the U.S. Army definition of the operational art. An example would be the conduct of the United States Central Command (CENTCOM) in the Gulf War to organize the blockade of shipping, the conduct of the air campaign using both U.S. Air Force and U.S. Navy aviation assets, and the defense of Saudi Arabia.

Operational strategy, the third level of strategy, governs the functions of what is done and not done tactically. These events may be large in scale but not autonomous. The air war during Operation Desert Storm is an example of the operational level of war.

Tactical strategy is a series of engagements and battles that supports the operational campaign and governs the actions at the technical level. These actions are conducted primarily by a single service, though multiple arms may be employed. This means that the dominant player is one service, though support from other services may play an integral role. One example is the battle of Goose Green in the Falkland Islands War, where naval gunfire played a significant fire support role in a British army battalion-sized attack.

Technical strategy, the lowest level, is the interaction between pieces of equipment or weapon systems. An example is the manner in which one tank maneuvers to engage and destroy another tank.

At each level there exists the counterintuitive logic of strategy. Weakness and strength may also vary at each level of strategy. An army can be technically, tactically, and operationally strong but weak in terms of grand strategy, as was the American army during the Vietnam War. Ancient Chinese strategist Sun Tzu suggested that to defeat an enemy one must strike where the enemy is weak. This also implies that an adversary does not strike where the opponent is strong. This paradox means that future adversaries of the United

States will not fight a technological war of disintegration. Instead they will seek to fight a war of attrition within the streets, jungles, and narrow roads of their homeland against U.S. military forces, or they will target the will of the American people with terrorist attacks within the borders of the United States. The American people and many American political leaders are not prepared for this paradox. The lack of preparation is due to erroneous assumptions about how nations fight.

Each of the battle analyses included in this book deals with the affecting or affected elements of each level of strategy. The analyses serve to put the various battles within a context, from the highest level to the lowest, which is critical to understanding their significance. The Maginot line is once again an appropriate example. At the technical and tactical levels of war, the barrier was deemed impregnable. At the operational and theater strategy levels, however, the Maginot line was simply the avenue to be avoided, and the German army went around it.

The key is understanding the fluid nature of strategy. One level of strategy may rapidly transform into another. In the era of modern media attention and almost instantaneous transmission of information, the levels of strategy are becoming compressed. Evidence of this compression was seen by the events of four U.S. soldiers in Haiti returning the fire of a few individuals opposed to the American presence and the rule of law the U.S. soldiers represented. The deaths of the Haitians and the almost immediate broadcast of the event evoked a response from a White House spokesman. This transfer of results from what could be argued as technical strategy (soldiers reacting to incoming small-arms fire) to the grand strategy level is more common now than ever before. Compression has caused a further confusion of strategic vision, because soldiers have to be concerned about the impact of their actions on the highest levels of decisionmaking.

Waves of change have swept over the globe many times and created and destroyed a variety of international security arrangements. Chapter One explains the changes in the context of conflict, focusing on the exploding cost of military hardware. Chapter Two describes the methods that lower-tier nations use in attempts to defeat higher-tier nations. Chapters Three through Seven describe five battles as case studies of the methods outlined in Chapter Two. Chapter Eight is a summary of the lessons from the battle analyses. Chapter Nine explains the thoughts of military futurists on the current path being taken by the U.S. military and possible dangers presented by numerous lower-tier nations.

The last chapter offers conclusions and recommendations. The dangers presented by the cross-tier conflicts that loom on the horizon for the United States require a more flexible, less expensive, more deployable, and more easily maintained force, which I term *Force 1944*. This name indicates the multipurpose function of the major systems used by the U.S. military at that time. For example, the ability of the Sherman tank to function in its primary role as an infantry support vehicle yet still defeat some opposing tanks is a function that must be included in any force that America plans to have. This recommendation and others about training and leader development are critical to the success of the United States' interests in the conflicts of the twenty-first century.

Chapter One
A New National Security Focus

This chapter provides the framework that demonstrates the alteration in the very nature of ground conflict. This is to say that the context in which any ground conflict may be conducted is significantly different from such conflicts fought in the pre–World War II era— the era of industrial-age warfare.

First, to explain the evolution in warfare: During the period 1795–1945, the world witnessed a series of struggles among the great powers. Most of these wars were fought with alliances and coalitions and covered several regions of the globe. This period culminated in two major world wars. The last two wars clearly demonstrated the concept of total war, in which a nation invests all of its resources to achieve its war aims. In the early part of this period, during the Napoleonic era, the world saw the growth of the army from a relatively limited structure of wealthy nobles and their retainers to one of large, conscripted land forces numbering in the millions. The combination of total war and massive armies required long, drawn-out struggles that sought to exhaust the abilities and assets of the opposing nation. These three concepts—total war between nation-states, massive armies, and protracted conflict—have become, for the current time and into the foreseeable future, less likely than anytime in the post–World War II era.

In many respects this is not a new phenomenon. Immediately following World War II, the combination of total war, massive armies, and protracted conflict between two relative peer nations was just as unlikely as it is today; however, the Cold War struggle clouded our ability to see the change in strategic affairs with clarity.

The end of the Cold War further magnified the changes already taking place. The use of military force extends from support of domestic disaster relief to strategic nuclear war. After the end of the Cold War, the preponderance of military deployments shifted from a war or near-war focus to what are often referred to as operations other than war (OOTW). The reasons for the departure from the traditional view of conflict are the focus of this chapter.

In the 1990s, two terms seemed to dominate articles written about the future of the military or about national security affairs. These terms are *Revolution in Military Affairs* (RMA) and *Military Technological Revolution* (MTR). These terms are nearly synonymous and focus on the technological changes that the U.S. military infrastructure has promoted. The focus on newer, bigger, faster, and apparently better weapons has driven a technology-focused improvement rather than an idea-, threat-, or people-driven one.

The most dominant term in the national security arena was RMA. One could hardly read an article about the future of national security or the military without running across this term. It is defined as "a major change in the nature of warfare brought about by the innovative application of technologies which, combined with dramatic changes in military doctrine, and operational concepts, fundamentally alters the character and conduct of operations."[1]

Are technological innovations changing the nature of warfare? This question is at the heart of the views between this book and many writers in the national security arena. The details of the debate between definitions are beyond the scope of this book, but clearly RMA is too narrow a definition for the change in the overall context of military operations just described.

The definition of MTR is even more technically based. It is "a technical development that when properly exploited through equipment, training, organization and doctrine provides a decisive (although temporary) advantage."[2] This definition focuses even more on technology and its impact on conflict and is even more narrow than that of RMA. Referencing the five levels of strategy outlined in the Introduction, RMA and MTR focus more on the tactical and technical levels of strategy. RMA has been shown to improve capabilities at the operational and theater strategy levels, but not to the degree of changing the nature in which these strategies are conducted.

The Geostrategic Revolution is the phenomenon that most national security and foreign policy writers discuss when talking about the context of these rapid changes in policy and the global framework. In some respects this term is actually too large. It tends to focus on the diplomatic and economic elements of national power.

The 11 September 2001 terrorist attacks combined with the geostrategic changes of the last fifty years should lead those who are concerned with national security and military issues to see the world in a completely different context (economic, diplomatic, and military) in which future conflict will be conducted.

The world and military conflict must be considered in light of the changes occurring in national security and with an understanding that they are not limited simply to the technological changes of placing computers in armored vehicles or the use of satellites to assist in the improvement of situational awareness; nor are they just about the changing global framework. These are all useful developments and have the potential to create evolutionary change in the future of conflict, but clearly they are not the main reason that conflict is now revolutionarily different.

A major part of the current national security environment is the fundamental shift in geopolitical alignment. Alignment has changed from multipolar (pre–World War II) to bipolar (Cold War). Now the geopolitical alignment is becoming multipolar again. As is the case in any multipolar organization, no two elements of power are dominated by the same nations. In the evolving world situation, there are different dominant powers in each element. Here is a simple example of the various dominant nations:

Form of Power	Dominant Nations
economic power	United States, Japan, China and the European Union[3]
diplomatic power	United States, the European powers (Britain, France, and Germany),

Form of Power	Dominant Nations
	the People's Republic of China, and Russia
military power	United States (defined as global power projection ability)

The United States remains a superpower in that it is the only nation that is a leader in all areas of power and therefore wields the most influence. The diversity of power "is a unique phenomenon of [this] era [in] that economic and military might tend to be in separate hands."[4] This statement is especially true when considering the current Russian economic position.

The economic revolution has taken the primary position among the elements of power: "Economic strength will become an increasingly important aspect of national power, and in many cases the decisive aspect, in what promises to be a more competitive global commercial and financial environment."[5]

Economics occupies this position for several major reasons. First, the world has become more interconnected through globalization. Second, the United States is losing economic dominance in comparison to other nations; this causes a greater level of concern and thereby further elevates the economy. Third, warfare has become so astronomically expensive that the ability to afford the new technology is more important than the number of systems that can fight with trained crews.

Expense of Modern War

The factor most affecting the ability of nations to be in a position to wage any significant future conflict is the monetary cost of military and diplomatic adventurism. The enormity of the expense of Operation Desert Storm was beyond comprehension; it cost billions of dollars to keep the coalition force deployed for a single day. Even the cost of noncombat operations is expensive; enforcing the Dayton Peace Accords in Bosnia for the first half-dozen years is going to cost an estimated $6.5 billion.[6]

When the RMA and MTR are discussed in any format, the discussion eventually centers on the cost of the weapons and military systems that make both the RMA and MTR possible. Examples of this include the U.S. Air Force's B-2 bomber, which was reported to cost an average of $2 billion per aircraft, and the U.S. Navy's SeaWolf submarine, which was budgeted at more than $2 billion for fiscal year 1998 alone.[7] The expense of modern "information-age" warfare becomes clear with even a cursory analysis of Desert Storm. It cost "about $500 million" a day for the conduct of the air campaign alone. The initiation of the ground war pushed the cost over $750 million per day.[8] Desert Storm represented only a single theater of war. World War II was fought in at least six separate theaters. If a similar-sized conflict were fought today, the cost would exceed $5 billion per day; over the course of a three-and-a-half-year war, the total cost would exceed $7.7 trillion. This is more than seven years of the entire current U.S. budget. These numbers include only logistical concerns, not the necessary increase in hardware to fight in six geographical theaters simultaneously.

A graphic example of the rise in the cost of warfare is that of tank prices. An average tank in World War II cost slightly over a half million constant dollars. (A *constant dollar* is an economic term designed to demonstrate cost equivalence.) In 1997 the United States paid $3.7 million for the only tank in the inventory (the M1 series), which is even more expensive today. This is a 7:1 difference. The Bradley infantry fighting vehicle, a tank by World War II standards, costs three times as much as the World War II tanks. The canceled light tank, the armored gun system (AGS), is a 5:1 ratio in price.[9] The increase is for a variety of reasons—computer fire control systems, thermal night vision, laser range finders, etc.—all of which add significant expense and in turn make the equipment much more effective. This rise in expense continues as the prices of Cold War aircraft versus the airframes proposed for the twenty-first century increase more than threefold.[10]

It is obvious that the economy of 2003 is dramatically different from that of 1937 or 1942. At the end of the Depression era, there were at least two factors that allowed for the World War II boom: first, the massive available workforce; second, an economic depression that had significant room for improvements in efficiency. Today we have room for only minor corrections. The U.S. economy could not absorb the level of change of more than a half century ago. As an example, the United States could not afford to buy nearly 30,000 tanks in one year, as it did in 1942.

The additional problem is that with all of the technology and expense comes a tremendous maintenance and logistical burden. Many nations do not have the infrastructure to even attempt to make the change toward a technocentric military, and many do not have the desire to attempt to outplay an opponent—in this case the United States—at its own game.

The expense of technologically enhanced weapons has the impact of minimizing the number of top-tier national armed forces. Not only can very few afford to have the newest, high-technology conventional equipment, even fewer want to. This separation between the very top nations and those just below can be seen even within NATO, where the United States has the possibility of fielding computerized communications a generation ahead of other NATO nations.[11] The technological expansion also increases the importance of a strong gross domestic product (GDP). This expense should create a four-tier system. The Introduction effectively identifies the characteristics of these four groups. In addition to previously stated definitions, these groups represent conventional military capability. The nonconventional, or asymmetric, military capabilities are not as cost dependent and therefore do not relegate nations who possess them into neat definitional boxes. These are artificial constructs to assist in explaining how economics has a dramatic impact on the conventional battlefield, but there is significant fluidity. For example, a tier-two nation may possess or have access to some satellite imagery of a specific region that may be equal to or even surpass a tier-one nation's capability. This does not make the tier-two nation a tier one.

These groups have always existed to some degree, but the level of modernization and expense will further increase the separation between nations and hasten globalization as smaller, poorer nations seek wealthy, powerful patrons to protect them. These patrons are fewer now, because many seem to be heeding the advice of economists to avoid the use of militaries, both as a stimulus to growth and in the hope of bringing greater world stability.[12]

The previous comments focus on the technological military developments and the economic impact that they cause. However, this cannot be separated from the ability of a national military to employ this technology to its maximum advantage. One example, from the battle of Hill 219 in the Korean War, illustrates this point. The American army possessed the technology in the form of communications, direct firepower, and indirect fire support to defeat the numerically superior Chinese forces. However, the failure of the American soldiers to properly maintain their equipment and to position and integrate their tanks, and the lack of training to effectively bring in indirect fires, resulted in a hard-fought withdrawal rather than a dominant victory.

The diplomatic changes to our national security focus are arguably the most dramatic. The previous comments on geopolitical polarity shifts are at the heart of the drama. The change in dominance following the collapse of the Soviet Union has the world still attempting to regain diplomatic equilibrium. American political extremes of Pax Americana and complete isolation are discarded, but where on the spectrum between the two will America finally end is the most critical question. President George W. Bush's declaration of war against terrorism has many unanswered questions concerning how the United States will seek to achieve victory; however, it is clear that the United States will be much more involved in the world community because of the terrorist attacks of 11 September 2001 than it would have been otherwise.

Among the factors that will influence the U.S. role in the world, three are identified here as the most critical in impacting future conflict:

- change in diplomatic focus
- diplomatic culmination in Operation Desert Storm
- diplomatic/political reaction to media pressure

The following illustrates the importance of balancing our diplomatic responsibilities, but one must always remember that what a democratic nation can do is determined by what the voting populace is willing to do. Walter Lippmann once cautioned that American foreign policy "consists in bringing into balance, with a comfortable surplus of power in reserve, the nation's commitments and the nation's power."[13]

Former U.S. Secretary of State Dr. Henry Kissinger clarified this by pointing out: "What *is* new about the emerging world order is that, for the first time, the United States can neither withdraw from the world, nor dominate it."[14] Despite the challenges faced by the diplomats, their role has become increasingly more critical. Nearly every nation is decreasing its defense budget, yet many nations have enlarged interests created by the globalization of the economy. United States diplomats have the critical function of trying to "galvanize political, economic and military forces outside its borders to address the challenges that confront us now and will only multiply in the years ahead."[15]

Change in Diplomatic Focus

This dramatic transition in diplomatic power has caused great difficulty in U.S. adjustment. The U.S. government has not completely left behind the concept of NSC-68—the document drafted to assist in dealing with the spread of communism and an expansionist USSR; it was the foundation of the containment policy. Government officials still talk in terms of Cold War philosophy. American soldiers are fighting and policing around the world in support of Cold War agendas; Bosnia and Kosovo are the most significant examples of this adherence to a Cold War policy.

The United States has yet to completely shift from a world balance of power mentality to a regional balance of power concept. The difficulty in making this change began in the Korean War, which was a fight for nationalism, for imperialistic and totalitarian purposes that then included the desire of an emerging nation to demonstrate its newfound power. The Soviet Union was aware of the desires of the North Korean forces, but it approved the North Korean attack to defeat South Korea only as a low-cost venture.

The Soviets did not see any significant downside to allowing the Koreans to do all the fighting. This was not the East-West showdown that many feared, or even the most remote rumblings of a third world war, though many saw that possibility in the crossing of the thirty-eighth parallel. President Truman stated, "Every decision I made in connection with the Korean conflict had this one aim in mind: to prevent a third world war and the terrible destruction it would bring to the civilized world. This meant that we should not do anything that would provide the excuse to the Soviets and plunge the free nations into full scale all-out war."[16]

United States diplomats saw in the Korean War a grand scheme for world domination led by the Soviet Union; the smaller nations involved were simply mindless puppets of the Soviets, doing as directed. This mind-set led to a series of critical decisions to prevent any escalation of the war beyond the borders of the Korean peninsula. Additionally, it led to decisions about the amount of national effort to be deployed into the theater. These decisions confused the military establishment in place and confused the American people as well. Following World War II, the U.S. military and the American people were used to an all-out fight to achieve victory as rapidly as possible, rather than this new "limited" warfare.

A limited war created the need for a totally different type of thinking. "In a limited war, if military and political goals are not synchronized from the very beginning, there is always the danger of doing either too much or too little. Doing too much erodes the dividing line to all-out war and tempts the adversary to raise the stakes. Doing too little and allowing the diplomatic side to dominate risks submerging the purpose of the war in negotiating tactics and a proclivity to settle for a stalemate."[17]

With the creation of the iron curtain and the production of NSC-68, the conceptual vision of foreign policy became more focused than at any time before or since in this nation's history. America was going to contain and then wait patiently for the fall of Communist Russia.[18] This focus caused a cascade effect throughout our diplomatic efforts. Every relationship was now seen as a pawn in the Cold War game. No conflict was viewed as anything less than part of the global struggle between the forces of democracy and the forces of communism.

The impact of the Korean War and the attendant policy of containment are still visible today in dealings with China. The United States deals with China as though each issue has global overtones, when the Chinese probably use this global focus to gain concessions or greater influence within their own region. Policies must reflect the regional balances and the issues that drive these balances rather than seeking for global linkages. The change from Cold War policies to regional focus is a work in progress, and much has happened to improve this transition; yet there is still a great deal of improvement needed. Specifically, development of proactive policies is needed to reduce future threats. In dealing with Russian nuclear weapons and weapons sales has the United States been truly proactive. The fall 1997 purchase of MiG-29 fighters from the former Soviet Republic of Moldova is an example of such a proactive policy. This philosophy needs to be translated to all regions.

Changing foreign policy focus is still problematic, because there is only recent emphasis on some regions, providing for little institutional knowledge. The United States has had Russian experts for more than sixty years, but we have few Indonesian experts or Rwandan experts; these nations were not as critical to U.S. interests during the Cold War. Despite the lack of a single powerful adversary, "The need for an organized approach to U.S. security policy remains as valid today as it was after [World War II] or at any other time."[19]

As the United States changes from a focus on nation-states to a focus on terrorist networks and cells, the change must be as much cultural as policy based. The key departments in the executive branch of the U.S. government must seek to see the world in its regional, religious, and cultural context and not in a global terrorist picture along the global Communist model, with which the U.S. government bureaucracy is so familiar.

Diplomatic Culmination in Operation Desert Storm

Culmination is defined in U.S. Army doctrine as the point in time and space when the combat power of the attacker no longer exceeds that of the defender.[20] To take this to a diplomatic level, the diplomatic power of the United States reached its high-water mark in organizing and maintaining the coalition against Iraq in 1990 and 1991. Almost simultaneously with the collapse of America's Cold War antagonist was the first post–Cold War and first information-age conflict. The diplomatic power that was demonstrated was probably the most significant since the Korean War. In this case no member of the coalition was physically threatened, with the obvious exception of Kuwait and the assumed threat to the Saudi government. With nothing more than potential economic threats, more than a hundred nations participated in the coalition against Iraq. This economic danger was a significant benefit in assembling some of the major coalition partners; however, many of the minor players relied little on Persian Gulf oil. It has been stated that the Gulf War "inaugurated not American dominance but a new era of international cooperation."[21]

This participation was a direct result of the ability of the key U.S. leadership to promote this cause. The president personally contacted numerous world leaders, as did the secretary of state. These two men were not only working from their own vast experience and personal contacts but using the positive reputation of the United States, which was at a twenty-year high. To most nations it was clear that there was only one show in town, and they needed to play along. For this playing along, many nations received significant benefits, a quid pro quo. Even with the benefits, this was the first war in American history in which the United States sought foreign aid to assist in funding a foreign adventure.[22]

Despite the play toward national self-interest, the Gulf War coalition was still the most lopsided coalition in world history—more than 100:1. Though some nations saw an opportunity in thwarting the coalition (and certainly would have, given a longer embargo), the world showed unprecedented solidarity.

Because of the coalition's tremendous success, the world changed diplomatically. Nations assumed that the United States would continue to play a leading role in the United Nations (UN) and help quench the numerous other hot spots around the world. The events in Iraq immediately following the cessation of hostilities—namely, the Shiite uprising in the south and the Kurdish rebellion in the north, which received no U.S. support—were in essence cold water on the face for the rest of the world community. This "Bay of Pigs" scenario again revealed that the United States fought only those fights that were in its own interest.

The decline in the diplomatic power and prestige of the United States began with failure to support the Shiite and Kurdish uprisings and has continued to fall. The size of the world coalition that supported Operation Desert Storm and the votes conducted by the UN General Assembly, which were nearly unanimous, all reflect tremendous prestige. This was a result of the use of U.S. diplomatic power. More recent events—namely the Iraqi expulsion of weapons inspectors in November 1997, and the difficulty the United States had arranging any coalition support for military action in support of the UN inspection policy—dramatically demonstrate the lack of prestige. Clearly there has been a significant drop in America's ability to have its will enforced by the world community. Much of this is a result of a lack of urgency on the side of the world community, because of what were perceived as minor technical offenses rather than more grievous sins of invasion. Regardless of reasons, the prestige has diminished to such a degree that nuclear tests by India and Pakistan in the spring of 1998 could not be deterred by threats of economic sanctions.

Additionally, Operation Desert Storm was the culminating point, because this was the first time in American history where the secretary of state went cap in hand to numerous nations in search of financial support for a military operation. More than $53 billion was pledged and approximately $27 billion collected by the end of the war. This solicitation did not go over well with all nations involved.[23]

The bottom line is that there was a great deal of effort expended, and in the end Saddam Hussein is still in power and the world community is having difficulties with a nation defeated a decade ago. It is not a situation conducive for improving or even maintaining diplomatic capital.

Much has changed in light of the highly publicized and dramatic terrorist attacks against predominantly civilian targets. The real question is how long this change will last. This may present a turning point for the decline in U.S. diplomatic influence; however, this will occur only if the United States acts upon these events and leads the temporarily galvanized world community toward a tangible and attainable goal.

Diplomatic/Political Reaction to Media Pressure

In addition to the loss of political capital in Iraq, there is the lack of focus on what is and is not a national security threat worthy of military intervention. This is caused in great part by an overreliance on opinion polls and concern over media coverage. Former U.S. Army chief of staff Gordon Sullivan describes the impact of emotionalism this way: "There is an emotional temptation to want to 'do something' without first clearly understanding what political purpose that 'something' is supposed to accomplish."[24]

In 1995 the National Defense University indicated eight humanitarian emergencies that threatened more than a million lives in countries other than Somalia, Bosnia, Haiti, or Rwanda.[25] The United States did not deploy forces to assist any of them.

Attention to the media is not a unique phenomenon, but it has gained greater significance since the end of the Cold War. No longer does the media represent national power, and it truly does not represent any single nation. The media has become a global entity with virtually no national identity. The exception to this was demonstrated by the New York–centered media following the destruction of the World Trade Center. There was a high degree of nationalism and fervor no doubt brought on by a sense of personal vulnerability not experienced within the United States since World War II. In fact many in the media see themselves as watchdogs of government with a duty to criticize and point out shortcomings rather than focus on success. A *New York Times* reporter said, "A journalist who decides that his job is to help win a war, rather than just to describe it, is better off enlisting."[26] In another case, a reporter stated during a public television–sponsored roundtable discussion on ethics that he considered himself a reporter first and an American second. Imagine the results if a similar attitude were to have been displayed during the Normandy landings on 6 June 1944. American deaths were in excess of 3,000 on that day, yet the reports that were released then and later were supportive and emphasized the accomplishments rather than focusing on the losses. Would the United States have left the war or sued for peace had the media functioned then as it does now? What would have been the result of such an action? Imagine the horrors. One writer tells us that "a nation needs chauvinism to win wars, so mass enlightenment has the ironic property of steadily ceding all struggles to the morally primitive (e.g. Saddam Hussein)."[27]

Not only does the media criticize, it also seems to drive foreign policy. The most poignant example of this is the Tet Offensive of 1968. "For a number of military men in Vietnam during the Tet Offensive, it must have been ironical to win a military victory, have it reported by American journalists as a defeat, and have those reports accepted as fact by many Americans."[28]

The images of a Tet defeat assisted in providing significant political pressure on the presidency to begin the Vietnamization of the war. This media focus in foreign policy has continued and become more pronounced. The media was viewed as so important to foreign policy in the United States that when the Kuwaiti government in exile presented its case before the United Nations, it hired a public relations firm to prepare the presentation rather than having experienced diplomats or government bureaucrats deliver the request.

The media's hold on foreign policy was not something it achieved; it was given as foreign policy began to lose focus. James Schlesinger stated:

In the absence of established guideposts our policies will be determined by impulse and image. In this age image means television, and policies seem increasingly subject, especially in democracies, to the images flickering across the television screen. To paraphrase John F. Kennedy: a videotape is more potent than ten thousand words. National policy is determined by the plight of the Kurds or starvation in Somalia, as it appears on the screen. "If a tree falls in the forest"—or a catastrophe occurs, but is unrecorded on tape—it is unseen. Starvation continues in the Sudan or Mozambique, suppression in East Timor or India, ethnic war in parts of the former Soviet Union, but it is Somalia or Bosnia that draws the attention, because the cameras are there. . . . In the past it was said, "Trade follows the flag"; these days it seems more pertinent to say that "sanctions or the troops follow the TV cameras."[29]

Somalia is one example of media-inspired intervention. The suffering in Somalia because of the famine, drought, and constant conflict was unimaginable. Millions were dying or on the verge of death. This tragedy was played out on a nearly daily basis in the living rooms of almost every U.S. home. The news coverage from Somalia displayed and described the suffering in sometimes graphic detail. The horrors of war were provided in living color and with all the sights and sounds. This was truly a human horror story, and one that needed to be stopped.

Somalia was not a nation described by a president as presenting a "clear and present danger to the national security of the United States of America." It was not of vital, national, or even minor interest. This was a nation that had absolutely nothing of critical importance to the United States. Yet the United States arrived in dramatic fashion to relieve the suffering in Somalia rather than in the dozens of other countries that needed help just as badly.

When an American asks why U.S. soldiers and Marines were in Somalia, the answer is quite simple. They were in Somalia because the media was in Somalia and not in other needy countries. There was indeed suffering of enormous proportions. The intent of this commentary is not to say that the United States should not have helped but to simply be honest about why the United States did help. Were it not for media coverage of the starvation in that nation, the U.S. military would not have gone there.

Another example of media influence is Rwanda. The images of hundreds of thousands of people fleeing the reported brutality were again displayed on television screens across the United States.

Once again the U.S. military was deployed to the scene to establish centers for humanitarian assistance.

Again the questions abounded. The United States has no vital or national security interests in central Africa. This is a region where Americans have remained blissfully detached for almost all of our history as a nation, yet the United States responded. It did so because reporters were there. The news reports were so graphic and described such heinous atrocities that American sensibilities demanded participation.

The most significant involvement is that in Bosnia. The issue of interest is more confused in this situation. But the concern here is this: What are the national or vital interests at stake? Are these U.S. Cold War interests or post–Cold War interests? Many would (and have) argued that the interest in the Balkans no longer applies outside the framework of the Cold War. This powder keg is not a powder keg at all when the Russians are allies. Many U.S. congresspersons made an issue about this being a European problem, yet the United States never completely challenged the major European power, Russia, with the responsibility of fixing that problem.

There is a significant amount of discussion now about a "long-term" presence in the area. Long-term can only mean semipermanent, just as the long-term U.S. presence in South Korea has been semipermanent. It is clear that American military personnel are going to be in Bosnia for a considerable time, just as in Haiti. Still, the political leadership has not fully justified why.

Once again the answer lies in media influence. ABC News anchorman Peter Jennings broadcast from Sarajevo, and numerous other correspondents briefed from the trenches around the besieged capital, showing photographs of people running from sniper fire. A mortar round impacted in a marketplace in Sarajevo and every person with a television or magazine subscription saw pictures of the dozens of dead and wounded. Dozens. We are not talking about a holocaust, or even starvation or suffering on the Rwanda or Somalia scale. Still, images of these twisted and bleeding bodies on the cobblestone streets gripped the political decisionmakers and forced the United States to increase its efforts.

The NATO- and UN-established no-fly zone resulted in the downing of an American pilot and the loss of an aircraft. A dramatic rescue enthralled the nation and linked the United States through the bloodstream of the media to the war-torn nation of Bosnia. America had to do something. It sent an envoy and sponsored a peace agreement, resulting in the deployment of thousands of U.S. soldiers to the theater. All because American heartstrings were tugged by the atrocities of war.

Numerous other examples abound of such intervention following the media lights and cameras: the Kurds, Haitian refugees, the Bangladesh typhoon relief. This domination of U.S. foreign policy by what is emotionally disturbing is a significant change in the manner in which the United States or any modern democracy determines its national security interests.

The impact of the media is not a new phenomenon, but the degree of coverage and the increase of images and public opinion polls have raised the impact of media influence so much that the status is essentially a new phenomenon. With the explosion of microtechnology, the average reporter already has the ability to broadcast from nearly anywhere with lightweight, easy-to-handle equipment. The technological developments only serve to threaten an even greater media deluge with almost-real-time coverage of minor international events. This leads to a trend toward the shortening of "diplomatic" time. In the mid-nineteenth century, a diplomat might have a period of many weeks and probably months to resolve a conflict or so shape the conflict as to be beneficial to the nation's cause. Today, however, this time is measured, in some cases, in terms of hours and maybe minutes. As each of these events are discussed, look at the change in time from the Korean War, where days were lost for transportation, to the Gulf War, where Tariq Aziz and James Baker conducted their negotiations over CNN in a matter of minutes. The time to decide, strategically position pieces, delay, demand, and threaten has been so compressed as to create a tremendous burden on diplomats of the modern era and further lessen this form of power.[30] This shortening of the diplomatic time line also shortens the military deployment time line. Nations must act before

Americans begin the deployment process. It almost assumes a pre–World War I mentality of deployment schedules driving diplomatic decisions that are in turn influenced by media image–induced public opinion.

This book is dedicated to understanding the changes in military power from the present into the first quarter of the twenty-first century. This section identifies a few key issues that have dominated the changes from World War II to the present. The U.S. military dominance was one of the great achievements of World War II. America elevated itself from the status of a second-class combat power to the preeminent world military power. Since World War II, the philosophy of the use of force has also changed. The advent of the nuclear bomb had a significant psychological effect on the use of military power. No longer was conflict viewed in the sense of all-out war being a test of national resolve, manufacturing might, and quality generalship. Instead, all-out war was seen as a version of Armageddon or apocalypse; in this sense, the idea of war completely changed. Probably for the first time in world military history, the manner in which we were to wage war had a total realignment. I would classify this as the only true RMA (Revolution in Military Affairs). This new means of waging war has taken on many new names. Some of these are familiar, and most have negative connotations. Limited war, police action, peacekeeping, and nation building are all names that have described the new style of conflict.

Many military fiction writers have discussed a third world war, and in most of these stories the entrance of nuclear weapons was only a matter of time. In all of these scenarios of all-out war, it becomes problematic to prevent the entrance of these most devastating of weapons. They are the ultimate crutch; a nation without a strong conventional military need only promise the destruction of its enemy's major cities, and the prospect of war is significantly reduced. It is because of this mutual assured destruction that warfare will not soon return to its nineteenth- and early-twentieth-century past. The century and a half (1795–1945) of global or multiregional conflict has possibly left the face of the planet for good.

Despite the sound of this comment, this is not to say that the future is all rosy and pleasant. In fact, the past five decades have witnessed tremendous loss of life and property due to wars on a national and regional scale. It is important to remind ourselves that there has never been a true, all-out war. In truth, "All wars are limited."[31] Therefore one must understand ways that nations limit wars:

> Wars are limited by three means: by the territory on which they are fought (as in Korea or Vietnam); by the means used to fight them (no nuclear weapons in Korea; no massive mobilization for Vietnam); or by the objectives for which they are fought—the most significant limitation in political terms and therefore the limitation that is most often discussed and debated.[32]

The following issues have a great impact on how conflict is waged:

- weapons of mass destruction proliferation
- proliferation of arms
- low tech vs. high tech
- strategic deployability
- cost of war (previously discussed)

Weapons of Mass Destruction Proliferation
The decision to disregard General of the Army Douglas MacArthur's recommendations to expand the Korean War, which included possible use of the atomic bomb in the defense of UN forces in theater and to assist in the reunification of the Korean peninsula, was the single most important decision in changing the face of warfare. President Truman and his advisors changed how generations would and still do fight. Just as it was the act of George Washington handing over the presidency to John Adams rather than the act of his assuming the presidency that made our nation truly democratic, it was the non-use of a nuclear device rather than its use that developed the overwhelming nuclear aura.

Imagine the outcry of world opinion were the United States to use a nuclear device against even a military target in Iraq or Afghanistan. Yet how many different atrocities are now being committed and have been committed around the globe for which there has been no out-cry? And these atrocities have created much greater suffering and greater death than either or both of the nuclear attacks on Japan.

If the United States had continued to wage war in a total manner during the Korean War as it had in several previous wars, it is possi-ble that the atomic bomb would have lost its mystique and the ter-ror with which it was viewed. It is possible that the Army of the Peo-ple's Republic of China (PRC) would have developed techniques to deal with the horrific destruction, and shown the world that it is pos-sible to fight despite the crushing power of the blast. The bomb was not used, so this is all speculation, but still the atomic bomb is one of the only weapons in history to be used in one war and then never again, despite its presence in the arsenal. The message given in Ko-rea, and later in Vietnam, that the United States would not risk nu-clear war in conflicts for less than vital interests became a symbol of hope for newly emerging nationalists around the world. This was es-pecially true for Southeast Asia. It was here, just shortly after the con-clusion of the Korean War, that Americans refused to allow tactical nuclear weapons to be used in support of a French mountain garri-son in Indochina.

The existence of nuclear devices is the ultimate trump card for the nations that possess them. World War II would have been nuclear in 1935 when Japan invaded Manchuria, in 1940 when Germany in-vaded France and began the Battle of Britain, or in 1942 when Ger-man troops initiated Operation Barbarossa against the USSR, if the capabilities of today existed then. No global, total war will happen without the use of nuclear weapons. This drives the limited nature of warfare and has for more than fifty years.

Nuclear weapons are only one of three types of weapons of mass destruction. Chemical and biological weapons are even more wide-spread and dangerous. The national media's discussion of anthrax in the winter of 1997–98 and discussions continuing to the present demonstrate a reasonable concern about these weapons. More na-tions have access to them than to nuclear weapons, and they can cre-ate a greater effect. A specific example is that the downwind hazard effect of ten kilograms of viable anthrax is roughly equivalent to that of a ten-kiloton nuclear device. Chemical and biological weapons are less expensive, equally deadly, and much wider spread than nuclear weapons. Any war that remotely resembles total war must be expected to involve the use of weapons of mass destruction. Given the effectiveness of the 11 September 2001 terrorist attacks and the change in tactics, it is certain that the use of chemical or biological weapons is not far removed from the nonnational organizations that seek to thwart or disrupt American policy or practice.

Proliferation of Arms

In both Korea and Vietnam, the U.S. military faced weapons that were for the most part grossly inferior to our own, with the exception of the T-34 tank in the early months of the Korean War. These pieces of military equipment were of World War II and then of Korean War vintage. Air defense consisted of iron sight weapon systems with radar-controlled missiles protecting the most critical positions. Typically the United States was defeated mentally and emotionally before it was defeated physically, if that in fact occurred.

This history of developing and emerging nations being militarily backward is no longer the case. Even though this book divides nations into technological tiers, the point is that the disparity between adjacent tiers is less now than fifty years ago. Many nations now possess some amount of high-technology military equipment, some of which is technically superior to current U.S. military equipment. The G-5 and the G-6 are perfect examples of this. These are South African–made artillery pieces designed by a Canadian inventor, Gerald Bull. They both possess the longest conventional (nonrocket assisted) range of any artillery piece of similar caliber.

Weapons proliferation came to a pinnacle during the 1973 war between Israel and her Arab neighbors. The buildup for several years prior to the war was dominated by then-state-of-the-art purchases or leases from the Soviet Union and the United States. Egypt was able to develop, around the Suez Canal, one of the most sophisticated air defense networks outside of Europe. Israel, in contrast, had one of the most modernized air forces in the world. Numerous other pieces of military hardware were also present in theater, including antitank guided missiles (ATGMs). This was to be the first large-scale use of such weapons.[33] During the fighting, both the United States and the Soviet Union shipped hundreds and even thousands of tons of materiel and ammunition to the combatant nations. The U.S. shipments totaled more than $3 billion in weapons sales and direct shipments.[34] This tremendous influx of weapons actually resulted in better-armed nations after the fighting than before it. The ripple effect of such military might was the increase in weapons purchases throughout the region. The attempt to develop nuclear weapons by Iraq was a direct result of Israel's reputed possession of such weapons. This in turn led to a preemptive strike by the Israelis against the Iraqi reactor, which prompted a dramatic improvement in Iraqi air defense, the same air defense system that was dismantled by the U.S. Air Force during Operation Desert Storm.

The move to expand high-technology and modernized military equipment and train combined-arms operations highlighted this trend in the developing world in the 1980s and 1990s. One of the most significant results of the Gulf War of 1991 was the weapons improvement throughout the region. Nearly every nation in the region is seeking to upgrade its air force and naval assets.[35] Many former Communist nations and former Soviet Republics with struggling economies use weapons sales as a means to gain hard Western currency. Reports have circulated that the T-72 main battle tank and the BMP infantry fighting vehicle were for sale for tens of thousands of dollars in the early 1990s. Such extraordinarily low prices have made it possible for nations to improve their military-technical tier level without the historical expenditures.

The increase of former Soviet sales has pressured Western arms merchants to keep pace and maintain their market share. Competition for declining military dollars and a race for more and more high-tech equipment has caused a buyer's market. The majority of the sales are with little or no conscious effort to determine the ethics of the buyer. Certainly, those who sold weapons of mass destruction technology to Iraq did not concern themselves with the fact that the person in leadership had previously used such weapons on his own civilian population. This is further evidenced by the sales of weapons to the economically deficient nations of Eastern and Central Europe. This is brought on by their Western neighbors and the United States, which use the carrots of easier acceptance into NATO or the European Union to entice nations to buy equipment that may or may not be in their national interest.[36] Today there is not a nation that does not possess near-top-of-the-line aircraft, tanks, artillery, and air defenses.

The fact that nations possess high-tech or near-top-of-the-line equipment does not mean that they have them in great quantity. In fact, typically there are minor concentrations of the best equipment in a few units, with the rest of whatever forces outfitted in older equipment. This is both a positive and negative aspect of modern weapons. Fewer weapons means less expense, but it also means that potential adversaries need destroy fewer targets. Modern weapons are also a great deal more effective, which allows for fewer weapons creating the same effect. For example, one precision-guided munition in Operation Desert Storm accomplished what it took 170 bombs to do in the Vietnam War, or 9,000 bombs during World War II.[37]

Despite the movement toward more high-technology equipment, there is little movement toward a completely professional force. Such a force lends itself to the ability to maneuver rather than to provide relatively static firepower alone.

The ability to get moderate to high-technological-level equipment at a relatively cheap price has allowed many nations to rise to tier levels heretofore unpredicted. This is certain to continue. Business interests will outweigh ethical considerations. Future American conflict will be against quality equipment in the hands of people probably without the same moral convictions.

Low Tech vs. High Tech

The conflict in Vietnam clearly demonstrated the vulnerability of high-tech forces to the tactics used by low-tech armies. Specifically, tier-four nations and many tier-three nations have an advantage over a tier-one nation. In the Ia Drang valley of Vietnam in November 1965, there were two battles that clearly delineate both the strengths and weaknesses of this struggle. The first battle was called Landing Zone (LZ) X-Ray, in which an airmobile infantry battalion fought off two North Vietnamese Army (NVA) regiments—outnumbered nearly five to one—by using disciplined forces applying significant amounts of firepower with direct fire, indirect fire, and U.S. Air Force assets. The second battle was fought only a few miles away and just the day after the first battle ended. It was fought near a clearing called LZ Albany. The infantry battalion was caught off guard. The NVA forces attacked and almost immediately were completely intermixed with the U.S. infantrymen. This prevented the use of large quantities of indirect and U.S. Air Force close air support. The American forces suffered heavy casualties.[38] The low-tech forces masterfully utilized terrain and close combat skills to overwhelm the exhausted, unprepared American force.

Another historical example is from the Korean War. The Army of the People's Republic of China was successful in using the ridgelines of the Korean mountains to encircle the "road-bound" American forces. This technique allowed them to surround and effectively destroy numerous American units during the U.S. withdrawal from North Korea. The U.S. Army is more road-bound now than ever, because the M1A2 is one of the heaviest tanks in the world.

Reliance on technology requires significant training time. This time takes soldiers away from training more basic skills. High-tech forces have tremendous strength as well, which was clearly demonstrated in the battle at LZ X-Ray. These must not be ignored, but once again a trade-off is required. How much high-tech equipment does America want if the military loses basic soldier skills while becoming effective with gadgets?

Strategic Deployability

Following the expansion of advanced weapons throughout the developing world came the clash between a developing nation and a developed one. This occurred in the South Atlantic between Great Britain and Argentina. The politics of the struggle aside, this appeared to be a one-sided affair between one of the world's historic great powers and an agricultural, developing nation. This is true before one considers the fact that this conflict was waged 10,000 miles from the European shore and within 200 miles of the Argentine coast.

The impact was the obvious—yet not tested—fact that military power is power only if it can be projected. This was where Great Britain struggled. A nation that was able to deploy soldiers all around the world, the only nation able to do so besides the United States during World War II, now struggled to fight in the same ocean. The *Queen Elizabeth II*, a luxury liner, was pressed into military service as a troop ship, and container ships were used to serve as helicopter carriers. One of these ships was sunk by a torpedo, which destroyed more than 80 percent of the British helicopter force for the war. Once the soldiers were in the area, they had to seize a series of footholds on neighboring islands first, to allow for operations, because the once-great British navy was not large enough to allow for operations from the sea alone.

All of these difficulties were compounded by the fact that the Royal Air Force was also outgunned by an Argentine air force equipped with modern French fighters. Despite all of this, the British were successful for three primary reasons. First, they had a well-trained, professional army. Once they got on land, the outnumbered Royal Marine Commandos, British paratroopers, and British infantrymen were significantly better trained soldiers and more successful in ground combat. Second, the Argentine air force had some high-technology assets, including Exocet antiship missiles, but not enough. They were forced to use contact bombs to attack British troop ships once in between the islands. These bombs proved ineffective, because many skipped off the surface of the ships. Third, the Argentines were unable and politically unwilling to reinforce the islands once the battle became a ground conflict. This inability was a direct result of inexperienced antisubmarine warfare experts and the desire on the part of both nations to keep the conflict from escalating too far and involving commercial cargo vessels.

Britain succeeded in reasserting its position as a power, but only barely, mostly because the Argentines were unprepared for the nature of combat. It is not enough to possess the best equipment if a nation does not possess it in enough quantity to be effective throughout the actual campaign.

Most of America's forces are now based within the borders of the United States. This requires a tremendous amount of strategic lift capacity to allow forces to arrive in theaters within the first thirty days of a conflict. This mobility requirement is the primary criticism of the current policy of the Department of Defense: There is not enough strategic lift capability to fight two major theater wars simultaneously. In spite of this critical shortfall, there is no current funding to remedy the problem. Even within the context of a war on terrorism, much of the U.S. equipment is too heavy and cumbersome to deploy by air in any significant quantity, and landlocked nations present greater challenges to the strategic mobility equation.

A great deal of the strategic lift problem is planned to be covered by pre-positioned materiel. There are sets either on land or afloat in the Persian Gulf region and on the Korean peninsula. This allows a significant amount of combat power to be ready in less than a week in either theater. The dangerous issue is this: What if the conflict does not happen in either Korea or the Persian Gulf? Then the deployability problem remains fully intact. Even with the pre-positioned equipment, this supports only a limited number of units; Operation Desert Storm required eight divisions. Positioning the forces in Desert Storm took nearly seven months. Desert Storm required 538,606 short tons delivered by air in 15,893 missions and 5,035,387 short tons delivered by ship in 441 shiploads to CENTCOM from 7 August 1990 to 10 March 1991.[39] It requires between fifteen to sixteen days to travel to the Persian Gulf region by ship, and nearly thirty days to get the same equipment to the Pacific theater.

During the fall of 1997, the difficulties of the two-major-theater-war scenario was evidenced as both North Korea and Iraq posed security concerns at about the same time. The possibility of fighting two different conflicts is real, which brings up the question: The next time, will the United States have as much time as it did in Desert Storm?

Conclusion

The context of conflict is more different now than at any time in the past two hundred years. The backdrop of grand strategy is no longer the same. To properly deal with the new challenges represented by these changes requires a change in national security focus. The world now functions under significantly different rules as a result of the major points described. Economics is the dominant factor of national power. This multitiered system has different nations in different spheres of power. Diplomatic and military power has been reduced a great degree in how each is evaluated in terms of a nation's power. No longer does diplomatic pressure alone provide significant results. The manner of using the military is different. The possibility of global total war is highly unlikely due to the proliferation of nuclear and other weapons of mass destruction. If the trends continue, this possibility will become even less likely. The trend of armies around the world is toward modernizing and making forces compatible with the information age. This high-tech, high-cost force must, by necessity, be smaller. In the American case, the army looks significantly different than it did only a few years previously. Additionally, the United States no longer wages wars of total victory, but instead seeks to obtain limited gains without great sacrifice of life or treasure. Finally, the thousands of dead in the 11 September 2001 terrorist attacks have changed the focus of U.S. policy to one of addressing a terrorist network rather than one of fighting nation-states. This is a change that the American political, diplomatic, intelligence, and military communities are not prepared for. It is likely that they will seek to fight this war through more standard engagements with the nation-states that house and support the networks.

The future will see conflicts about the size of Desert Storm; Vietnam, and Korea are on the high end; the Falkland Islands, Panama, and Bosnia are the norm for this scenario. The U.S. preference is for the time frame of these conflicts to more closely resemble Desert Storm, the Falkland Islands War, and Panama than either Korea or Vietnam. Only a proper focus on regional issues at the diplomatic level and new proactive policies will allow the military to accomplish a manageable level of tasks with limited resources.

The factors of the new environment work to compress the levels of strategy. During World War II and into the Korean War, the infantry squad member made decisions that had virtually no impact on any level above the technical and tactical levels of strategy. With the modern media and the speed of communications in- and outside the military, a private now makes decisions that may require further decision and reaction from national-level leaders.

The nations of the world must now survive in this new environment. Not only the nations, but the militaries, and most specifically the armies of these nations, must change to provide the security required from their parent nations. The nations that adapt to the new rules will be the ones that carry power into the second half of this century. The nations that draw the wrong lessons from history will be like the French army of 1940, without the flexibility of thought and action to stop the numerically inferior yet maneuver-superior German force; or the Argentine forces guarding Port Stanley who were poorly trained, poorly disciplined, and poorly led, and were subsequently defeated by the more disciplined British paratroopers, infantry, and marine commandos.

Chapter Two
Cross-Tier Conflict Methods

When asked why he robbed banks, a famous thief answered, "That's where the money is." We will fight in and around cities because that's where the people are. . . . Cities are also where the wealth, communications, infrastructure, governments, religious seats and national symbols are. They are the ultimate killing fields. The age of grand maneuvers on green fields is over.

—Ralph Peters, *Army Times*, 11 May 1998

In the previous text, the dangers and inevitability of the U.S. military fighting against a lower-tier nation or nonnational organization or network is identified as being very high. The fact that most developing nations have large, land-based militaries, reliant on mass human attacks to achieve success, leads to one of the major underlying questions of this entire book: How does a technologically advanced nation deal with a people's army that so dramatically outnumbers its own army? In a general sense, this chapter introduces the reader to the methods that low-tech nations have sought and used to sometimes achieve victory against higher-tier nations.[1]

Technology and information dominance can give a significant edge to those who possess it in the proper environment, but will the U.S. Army fight in this environment? The talk of expanded area of influence[2] is mute if units fight in urban terrain.

Technology, in war, has an effect very similar to that of an explosion. If an omnidirectional explosion occurs in a zero-gravity environment, the effects of the detonation are felt equally at equal distances in any direction. This same blast, placed in the air above the Earth's surface, is now affected by atmospheric anomalies and gravity, yet it is relatively unencumbered. A similar, though still greater, constraint is placed on this blast when placed at or below the surface of the ocean. Despite the impact of water, currents, and gravity, there is still a relatively similar effect at similar distances from the blast site. This same blast placed at or very near ground level of a featureless plain or desert again has a similar effect, though the ground itself significantly impacts the power of the blast traveling in that direction. Once terrain, buildings, and vegetation are figured into the equation, our omnidirectional explosion is now radically different at similar distances in various directions. Some areas feel no impact whatsoever, and others allow for the effects of the explosion to travel a significant distance.

Technology will behave the same as this explosion in the various types of terrain. Terrain is divided into four categories: unrestricted (northern Saudi Arabia and southern Iraq), restricted (Falkland Islands), severely restricted (tropical triple-canopy jungle or Korean mountain terrain), and complex (urban sprawl). Each of these categories has an increasing impact on the power of technology, just as with the explosion. Lower-tech nations or other adversaries will attempt to exploit this effect of terrain on technology throughout any future conflict.

Various methods are explained as ways in which a low-tech nation will attempt to achieve victory over a high-tech nation. Each method discussed deals with combat on the ground. This was done for specific reasons. It is not to insinuate that the future of conflict will not involve air or naval forces; in fact, the opinion of this author is entirely the opposite: Future combat must and should be a seamless integrated whole, from the initial preparation of the targeted area by sea- and air-based platforms to the protection of the materiel as it transits along sea and air routes, and the continued protection from ballistic missiles by an overlapping redundant system involving platforms in all environments. This must not have any service rivalry, but instead be a unified capabilities-based force. The references in this book to the army are done so out of experience and where the material was gathered rather than as a judgment in favor of the army over other ground components.

Additionally, this ground component is the force that must eventually determine the success or failure of national objectives. Finally, the ground commander is the single most vulnerable element in the U.S. military power arsenal. This person is placed within the hostile territory throughout the length of the engagement and may be there for a significant time preceding and following the engagement. This time on the ground is both the strength and the vulnerability of this particular asset. It is a strength because the ground element is a twenty-four-hour, day and night, all-weather presence; it is a weakness because the ground component is a target for the entire time it sits on the ground.

This chapter creates a picture of the manner in which nations and other entities in the future will attempt to achieve their aims despite, and in direct opposition to, the interests of the United States. There are many reasons for this focus on ground combat:

- This is the venue that the entire book addresses in terms of future warfare.
- United States superiority in the air and at sea is so dominant that few futurists predict significant challenges within the next half century.
- The majority of nations—in fact, probably all nations—cannot and will not attempt to challenge U.S. superiority in the air or on the water; therefore, their only option is to challenge U.S. power on the ground. In support is the fact that this is also where the majority of raw materials and resources are located; therefore, a person who controls the ground controls the nation.
- Ground combat is the strength of tier-two and tier-three nations. They have large populations, which allow for large standing armies, and they may also have limited resources, which forces them to focus on the most cost-effective form of defense—an army.

• In every conflict there comes a time where either the threat of or the conduct of ground combat operations is necessary to ensure the success of the national interest.

• Ground combat is also, seemingly, the least understood in the U.S. media and among the majority of the American populace.

Before the specific methods can be explained, it is important to understand the nature of the world into the early part of the twenty-first century. The population growth being experienced will continue, bringing the total global population to more than 8 billion people by 2020. The majority of these people, nearly 70 percent by 2014, will live in urban or semiurban areas.[3] The associated urban sprawl will become the primary venue for conflict as explained: "The new century will be one of street fighting, uncontrollable masses, shortage, disease and immeasurable hatreds—all concentrated in the decaying urban landscapes in the world's least successful states and regions."[4] Unrest and tension in the population centers will become the breeding ground of war.

The expanded global population will further tax the ability of governments to provide for critical human needs. Just as in Maslow's hierarchy of needs, when the more base needs—food, shelter, clothing—are threatened, the average person will become more rebellious and less stable. Current systems of government within the developing world have proven inefficient for dealing with the basic needs of most citizens. As the populations expand, the systems, already shown to be inadequate, will break down. As they break, people will turn to other sources for their basic needs. In some cases, global corporations can meet these needs; in other cases, people will turn to less legal means: piracy, terrorist organizations, warlords, factional violence, open revolt, and rebellion.

The environment of the first quarter of the twenty-first century is the time frame focus. The bleak descriptions of the previous paragraphs show a world in potential chaos. The developing nations of the world that are most effective will seek solutions. Solutions will come in the form of resources. The nations most affected will be the ones with the greatest populations. These are also the ones currently stressed. The stress will continue to grow until the nation either dissolves into chaos, or extraterritorial attempts are made to secure greater resources. The military that is used to accomplish this will of necessity be relatively inexpensive and dominated by people. To accomplish their aims, these people's armies will face technologically higher-tier nations. They will seek victory through a series or combination of methods. Each of these are described in succeeding sections.

Mass Human Wave Assaults

First is the method toward mass human wave assaults; this was used by the Chinese to great success during the 1950–53 Korean War, and by the Iranian army during the 1981–88 Iran-Iraq War. The point here is that the emerging nations are also the fastest-increasing population regions in the world. This increase in population is the largest drain on the economy, the largest national resource, and the single greatest reason for the current instability the nation is facing. Therefore, it makes the most sense to employ this resource in a military fashion.

Mass wave attacks are an element of military operations as old as war itself. Whether it was the "Fuzzy-Wuzzies" outside Omdurman, Sudan, fighting the British army of Lord Kitchener or the Zulus against the British in the Natal, the intent is to sweep over the higher-tech force with sheer weight of numbers.

The Iranians in the 1980s used tens of thousands of people to sweep across marshes against Iraqi positions. Sometimes the back ranks had no weapons but were expected to pick up weapons of the forward elements as they fell. The economy of such measures is obvious. Little training is needed, and previous successes showed that little coordination was needed; the Chinese forces in Korea used bugles, horns, and bells to coordinate and signal movements.

These forces are poorly disciplined, as a general rule, and have difficulty conducting intricate maneuvers; however, they have shown remarkable success, even against significant firepower. The reason for this success is discussed in the next section.

Closing with High-Tier Forces

The second method is the desire of low-tier nations to move in close proximity with high-tier forces to intermingle personnel and therefore negate precision, long-range firepower. A specific example is the battle of Landing Zone (LZ) Albany from the Vietnam War. This is also demonstrated by the engagements in Grozny, Chechnya, and the 1973 Arab-Israeli War.

As a people's army attacks, the goal is like that of a prizefighter: Get inside the reach of the opponent to strike at his weaker portions without being hit. The human waves accomplished this in numerous historical scenarios. As the people closed, they became more effective, and the higher-tier force became less effective as firepower was denied to them for fear of friendly casualties. Within fifty meters there are few fire support means available to a ground commander. In fact, some of the direct fire capabilities are denied for lack of arming range. The loss of firepower reduces shock and devolves the fight into one of human against human. Once at the level of personal survival, the more personally hardened and desperate have the advantage. It is difficult to imagine any high-tier nation producing soldiers that have hardening or desperation equal to those who grew up in a survival mode from their earliest recollection.

Extending to Extreme of Power Projection Capability

The third method is to draw the higher-tech force away from its logistical support. Extending the high-tech force to the edge of its power projection capability allows the low-tech force to lower the overall technology level of the conflict. This was specifically demonstrated in the Falkland Islands War.

This is a difficult option for a nation to use against the United States. A potential example occurred during Operation Desert Storm. Had North Korea attacked South Korea during this time, it would have had a great chance for success. The United States was occupied with a major engagement in one region, with most of the transportation assets occupied. How quickly American forces could have repositioned from one theater or supporting one theater to the next is difficult to say; however, time lines for defending South Korea would have been significantly degraded, possibly long enough to allow the North Koreans to achieve initial successes and make the American position extremely difficult and costly, possibly prohibitively so.

The danger is that as the distance and dispersion increase, each problem is magnified geometrically. In the case of the Falklands, the distance required the transport of helicopters aboard a converted containership. The subsequent loss of this ship forced a dramatic change in the operational plan. A similar possibility is that of the United States engaged in two or more crises around the world. Each one demands the attention of one or more aircraft carrier groups. Realities such as sailing times, required maintenance, and unscheduled repairs all conspire to place a great deal of friction into the movements. Now, imagine the loss of one of these carriers to enemy action. How much harder does it become to support an additional crisis? Maybe something now falls through the cracks, and some nation gets away with an otherwise intolerable act.

This loss of the carrier has a ripple effect for the commander on land. The commander now requests additional air force assets to make up for the loss of the naval-based aviation. Maybe the commander needs additional fire support assets because there is an attendant loss of cruise missile support with the carrier group being delayed. With a world of ever increasing chaos, there can be expected a multitude of simultaneous crises, which will all assist future world leaders in opposing the will of the United States.

An additional consideration is the challenge of the United States to react against a military target in a landlocked nation. This poses significant logistical problems. How does the U.S. Army or Marine Corps get its tanks, field artillery, and other ground-based firepower into theater? Airlift is faster than ships, but the quantity of materiel is low. Ships can bring in large formations worth of equipment, but how does the equipment get from the port of debarkation to the area of operations? Most nations do not have sufficient road or rail networks, and special railcars are typically necessary to move the heavy American equipment. The Falkland Islands War is analogous to the American military when viewed in light of seeking to conduct military operations against a landlocked opponent nation or organization.

Conventional Engagement

The fourth method is to face the high-tech force in a conventional battle in open terrain. This is typically an unsuccessful technique, as demonstrated in Operation Desert Storm and in the 1967 Arab-Israeli War. There are those nations who will either be forced by events or by poor decisions to engage higher-tier forces in a purely conventional struggle, though most nations will completely avoid this option. There really is no other way to put it: This will fail. Without effective use of the other methods described, the results of Desert Storm are certain to be repeated. Even with weapons of mass destruction or the use of limited high-tech equipment, defeat is inevitable for the lower-tier enemy without the assistance of another method.

Complex Terrain Conflict

The fifth method is to engage the higher-tech force in an urban environment. The demographics over the next thirty years point to an explosion in the size of large cities all over the world. This "urban sprawl" is the environment in which a high-tech force is the most vulnerable. The former head of the U.S. Army's Dismounted Battle Space Battle Lab worded it this way: "An urban fight degrades our sensor platforms, makes situational awareness more difficult, impedes our communications, degrades precision fires and takes away what we do best—maneuver warfare."[5]

Overhead imaging, precision munitions, and armor protection are all greatly reduced in the close confines of the city. Mogadishu, Somalia, is the single best example of this, but operations in Bosnia and Chechnya are further examples of this tactic. Within the confines of the city, the benefits of technology are significantly reduced.

The example of the explosion is one reason for this difference. The benefits and possibilities of future technologies are reserved for Chapter Nine, but let it suffice that, until greater technologies are invented and fielded, warfare within urban environments will remain a costly endeavor in terms of blood and treasure.

When a ground commander moves into an urban environment, the force is faced with ground direct fire danger in the entirety of three dimensions—not just to the left and right, forward and backward, but also up (multiple-story buildings) and down (sewers and subways). This places the heretofore most survivable systems at great risk. Tanks are notorious for relatively weak top armor. The extreme angle of engagement created by short engagement distances and higher threat areas means that many systems cannot engage within the confines of the city.

The previous difficulties are entirely military, but what about the political and moral difficulties of fighting in such close proximity to large civilian populations? Many of the civilians are certainly hostile. Intelligence gathering and terrorism are constant dangers. Security of the force is nightmarish without the extermination or removal of the nearby civilians. Hostile and nonhostile civilians are all potential collateral damage when an engagement eventually begins. This is a professional way to excuse the indiscriminate killing that will always take place in a war zone. The political and public-relations fallout is enormous, as demonstrated by Israeli military actions within Palestinian refugee communities in early 2002.

All these reasons combine to make this the perfect venue for a low-tier force.

Using Terrain

The sixth item is one that runs in conjunction with the previous five and is a larger discussion than the focus on complex terrain alone: engaging high-tech forces in severely restricted terrain. Only as a last resort will any future adversary attempt to engage U.S. forces in open terrain. The primary reason for this change is that in unrestricted terrain technology can have the full impact. This is why the U.S. military dominates the oceans and skies: the mitigating impact of terrain is nearly nonexistent in these areas.

The use of terrain is one of the oldest and most repeated dictums in the military profession. Sun Tzu stated the importance of terrain thousands of years ago when he included it among his "five fundamental factors"[6] and then summarized: "Know the enemy, know yourself; your victory will never be endangered. Know the ground, know the weather; your victory will then be complete."[7]

No military commander disregards the impact of terrain and is successful. The U.S. Army's most common and repeated acronym for assessing a situation includes terrain.[8] This is one of the few true constants of the military art. Terrain dominates the thinking of a ground commander almost as much as, and sometimes more than, the actual enemy. Success against higher-tier forces has always come through an effective use of terrain.

Attrition vs. Disintegration

The seventh item is the constant struggle between attrition and disintegration purposes of combat. Attrition is the method that attempts to achieve victory by grinding down the opponent. Pure attrition warfare is the ancient goal of not leaving a single enemy alive. Disintegration involves using various assets, including maneuver forces, to cause the breakup and collapse of the opposing force. Pure disintegration is winning a battle without firing a shot. The struggle between these two will be a constant trend that requires the United States to be able to fight both. Attrition and disintegration are inseparable; neither exists in its pure form, and success in either one requires the use of the other.

The best way to explain the difference between the two is to use the game of chess. Disintegration is the ability to place the opponent in checkmate with few losses. As the following clearly explains: "Imagine you've been beaten in a lightning round of chess by a highly-skilled and aggressive opponent. You wanted to play a defensive game to wear your opponent down while looking for openings to attack. The opponent, however, had other ideas and, seemingly, access to your thoughts. Your king, queen, bishops and knights were captured or neutralized in a series of swift, uncanny moves. Checkmate stared you in the face. Dazed and confused, you had but one choice: surrender."[9]

Even in this scenario, attrition is used in a limited fashion. The opponent has effectively removed other pieces of the set. What if a player achieved checkmate without any losses occurring? This is true disintegration. The accomplishment of checkmate with the loss of all pieces is pure attrition. Obviously, reality is somewhere in between. Ever since World War I, abhorrence of attrition warfare has been part of Western political and military training. Most developing nations do not necessarily share this view. The North Vietnamese willingness to suffer significant casualties in pursuit of its goals is an example.

It has already been identified that future low-tech opponents will use their large populations as a military resource. This allows for a form of attrition warfare that will essentially defeat high-tier nations through moral disintegration. The American people and political leaders are moving toward an extreme position where the loss of human life for anything other than national survival is unacceptable. Even during the recent battles in Afghanistan, after the Bush administration warned there would be casualties, there has been significant criticism over the loss of military personnel in combat. This gives a tremendous advantage to future opponents.

Burst vs. Protracted Conflict

The eighth item is truly all encompassing. It is the element of time. The increase in the most technologically advanced observation devices has effectively reduced time in the decision cycle. The decision cycle as communicated by Col. John Boyd comprises four components: observe, orient, decide, act.

Even with the shortening of the decision cycle, time has a dichotomous nature. Nations seeking to defeat a higher-tier force will move rapidly to seize objectives, typically within an urban sprawl, then consolidate the gains while the high-tech force deploys into theater. The other option is to operate an insurgent campaign that seeks to expand the campaign in an incremental fashion, and thereby never truly face the brunt of the high-tech force. Either technique seeks to extend the casualty-producing nature of the actual fight and dramatically increases the expense of the conflict.

Sun Tzu states: "A speedy victory is the main object in war. If this is long in coming, weapons are blunted and morale depressed. If troops are attacking cities, their strength will be exhausted. When the army engages in protracted campaigns, the resources of the state will fall short. When your weapons are dulled and ardor dampened, your strength exhausted and treasure spent, the chieftains of the neighboring states will take advantage of your crisis to act. In that case, no man, however wise, will be able to avert the disastrous consequences that ensue. Thus, while we have heard of stupid haste in war, we have not yet seen a clever operation that was prolonged. For there has never been a protracted war which benefited a country."[10]

The philosophy espoused by Sun Tzu is the philosophy of the U.S. government. In fact, it has been stated in proposed future doctrine: "The cost of war to modern societies is such that military campaigns will not be undertaken unless the result can be quick and decisive. Only short and decisive campaigns will be considered 'winning' ones."[11]

Future and past American adversaries have understood this as well. The following is an example of North Vietnamese thinking on American national patience: "According to Truong Chin, the pre-eminent North Vietnamese theoretician, 'The guiding principle of the strategy of our whole resistance must be to prolong the war.' This would lower enemy morale, unite the North Vietnamese people, increase outside support, and encourage the antiwar movement to tie the enemy's hands. 'To achieve all these results, the war must be prolonged, and we must have time. Time works for us.' This strategy worked against the French and, with time, it would be effective against the Americans."[12]

No benefit from protracted war is true from a wealthy industrialized nation's viewpoint, but this is not true from that of a severely disadvantaged and poor nation with a large disenfranchised population. These nations, like the North Vietnamese, see protracted conflict as a means to achieve victory against those nations that follow Sun Tzu's dictum. Time is the single greatest weapon a nation or any entity can use against the United States or any high-tier nation at the grand strategy level.

The unique nature of time is that at the technical, tactical, and operational level of strategy, time of conflict needs to be as short as possible for the lower-tier force, with a few exceptions. For example, it is worthwhile to have a tank sit a long time, with its engine running, to diminish the fuel, then attack the logistics as they come to resupply. The tank can be dealt with in turn. However, if the tank is attacked directly, it must be reduced as quickly as possible to deny the use of the superior firepower. This technical strategy level example portrays a concept that is true across the tactical and operational strategy levels as well.

Lower-tier nations will constantly seek to achieve dominance in this fashion: rapid strikes against the American center of gravity at the technical, tactical, and operational levels—logistics—and extending the length of the conflict at the theater and grand strategy levels to attack the center of gravity at those levels—American national will.

Conclusion

Each of the following five chapters explains in a tactical-level case study the dynamics of the first five methods. Within all the case studies, the sixth, seventh, and eighth methods are discussed as a common thread. The following are the case studies and the method emphasized:

Chapter Three: Battle of Hill 219 (Korean War) mass human wave assaults.
Chapter Four: Battle of LZ Albany (Vietnam War) closing with high-tier forces.
Chapter Five: Battle of Goose Green (Falkland Islands War) extending to extreme of power projection capability.

Chapter Six: Battle of 73 Easting (Operation Desert Storm)—
conventional engagement.
Chapter Seven: Battle of Mogadishu (Operation Restore
Hope)—complex terrain conflict.

The case studies give a complete battle analysis of the engagement. The battle analysis discusses each level of strategy to define
the context, identifies the key personnel with a short biographical
notation, explains the terrain and weather constraints, and includes
a brief narrative description of the tactical level of strategy. The analysis concludes with a discussion of the framework discussed previously—identification, isolation, suppression, maneuver, and destruction—and lessons learned about the impact of leadership and
training.

Chapter Three

Battle Analysis: The Battle of Hill 219
Korean War, 25–26 November 1950

The battle of Hill 219 is a demonstration of one of the primary means that lower-tier nations use to fight and defeat higher-tier nations: overwhelming the superior firepower and technology with the use of mass human wave attacks. The use of these human waves is a result of a nation's using the most functional resource available. Human beings in combat are the lowest common denominator. When everything else fails, the human with a will to fight and die is the reason why battles are won and lost.

The Korean War is a demonstration of human wave tactics used against U.S. forces at the tactical level of strategy. Early in the Chinese Communist forces (CCF) intervention, the CCF used maneuver warfare at the operational strategy level. Later, as the terrain became less restricted, they turned to the use of human wave assaults as the basic strategy from the operational level and below. The Iranian army demonstrated this tactic to an even greater extent against the Iraqi army in the 1980s; however, the differences in the use of technology between Iran and Iraq were not as significant as the differences between the armies of the CCF and the United States.

The Korean War featured a tier-three force (China) pitted against a tier-two power (the United States) in rugged, mountainous terrain. The CCF came into Korea following the recent completion of their own civil war, which resulted in the ousting of Chiang Kai-shek and his Chinese Nationalist forces to the island of Formosa. Now, in an effort to demonstrate its newfound national power, the People's Republic of China (PRC) began to flex its international muscle. A great many warnings were issued about the advance of the United Nations forces into North Korea. For the most part, these warnings were initially ignored, mostly because no direct diplomatic channel existed between the United States and the PRC. They were also discounted because the CCF had little equipment and even less technologically advanced equipment.

The discussion here is focused primarily on a single engagement in the Korean War. No battle can be completely isolated from those of surrounding units, but the battle of Hill 219 demonstrates in a nearly isolated context the struggles of the cross-tier conflict in microcosm. These are the struggles to understand terrain, the difficulties in logistical support, the failure to coordinate massive firepower, and the lack of preparation by the higher-tier forces. These issues were faced and overcome through the loss of soldiers' lives on Hill 219. The lower-tier force faced the difficulties of coordinated attacks and seizing opportunities for exploitation. This resulted in a complete, though not overwhelming, victory that led to a more significant victory in the attack on the withdrawing UN column.

The attack on these columns was the end result of all the success. The CCF forced a stampede, then killed the cattle as they went through a chute. The attacks on the Republic of Korea (ROK) units, then the success against the 2d Infantry and 1st Cavalry Divisions led to, first, a shift from the offense to a consolidation, then to a withdrawal, and finally to a complete retreat. The resulting retreat had units traveling through a narrow pass where the CCF effectively closed the exit to the pass and caused a significant amount of carnage as each unit ran a gauntlet of direct fire in the hopes of escaping. This retreat is beyond the scope of this chapter but must be understood in order to gauge the larger results of what is to be described on the slopes of Hill 219.

In the discussion of future conflict, this battle paints a vivid picture of the dangers faced by a higher-tier force when they extend beyond its ability to understand the conflict. The current technological reliances are even more area focused. What this means is that the communications architecture needed to support the most advanced information-age systems is confined to a footprint defined by the limits of various signal nodes. Once an element moves outside the footprint, the benefits of the system are nonapplicable, because the system no longer exists. Eighth Army had moved beyond the boundaries of its "information-age" web in November 1950.

This chapter makes many references to S. L. A. Marshall's book *The River and the Gauntlet,* the one book that focuses on the engagement at the company level. It is widely recognized as the definitive work done on this portion of the Korean War. Additionally, this chapter discusses racial issues. The Korean War began with a segregated American army and ended with an integrated one. The battle of Hill 219 encompasses some of the best qualities of this integration. This is one of the few times in this book that racial issues are mentioned.

Geographical Setting

Location

To understand the dynamics of this particular engagement, the reader needs to understand the geography and terrain. Following the successful Inchon landing and the breakout from the Pusan perimeter, the UN forces crossed the thirty-eighth parallel in fall 1950 and entered North Korea in pursuit of the fleeing North Korean People's Army (NKPA) with the intent of reunifying the Korean peninsula. When the UN forces did this, they also entered a more rugged phase of the campaign. The terrain increases in relief northward along the peninsula. The mountain ranges run essentially north-south. This provides relatively good mobility moving north but poor east-west lines of supply and communications. The Chongch'on River is one of the few rivers that runs east for any significant distance before turning north. It is along this river, deep in the country of North Korea, that this engagement took place. Hill 219 is one of an innumerable host of hills that stretches along the Chongch'on River. Most rise higher than 219 meters. The hill is situated on the east side of the river, less than a mile north of a small village called Sinhung-dong and more than sixty miles north-northeast of the North Korean capital of Pyongyang. The hill was of little consequence in and of itself, but it was a place where the CCF was identified. As in most of the battles during the Korean War, the control of the hills and ridges was the key to success.

Terrain/Vegetation

The terrain around the Chongch'on River is a rugged collection of rolling hills and folded ground, with sharp cliffs and sloping sides as well. The hills are sparsely covered with low scrub brush. The hill itself has two summits. A soldier approaching from the west would encounter the lower summit first, then a saddle with a small copse of trees, followed by the hill's primary summit. On the south side of Hill 219, the slope is essentially a cliff. On the west was the primary road, on which the attached tanks and quad-50s were located. Most of the tank fires were masked by another low-lying hill that lay between Hill 219 and the road.[1]

Weather

The weather in November 1950 was consistently below freezing. The temperatures on the night of the battle were in the teens. The windchill factor was below zero. This had a significant impact on the technology of the U.S. Army, specifically its equipment and weapons. For example, vehicles failed to start, mortar base plates cracked during recoil, radio effectiveness was significantly reduced, and submachine guns had difficulties in cycling.[2] Prior to the attack, many soldiers had discarded their steel helmets in favor of the cold-weather pile cap. The pile cap prevented frostbite but was extremely uncomfortable to wear underneath the steel helmet.[3] Soldiers also were on watch while partially in their sleeping bags.[4]

Units Involved

American Forces

The primary unit involved in this battle analysis is B Company, 1st Battalion, 9th Infantry Regiment of the U.S. 2d Infantry Division; it consisted of 129 personnel. B Company began the war as an all-white unit as part of the American army's segregation policy. Informally, commanders within the Korean theater of operations began to desegregate the regiments. B Company was one of the units that became integrated. When the battle began, the unit was 30 percent black, 60 percent white, and 10 percent Republic of Korea (ROK) troops. This integration was carried over to the officer arena, where a white commander was supported by a black executive officer.[5]

B Company began its offense from the Pusan perimeter and had been moving north ever since. The unit's time in country had fostered a battle-hardened mentality that would be evident during the battle, but it had also created complacency about the quality of the opposition and the discipline needed to achieve victory. The unit had been moving north for several weeks, and the soldiers were taking expediency to the limit that only a soldier would push. They discarded helmets and entrenching tools; only two soldiers carried bayonets. The average on the day of the battle was less than one grenade per person, and most had fewer than thirty rounds of ammunition for their rifles. The platoon and squad radios had been destroyed when one of the supply trailers rolled over a few days previously. In short, the unit was unprepared for a long fight.[6]

Within the company was the organic mortar section that traveled as part of the 4th Platoon. The company was also given the assistance of four tanks and two quad-50s. The quad-50 was designed to serve as an antiaircraft weapon. During the fighting in the Pusan perimeter, the Americans began to appreciate what the four .50-caliber barrels could do to massed waves of infantry attacking prepared defenses. The lack of NKPA or CCF airpower turned the weapon to one of almost exclusive ground support. Typically the four-barrel turret was mounted on the back of an M2 half-track of World War II fame. Despite the firepower represented by the tanks and quad-50s, the company fought at Hill 219 as unsupported infantry. The terrain and positioning of the assets conspired to reduce the effectiveness of the more powerful weapons systems to practically nil. During the course of the battle, a close air support napalm strike proved extremely useful, but few other nonorganic fires were involved.[7]

Chinese Communist Forces (CCF)

The CCF had approximately one understrength company (unknown number, but estimated at approximately fifty soldiers) defending Hill 219 at the beginning of the attack. This was reinforced by elements of the 13th People's Army,[8] estimated at about a battalion or more. The specific units are not known. The disposition during the initial defense was one understrength platoon with machine guns in the copse of trees in and around the saddle. Additionally, there was probably more than a platoon positioned on the summit with effective fires covering much of the intervening ridgeline. Most of this is deductive analysis rather than conclusive fact. During the attack on the night of 25 November 1950, approximately a battalion attacked from the north through the saddle and against the main defensive strongpoint. A secondary attack of approximately eighty personnel or an understrength company attacked from the southwest against the lesser strongpoint.[9]

Key Leaders in the Battle

American Forces[10]

- Capt. William C. Wallace—commanding officer of B Company, 1st Battalion, 9th Infantry Regiment, 2d U.S. Infantry Division. He was injured early in the attack and self-evacuated to the supply column, where he was ordered to the battalion aid station. While he was at the aid station, it was attacked, and he led a makeshift group of patients and medical personnel in defense of the position. He was awarded the Distinguished Service Cross for his actions.
- 1st Lt. Ellison C. Wynn—executive officer of B Company, 1st Battalion, 9th Infantry Regiment. A black officer whose actions during the course of the battle would result in his receiving the Distinguished Service Cross.

Grand and Theater Context

Grand Strategy

Decisions in war are not always the most clearly understood later, yet they nearly always make perfect sense at the time. In particular, this statement applies to the decision to cross the thirty-eighth parallel during the advance to the north in late 1950. The UN forces were conducting a pursuit operation as the NKPA fled north. No one seemed to be concerned with the rising volume of criticism of UN action coming from the new People's Republic of China (PRC). Most attributed this criticism to a flexing of political muscle and an attempt to gain relevance within the region. PRC support of the NKPA was not even seriously considered. Even if the UN member nations who were contributing forces to the conflict had called for a stop and prevented their militaries from crossing the parallel, the ROK army would have crossed anyway:

> Regardless of whether the UN forces did or did not cross the 38th Parallel, there was always the strong probability that the ROK troops would. Syngman Rhee had often stated his intention of halting the South Korean Army only at the Yalu. Speaking at a mass meeting at Pusan on 19 September he said, "We have to advance as far as the Manchurian border until not a single enemy soldier is left in our country." He said that he did not expect the UN forces to stop at the 38th Parallel, but if they did, he continued, "we will not allow ourselves to stop." And stop the ROK troops did not.[11]

Intervention by China was dismissed at virtually all levels of the conflict—from tactical strategy through the grand strategy levels and including the international community. Most thought the PRC would become involved if the UN violated the sovereign territory of the nation. In retrospect, the CCF crossed into North Korea one week after the UN forces crossed the parallel.[12] General of the Army Douglas MacArthur consistently discounted the intervention of the CCF even after the late October CCF offensive. He, backed by his key staff officers, painted the intervention as simply a few volunteer units totaling not more than 30,000 to 40,000. This was significantly different from the actual force in country—by late October, the CCF had more than 350,000 forces in North Korea—and these represented significant combat power; the ratio of combat elements to support elements was much higher in the CCF than in the UN forces.

Theater Strategy

Following the landings at Inchon, it was expected that X Corps would be brought under the control of Eighth Army. Instead, General of the Army MacArthur retained X Corps under his direct control. The Eighth Army units, tired from the pursuit up the peninsula, were told to continue the attack north, while the X Corps units were reloaded onto ships and moved around the other side of the peninsula to make a second amphibious landing. Neither of the two major formations received enough supplies to complete the assault without exceeding their logistical support. The Eighth Army, in particular, was ill equipped for the rigors of a Korean winter. This lack of logistical support would prove critical in the upcoming events.

Time Line

Date	Event
8 Oct	Eighth Army crosses the 38th Parallel
19 Oct	Eighth Army forces capture Pyongyang
26 Oct	Reconnaissance Platoon, 7th Regiment, ROK 6th Division reaches the Yalu River
25 Oct–1 Nov	CCF elements counterattack II ROK Corps
24 Nov	Eighth Army begins the attack

Source: Roy E. Appleman, *South to the Naktong, North to the Yalu (June-November 1950), United States Army in the Korean War* (Washington, D.C.: Center of Military History Press, 1956).

The UN forces continued a drive north, designed to return the entire peninsula to a unified country. This drive was conducted in a headlong rush for the Yalu River that at times was more a race than an organized military operation. The drive to the Yalu River was conducted as a pursuit operation, with little thought for security and very little conservative thinking. Every commander was pressing to reach the border and end the war. This attitude filtered down to all levels of the command. Logistic stockpiles were not available north of

Seoul, and there was no significant airfield north of Kimpo airfield, also near Seoul. Soldiers discarded equipment as they moved north. Helmets, made of steel and very heavy, and considered of little use during the chase, were tossed to the side to lighten the load. These attitudes would have a significant impact in November.

The exploits of the 7th Regiment of the ROK 6th Division are evidence of this. The regiment raced along a branch road from the main Chongch'on valley and encamped in an assembly area, then sent its reconnaissance platoon the next morning into the Yalu River valley. It was dozens of miles forward of the rest of the division and completely out of physical contact with any other friendly element. To rejoin its division required fighting through CCF roadblocks.

The mad dash for the Yalu River by the UN forces was halted by the CCF offensive that began on 25 October. The CCF were of a completely different mind-set. They were moving into the Korean peninsula to meet and destroy the Western forces and establish a united Korea under northern control. The armies moved in quietly at night, using sunken bridges across the Yalu River to avoid detection by American reconnaissance aircraft. They sought to occupy a series of concentration areas where they would be able to effectively defeat the attacking UN forces. The infiltration and staging techniques were selected specifically to defeat the UN air and technological superiority.

A combination of attacks by at least four CCF armies crushed the II ROK Corps and badly mauled several U.S. regiments. Even with captured prisoners who identified their parent units, the primary intelligence officers failed to recognize the signs of major intervention. An I Corps estimate from 30 October 1950 states, "There are no indications at this time to confirm the existence of a CCF organization or unit, of any size, on Korean soil."[13]

This was to change over the next six days to indicate CCF totaling approximately two regiments' worth.[14] The estimates would rise as high as 70,000 by intelligence analysts in Washington, D.C., but never near the real figures. United States intelligence and commanders were seeing what they wanted and expected to see. Western armies fought in a manner similar to that of the U.S. Army, so all opponents were evaluated using a common model. The CCF used a completely different model and were therefore able to move into the area of operations completely undetected. They used a doctrinal and ideological cloaking device.

Following the late October and early November fighting, there was a period of nearly three weeks of silence from the CCF. This tended to confirm the reports by most of the analysts that pointed at the CCF conducting a delaying action to allow the NKPA forces time to redeploy across the Yalu into Manchuria. During this time the II ROK Corps was provided replacements but no significant American augmentation. The X Corps to the east was beginning its attack north through the Chosin Reservoir and toward the Yalu. Eighth Army was about to begin its expected final attack to end the war before Christmas. The day prior to the attack, General of the Army MacArthur visited the peninsula, then gave the following comments to reporters:

> The three-week air offensive, he said, had isolated the battlefield and had "sharply curtailed" CCF manpower reinforcements and "markedly limited" the flow of supplies. After a series of "brilliant" maneuvers the "eastern sector" of his forces (X Corps) was now in a "commanding envelopment position" for "cutting in two the northern reaches of the enemy's geographical potential." The "western sector" (Eighth Army) of the "pincer" moves forward "this morning" in a "general assault in an effort to complete the compression and close the vise." He added: "If successful this should for all practical purposes end the war. . . ."[15]

Now the CCF commanders and the rest of the world were aware of the UN plan of operation. The attack was one that was doomed to failure by a lack of understanding of the data collected and the poor operational security by the theater commander.

Operational Context

The defeat of the 8th Cavalry Regiment of the U.S. 1st Cavalry Division during late October forced the Eighth Army to reach self-awareness in November 1950. There was more and more word that the Chinese would intervene. Lieutenant General Walton H. Walker developed a significant concern over the possibility of Chinese intervention as he viewed the icons on his battle map; they showed his army spread in an almost haphazard fashion. This resulted in a series of orders that were designed to bring the army back into a relatively traditional front with greater security. This initially brought most units back to the Chongch'on River. Despite Walker's caution, he was being directed to continue the attack north. He did so with I and IX U.S. Corps and II ROK Corps essentially attacking abreast. The newly arrived Commonwealth Brigade and 1st Cavalry Division were in army reserve. Within the IX Corps, the 25th and 2d Infantry Divisions attacked with five assault units. Initially, only slight or in many places no resistance was reported.[16] It was on the second day of the offensive when the resistance began to be heavy, and where the tactical portion of this chapter begins, with the 9th and 38th Regiments attacking abreast. B Company of the 9th Regiment had the lead and would be the first to be engaged.

The attack on 24 November would proceed only a few miles before the second CCF offensive would force the American and ROK forces into a disorganized retreat. This eventually resulted in the loss of millions of tons of equipment and thousands of American lives and would not stop until the army commander died in a car crash and the UN forces had once again lost possession of the South Korean capital.

Technical Context

The technical aspects, or rather the lack of technical aspects, of this battle are the most interesting. The most advanced army in the world was brought face-to-face with mortality by a "peasant" army. The soldiers of the CCF were poorly equipped; most used old weapons, and some had no weapons at all but waited for a comrade to fall, when they would retrieve the fallen weapon. These soldiers did not use advanced communications gear but instead utilized the oldest forms of battlefield command and control, the bugle or horn. These ancient means of fighting were in direct contrast to the advanced weaponry of the American soldier.

Despite the fact the American unit had tanks and quad-50s in support, these weapons played no significant role. The terrain made the use of such road-bound fire support nearly worthless. The fires were trapped on or near the roads while the battle raged on the hillsides.

In addition to the difficulties of using the more powerful fire support was the failure to utilize the other equipment provided. Most of the radios were either left behind or nonfunctional. The only means the Americans had to communicate was sending couriers back and forth. This lowered the American battle command to a level beneath the bugles of the Chinese.

American forces also suffered from the cold, because few had received the winter equipment being shipped from the United States. The Chinese forces, however, had a quilted coat and basic necessities to allow them to survive the cold weather, plus a familiarity with the harsh climate. The very nature of struggling through the weather and being a prisoner to the whims of nature seemed to flout the idea of a modern army's conquering the basics.

Tactical Chronology[17]

The order was received to move to and occupy Hill 219 to establish a portion of the regimental defensive line. The company moved up the hill with two platoons forward and one back, and a lead squad as the point element. At the lower knoll the lead platoon received a hail of grenades, and the soldiers farther away received rifle fire. Both platoons hit the ground. The company commander ordered his unit forward, trying to get the men to reduce the enemy position. As soon as soldiers crested the knoll, they received machine-gun fire from the small copse of trees in the saddle. As elements of the platoons attempted to work around the knoll, they were engaged and took casualties. The company commander leaped forward to lead a charge but was forced to the ground, where he was seriously wounded by a grenade blast that impacted close to his face. The commander was forced to withdraw, leaving his executive officer (XO) in charge.

Once on the ground near the tank column, the commander was informed for the first time that his 3d Platoon had also been in contact on the north of Hill 219. The 3d Platoon, led by a brand-new lieutenant, had conducted fire and maneuver up the side of the hill. As the men conducted this drill, they expended rounds, suppressing a nonexistent enemy. Once they arrived at the enemy trench line, they were almost completely out of ammunition. The platoon leader had his unit withdraw to replenish the ammunition and grenade supplies. The 3d Platoon returned to attack along the same route, this time with quad-50 support the majority of the way. The CCF had met them earlier on the slope. After a hail of grenades and gunfire, several enemy appeared with their hands upraised. A Chinese-speaking member of the platoon called for the Chinese forces to come down, but the platoon was instead greeted with more grenades. Eventually the 3d Platoon was forced to withdraw. The commander was going to send them back up again, but one of the soldiers stated that it would be suicide, so the commander had them reinforce the 1st and 2d Platoons.

The battalion operations officer ordered the company commander to the battalion aid station. The executive officer (XO) became the ranking person in the company and continued the attack.

First and 2d Platoons continued their duel on the hill. Each time they tried to silence the machine gun in the copse, something seemed to delay their attack. The company consolidated its positions on the lesser summit and a small knoll about 120 meters to the west. More ammunition and hot food were brought forward as they consolidated.

During the night the temperature dropped to about fifteen degrees Fahrenheit. Soldiers crawled partway into their sleeping bags for warmth. Others simply huddled in their shallow foxholes to avoid the extreme cold. One of the soldiers awake saw a figure approaching who was identified as a Chinese soldier, and they opened fire. This engagement would last until dawn. The small knoll was attacked by a rifle company equivalent, and the men were rapidly forced away from the mortar positions and their foxholes. About fourteen riflemen fought to another position. These fourteen would hold off the attacking company for the rest of the night. Several would spend much of the night throwing back enemy grenades that rolled near their positions.

The lesser summit was also being attacked, this one from the north. A battalion's worth of infantry (estimated at five hundred to six hundred soldiers) was attacking less than half of a company (approximately fifty soldiers). The American soldiers struggled to defend the high ground, mostly with rifle fire and grenades. This struggle continued all night. Eventually soldiers used the bodies of the enemy to form an additional protective wall. During the course of the fight, those on the smaller position nearly ran out of ammunition, until one soldier crawled up to the rest of the company and brought back a box of grenades. Despite its isolation, the smaller position actually enjoyed greater success. At dawn the enemy forces withdrew, leaving the fourteen victorious.

The higher position was being completely overwhelmed, though. The XO called for a fighting withdrawal to the lower position. The XO offered to cover the withdrawal by throwing rocks and food tins. Another soldier remained, using his rifle as a club. During this displacement, the XO was wounded by a grenade that detonated close to his face. Despite the pain he was able to evacuate himself. This allowed the displacement and the linkup between the two forces. Once together, the soldiers used their reclaimed mortars to prevent enemy machine-gun occupation of the small crest. Close air support dropped canisters of napalm, rockets, and machine-gun fire near the machine-gun position and the hilltop.

This silenced the majority of the opposition, yet still enough remained to prevent the seizing of the hill. Finally the limited ammunition was nearly gone, and regiment ordered the American forces to leave Hill 219. Once down they were ordered to the rear; the entire regiment was to begin the first steps in a withdrawal that would take them from north of the North Korean capital to south of the South Korean one.

Time Line[18]

Date	Time	Event
25 Nov 1950	1015	B Company begins attack on Hill 219
	1030	Initial contact with Chinese forces
		Capt. Wallace injured; 1st Lt. Wynn takes command
	1600	3d Platoon sent by Capt. Wallace to support main defensive position
26 Nov 1950	0400	CCF elements attack both defensive perimeters
	0700	Lesser summit abandoned
	0930	Close air support strike against lesser summit
	1300	B Company ordered off Hill 219

Battlefield Leadership

The battle of Hill 219 was a struggle in the classic movie genre. A small group of Americans is severely outnumbered and nearly annihilated; yet through bravery and courage the men endure until the arrival of the cavalry drives off the attackers. With the exception of the cavalry, this battle fits the melodramatic model rather closely. The fact that the American army began the longest retreat in its history would forever reduce this battle and the Korean War in general to relative obscurity. Despite this obscurity, there are some tremendous examples of leadership.

The first of these events is the transition between company commander and executive officer. When the commander left the field of battle, the unit did not waver or collapse. In fact, it continued for more than twelve hours against overwhelming odds. This is despite the fact that this newly integrated unit had an African-American executive officer. In a war when the color of skin within American units seemed to have rather significant impacts on unit cohesion, in this case there was no issue whatsoever. Lieutenant Wynn led and the company followed without hesitation.

The second event occurred at very close interval to the first. This was the decision by the wounded commander to redeploy 3d Platoon in support of the rest of the company. The redeployment would consolidate all elements under a single commander in an environment without radios.

The third event was the attempts to resupply ammunition, both from outside the company position and from within the position. Had this not happened, the entire element would have become completely overwhelmed.

The fourth situation occurred during the withdrawal. The move by Lieutenant Wynn to support the withdrawal by throwing rocks was completely unexpected and therefore successful. He was able to bring off the hill the remainder of his command.

Significance

The defeat of the American forces along the Chongch'on River and the intervention of Chinese forces was to change the context of conflict in Asia from that moment to the present. The Chinese were in the war in force, and all the questions about intervention were clearly answered. An overwhelming number of personnel entered the fight creating a perception of fighting a wave of humanity that was impossible to hold back. A malaise of defeatism and pessimism entered the American camp during this withdrawal. This would not be corrected until the death of the army commander, General Walker, and his replacement with Gen. Matthew B. Ridgway. At this point, the U.S. Eighth Army had been forced south of Seoul, and commanders were talking about a withdrawal from the peninsula. General Ridgway conducted a series of visits and gave clear, direct guidance about how the army needed to fight in this environment. His drive to look for opportunities for the offense and his dynamic personality were able to eventually change the attitude of the entire Eighth Army.[19]

The battles that followed Hill 219 were carnage created by the panic of the initial Chinese assaults. American and allied units were caught on the roads, trying to move through narrow choke points, while the dismounted Chinese moved along the ridgelines to get behind the forces and cut off their retreat. Numerous bloody battles resulted as logistics and medical units were caught without sufficient protection. These gauntlets went a long way toward creating the defeatism.

Hill 219 was a relatively small part of this greater loss. It has been made even smaller by the sheer numbers of other units engaged and lost during that night of battle. Despite the size of the engagement, Hill 219 is a microcosm of the challenges that future ground commanders face against the techniques that lower-technology forces will use.

Lessons Learned

The lessons from Hill 219 are among the most important and basic of all the battles studied. This battle demonstrated ways that the higher-tier nation will lower itself and how the lower-tier nation will attempt to even the future battlefield.

Identification: At no time did B Company truly understand the enemy force it was fighting. This was a failure of intelligence from tactical strategy to grand strategy. Even after the initial CCF attacks in October 1950, the UN and U.S. forces were unwilling to refocus their reconnaissance assets to identify the threat. The apparent reason was a lack of understanding of the enemy and the tactics and techniques they would employ as they sought victory. The intelligence officers within the U.S. Eighth Army would probably say they were looking for the Chinese. They directed reconnaissance flights over the north of the peninsula, and there was interrogation of prisoners; however, even when faced with information that ran contrary to their estimates, no one changed his estimate in any significant fashion. The challenge is to understand the enemy and to understand the methods they will employ in their attempts to defeat the higher-tier force.

Isolation: B Company and the 9th Infantry Regiment were unable to isolate the forces on Hill 219. The company there was reinforced with a battalion or more. The infiltration tactics used by the CCF carried from tactical to theater strategy. At no time was the U.S. Eighth Army able to isolate the battlefield. At the theater level, Eighth Army and the Far East Air Force failed to isolate the peninsula. At the operational level, Eighth Army and X Corps failed to isolate the area of operations that they were attacking through. This allowed the CCF to move at will during this offensive.

Suppression: The tactics used by the CCF denied effective suppression beyond the tactical level. In this battle the poor placement of fire support assets combined with the challenging terrain ensured limited suppression at the tactical or technical levels as well.

Maneuver: B Company did not achieve a position of advantage at any time in the attack. Only when the CCF attack occurred did the knoll and small hilltop function effectively as a position of advantage. Above the local engagement, the Eighth Army was denied bold maneuver by the lack of understanding of the enemy's tactics.

Destruction: Failure to understand the enemy, their techniques, and their objective resulted in Eighth Army being completely unprepared and unable to destroy the CCF. Failure of the company to accomplish effectively any of the preceding four elements ensured that B Company would not be able to destroy the enemy. The company fought from disadvantageous positions throughout the day, then changed to fighting for survival all night as the CCF attack nearly overwhelmed its positions.

Conclusion

Hill 219 was a testament to arrogance and false pride. The failures of the intelligence community to inform and prepare the fighting units resulted in one of the greatest success stories in the history of cross-tier struggles. The most advanced nation on Earth was caught completely off guard by a peasant army, which drove it back several hundred miles. The use of the oldest techniques to successfully elude the high-tech gadgetry of the West is a great lesson for high-tech nations in the future.

The Chinese used the terrain to their extreme advantage. American forces were interested in bridges, fords, and roads, not in the valleys and ridges far from these major transportation networks. This allowed the completely dismounted Chinese army a sanctuary within a few miles of the route of advance. Today there are many more assets available to the U.S. Forces Commander, Korea; yet the fact is that the intelligence assets of today still cannot look everywhere. A potential adversary needs to be able to move where the high-tech force will not, and therefore the odds are in favor of the high-tech force not looking there. The use of terrain is an integral part of success of any lower-tier force against a higher-tier one.

The failure of strategic air campaigns to isolate and destroy the enemy forces—they could not even identify them—was a fact that seems to be both obvious and intangible at the same time. In predictable cycles, Americans become enamored with the idea of destroying an enemy from hundreds of miles away or from thousands of feet:

> Americans in 1950 rediscovered something that since Hiroshima they had forgotten: you may fly over a land forever; you may bomb it, atomize it, pulverize it and wipe it clean of life—but if you desire to defend it, protect it, and keep it for civi-

lization, you must do this on the ground, the way the Roman legions did, by putting your young men into the mud.[20]

In addition to the effective use of terrain, the lower-tier force also sought to use sheer weight of numbers to defeat the greater weapons capabilities. In this case, the tactic was virtually a complete success. The forces were able to destroy the majority of the company and push them off the entire hill. That the company made a fighting withdrawal does not negate the fact that it still lost possession of the terrain. This tactic was to prove useful throughout the entire theater, until the terrain changed to being more open and the use of advanced firepower was able to be used to full effect.

Chapter Four
Battle Analysis: The Battle of LZ Albany
Vietnam War, 17 November 1965

The battle of Landing Zone (LZ) Albany from the Vietnam War demonstrates one of the tactics that lower-tier militaries use to defeat a higher-tier force. In this particular case, the lower-tier force closed with the higher-tier force to negate the effective use of the mass casualty-producing firepower. This technique proved successful; the American force suffered significant casualties, which demonstrated the tactic that would dominate the majority of the conflict in Southeast Asia. The Vietnam War is the classic cross-tier conflict between a tier-two nation (the United States) and a tier-three/-four nation (Democratic Republic of Vietnam)[1] in a guerrilla war that the United States was trying to make conventional. The very nature of this cross-tier conflict was such that it was a soldier's war, meaning that it was fought on a one-on-one basis because of the terrain and the tactics utilized by the North Vietnamese Army (NVA). The battle of LZ Albany reflects this extremely personal aspect of war.

When discussing this battle, it is nearly impossible to separate it from the other battle of the Ia Drang valley operation, LZ X-Ray; a brief discussion of LZ X-Ray is included in this analysis. The focus of the chapter is on the experiences of 2d Battalion, 7th U.S. Cavalry (2-7 Cav), and the individual soldiers who fought. Additionally, this discussion describes the thought process of the North Vietnamese commanders in planning the strategy for fighting the American force in the first large battle of the American portion of the war. The entire struggle of the Vietnamese military is about how a lower-tier force seeks to gain advantage over a higher-tier force. The advantages were gained primarily by the use of terrain and guerrilla tactics at the lowest levels.

No discussion of the battles in the Ia Drang valley is possible without extensive references to the writings of Harold Moore and Joe Galloway. Harold Moore was the battalion commander of the 1st Battalion, 7th U.S. Cavalry (1-7 Cav). It was his battalion that successfully fought at LZ X-Ray. Joe Galloway was a United Press International correspondent who was also present at LZ X-Ray. These men cowrote a book about the battles in the valley, and a series of articles and after-action reports. Most of this chapter is written through their words, because there are virtually no other significant sources available. This gives a somewhat skewed view; however, Moore and Galloway do provide tremendous detail and description.

Landing Zone Albany provides insights about severely restricted terrain combat. The majority of writings today focus on future battles conducted where the full brunt of American technology can impact the battlefield. Yet this is probably not reality. A former commandant of the Marine Corps states, "I am not going to fight the son of Desert Storm."[2] The jungles of Vietnam conspire against the use of precision weapons and satellite imagery. Soldiers and scholars need to understand these facts to better appreciate the potential future of war.

Geographical Setting

Location

The Ia Drang valley runs east-west toward the Cambodian border in the Vietnamese highlands. This was a major staging ground for the NVA because of its proximity to the border and the relative protection this provided against the American army. The landscape is relatively rugged, with almost no roads throughout the majority of the highlands region. The lack of roads prevented American (and, previously, French) entrance to the area. The U.S. operational concept was to utilize the newly developed doctrine and practice of vertical envelopment through the use of airmobile infantry. The ability to vertically envelop a force allowed for the introduction of military forces to oppose NVA operations and essentially end "safe havens" within the borders of South Vietnam.

The difficulty in execution of airmobility was the need for landing zones (LZs) or places where helicopters could set down to disgorge their occupants. In the Ia Drang valley there were six such locations. These LZs needed to be clearings with relatively limited obstructions. One of the possible LZs could accommodate only two helicopters at a time; another was covered with stumps, making any landing too unsafe to attempt. Another—designated LZ X-Ray—was used for the landing of 1-7 Cav for the fight on 14 and 15 November. Yet another, designated LZ Falcon, was used by the field artillery battery that supported the LZ X-Ray fight. The fifth was LZ Columbus, where 2d Battalion, 5th U.S. Cavalry (2-5 Cav), a supporting participant at LZ X-Ray, was being extracted. The sixth, LZ Albany, was where 2-7 Cav was supposed to link up with its aviation support and be returned to the rear.

Terrain/Vegetation

As 2-7 Cav moved from the relatively clear area in and around LZ X-Ray, it entered the jungle of the Vietnamese highlands. This was initially relatively clear with low grass and trees. As the battalion turned off 2-5 Cav's route and headed toward LZ Albany, the grass became thicker and higher and there were many felled trees. The restrictive terrain forced a battalion column nearly six hundred meters long. As the men continued, "The elephant grass was chest high, the vegetation was greener and thicker, and the trees higher."[3] Near Albany the vegetation became even thicker, forcing the formation tighter and the security elements even closer. Landing Zone Albany was identified as a clearing big enough for one helicopter yet was also described as being as big as a football field. It was in fact two clearings separated by a few trees. The battle took place near the edge of the first clearing. In addition to the elephant grass, there were large termite mounds and anthills dotting the terrain. These hills could be as high as eight feet tall and several feet thick—more than enough to conceal a person. This terrain so constricted the American forces that the flank security elements were driven closer and closer to the main body. This happened to such a degree as to completely negate any effective security—meaning early warning— from these flank security elements. The terrain, in fact, made the surprise attack possible.

Weather

The weather in November 1965 was extremely hot and humid. The heat and humidity sapped energy reserves and played a significant role in fatigue; this in turn increased the breakdown in individual discipline, which led to the NVA success. Some of the soldiers had been on 100 percent alert for more than fifty-two hours. This prompted commanders to direct the use of aspirin with caffeine tablets to increase alertness.[4]

Units Involved

American Forces

The primary unit was the 2d Battalion (Infantry), 7th U.S. Cavalry. This is a unit whose distinguished history dated back to the post–Civil War expansion of the cavalry in 1866 and continued through World War II and Korea. During the early 1960s the army sought to develop a way to utilize the helicopter to assist infantrymen in mobility and to free soldiers from the constraints of terrain. This concept was developed using a test division, which was renamed the 1st Cavalry Division upon the completion of the test phase. Vietnam was deemed the perfect venue for a trial of this concept. The division deployed to the Vietnam highlands and set up headquarters at Pleiku, the regional capital. From this base of operations the various battalions, with the assistance of the division's hundreds of helicopters, conducted missions to search for and destroy the Vietcong. These search and destroy missions frustrated American commanders, because little enemy contact was being made.

Then came the Ia Drang battles. The battalion was sent in to support its sister battalion, 1-7 Cav, at LZ X-Ray. The battalion consisted of four line companies and a combat support company, which included the mortars and medium machine guns. One of the organic companies that had supported 1-7 Cav for three days was replaced with an attached company from 1-5 Cav during the LZ X-Ray fight. The battalion, at 550 men, was understrength by more than a hundred personnel.

Support from the field artillery at LZ Falcon and U.S. Air Force aircraft was critical throughout the battle for those who survived. The nature of the fight limited the effectiveness of the firepower. The same instruments of death used only a day previously were completely ineffective during the opening phases of this fight. Not until the fight stabilized did supporting firepower become effective.

North Vietnamese Army Forces

The 33d NVA Regiment had been severely depleted by the engagements at Plei Me and later at LZ X-Ray. Of this regiment, the 1st Battalion and the Headquarters of the 3d Battalion were among the forces engaged around Albany. Additionally, the 8th Battalion of the 66th NVA Regiment was also engaged. This was a reserve battalion, fresh from the trip down the Ho Chi Minh trail.[5] Its soldiers were battle hardened and ready for a fight with the American soldiers who had killed so many of their comrades in the previous days' battle. The 33d Regiment commander watched the American units depart from LZ X-Ray. He gave guidance about grabbing the Americans by the belt and getting in close to negate the awesome firepower witnessed at LZ X-Ray.

The 8th Battalion was a unit of more than five hundred soldiers. They moved early in the morning of 17 November 1965 and set in a position just east of the Ia Drang:

> The column had halted, dug in hasty positions and generally was in a relaxed posture (some soldiers were eating their noon rice) when outposts brought word that a large American column was headed directly toward them. The battalion commander had little choice but to organize hasty positions and prepare for a meeting engagement at close quarters in the

dense jungle. In some cases his machine guns had to be fired from unprotected positions and many soldiers were thrust into battle still wearing their heavy forage packs.[6]

This battalion was thought to be moving toward the field artillery position at LZ Columbus. If this was the case, the unit was significantly delayed by the engagement at LZ Albany. In fact, Columbus was attacked on 19 November 1965, but the battalion was several hours late and did not have the numbers to pose any serious threat to the base. The NVA actions demonstrate a broad view of engagements: that each engagement supports a larger scheme. This is in contrast to the U.S. Army approach of seeking engagements where possible to wear the enemy down through a series of disjointed battles.

Key Leaders in the Battle

American Forces[7]

- Lt. Col. Robert A. McDade—commander of 2-7 Cav. Formerly the division G-1 (personnel officer) and battalion commander for only three weeks. The division commander "had sent his personal aide, MAJ Frank Henry, to serve as . . . second-in-command and to keep things going till McDade could get his feet wet."[8]
- Capt. Joel Sugdinis—commander of A Company, 2-7 Cav. He had previously served in 1-7 Cav and was nominated to take command of A/2-7. He was a twenty-eight-year-old West Point graduate. He possessed a great deal of experience, having previously served as an infantry advisor to the Army of the Republic of Vietnam (ARVN). He had spent more than two years in the division from the test phase of airmobile operations to the present situation in the Ia Drang.
- Spc. Jack P. Smith—a twenty-year-old college dropout who joined the army and became part of the air cavalry. He was an assistant machine gunner in C Company.
- Capt. George Forrest—commander of A Company, 1-5 Cav.

He was an ROTC graduate from Morgan State University and in command for three months. His unit was an attachment. The B Company of 2-7 had been used extensively as an attachment for 1-7 Cav during the battle at LZ X-Ray. A/1-5 was the replacement for B/2-7.

North Vietnamese Army Forces

- Sr. Lt. Col. Nguyen Huu An—battlefield commander.
- Lt. Col. La Ngoc Chau—commander of the 66th NVA Regiment.

Grand and Theater Context

Grand Strategy

The United States was concerned with the spread of global communism. The stated policy was designed to contain this spread and prevent the fall of the neighboring Southeast Asian nations. The policy of containment was the driving factor behind the U.S. involvement, because no president wanted to be the one to lose a nation to communism. In addition to containment, there was a significant fear of Chinese intervention. The policy toward Vietnam was governed by a limited posture designed to prevent Chinese intervention as had happened in Korea. Little was made of the statements of regional scholars about the historical animosity between the Vietnamese and Chinese. This fear prevented major ground action north of the demilitarized zone.

Prior to November 1965, there had been no major ground engagements between U.S. and NVA forces. The U.S. policy had been to win the hearts and minds of the local populace and assist the ARVN in defending itself. American Marines and Special Forces units were the only deployed combat forces until the arrival of the 1st Cavalry Division. This was the major turning point of the war. No longer was the United States going to be simply an advisor. It was now going to enter battle with the NVA face-to-face. This shift in focus was decided at the highest levels, based on advice from the Military Assistance Command-Vietnam (MACV) commander, Gen. William Westmoreland.

Theater Strategy

The entrance of the 1st Cavalry Division meant that now the U.S. military shifted from the advisory to the major combatant level of the war. No longer were the soldiers simply staying in Saigon or protecting convoys along Highway One. They now began to conduct a new type of engagement, termed "search and destroy." This meant that U.S. units would identify an area, seal it off, and sweep the entire zone in search of NVA or Vietcong forces or supplies. Once they were located, U.S. soldiers would destroy all enemy in the zone. This approach was specifically designed to bring the NVA to battle. There was a great deal of impatience manifested in this policy. The United States had no stomach for the kind of guerrilla campaign being waged against it. The soldiers and their political leaders wanted a "stand-up" fight, where the power of the most advanced military could be brought to bear against the backward foe. When combined with the bombing campaigns against the logistical supply lines of the NVA, commonly referred to as the Ho Chi Minh trail, this would bring ultimate victory. Or so many thought. The problem was the fact that the Ho Chi Minh trail was literally a moving target, because it was a series of dozens of trails that were active or dormant at different times, and sometimes shifted tens of miles based on the current trail network.

Additionally, the average NVA soldier needed only a few pounds of supplies a month to keep him fighting, whereas the U.S. counterpart needed hundreds of pounds. This is one of the most significant differences between lower-tier and higher-tier forces—logistical requirements. There is also the fact that bombing through triple-canopy jungle is problematic and has been shown to be ineffective. All these factors led to an actual increase of materiel flowing south and an increase in the number of NVA personnel.

Operational Context

The 3d Brigade (BDE) of the 1st Cavalry Division was conducting search and destroy operations during November 1965 in the western portions of South Vietnam. These operations were providing only the most limited contact, thus defeating the entire purpose of the missions. During these operations, the Plei Me Special Forces camp came under attack from an NVA regiment. This attack was similar to the developed standard pattern for the NVA. They would identify a geographically isolated post, then surround and completely cut off the position from outside support. Ambushes would be set for resupply or relief columns with the intent of achieving a significant victory without a major engagement. In the Plei Me engagement, the relief column, accompanied by Maj. H. Norman Schwarzkopf, was successful in breaking through, and aerial firepower was able to break the siege. The NVA units then began a withdrawal to the east.

Ia Drang Chronology

Date	Event
14 Nov	1-7 Cav air assaults into LZ X-Ray
17 Nov	2-7 Cav and 2-5 Cav move from LZ X-Ray
18 Nov	2-7 Cav reinforced and evacuated
Apr 1966	Col. Moore and Capt. Forrest retrieve the last bodies from the Ia Drang; all accounted for

Source: Harold G. Moore and Joseph L. Galloway, *We Were Soldiers Once . . . and Young: Ia Drang, the Battle that Changed the War in Vietnam,* Paperback Edition (New York: Harper Perennial Publishers, 1993).

During this withdrawal, the 1st Cavalry Division commander planned to air assault in a battalion to block and destroy the escaping enemy units. This battalion was 1-7 Cav. It was sent into LZ X-Ray to find and destroy the remnants of the regiment that was retreating from Plei Me. Instead, the unit came into contact with one full-strength regiment and two understrength ones. Outnumbered nearly ten to one, the battalion successfully defended for nearly three days, inflicting casualties greater than ten to one against the NVA. Companies from 2-5 Cav and later 2-7 Cav eventually reinforced 1-7 Cav. The final state had all three battalions fully involved. Finally the NVA ceased its attacks and the U.S. units began their withdrawal. The 1-7 Cav was airlifted out; 2-5 Cav moved overland, approximately two miles, to LZ Columbus to be extracted. The 2-7 Cav also moved overland, approximately four miles, to LZ Albany for extraction. All of this was accomplished under observation of the NVA forces located on the Chu Pong Massif. Lieutenant Colonel McDade, the commander of 2-7 Cav, commented: "I will tell you one thing that sticks in my mind: This was the least airmobile operation that occurred probably in the entire Vietnam War. It was right back to 1950 Korea or 1944 Europe. All we got were verbal orders: Go here. Finger on a map. And we just marched off like we were in Korea."[9]

Technical Context

During this entire engagement there were few significant technical advantages by either side. The engagement was fought at such close quarters that most of the technically advanced combat measures were not the slightest bit useful. This was an engagement between the most modern army on the planet against one of the most backward forces. The cross-tier nature of this engagement is the real reason for this study. Why was such a technically backward nation so successful? The reasons are relatively simple, though not all pleasant for Americans to understand.

The NVA were typical of tier-three/-four nations, which have extremely effective infantry forces. This is primarily because they have to. The NVA proved adept at the use of mortar fire in support of their operations. They also were effective in using individual and crew-served weapons as suppressive fire, to allow assaulting forces to close with the enemy. This was tested and proven during the struggle against the French forces, and most effectively demonstrated in the battle of Dien Bien Phu.

The strength of the United States was in its air and mechanized firepower, as well as the advantage of mobility by helicopter. These advantages were relatively negated once the infantrymen were on the ground under the canopy of the Vietnamese jungles. The effectiveness of airpower was reduced by the jungle but rendered even less effective by the proximity of the combatants during the course of the fight. Napalm and other air-delivered antipersonnel systems are not precision weapons, and some damage was inevitable to friendly forces when they were used during this battle.

The majority of technical improvements were negated by the fact that the light infantrymen's world has changed less than any other aspect of modern combat. Aside from the individual weapons they carried, the soldiers who struggled in Vietnam were not that much different from those who had struggled on Guadalcanal twenty-two years earlier, with the exception of how they were transported to the area.

Tactical Chronology

The reasons for the movement to LZ Albany are unclear. One known fact that all understood was that B-52s out of Guam were en route to drop nearly 20,000 tons of bombs on the eastern slopes of the Chu Pong Massif, and all U.S. units needed to be farther than two miles from the intended impact. That was considered a minimum safe distance. This was one of two primary factors behind the movement; the other was that the mission in the Ia Drang valley was not complete:

> My intentions were that Albany was just an intermediate thing, that McDade was to go on through to LZ Crooks. I wanted to move 2-7 on to Crooks rather than have them all (2-5 and 2-7 and 1-5) congregate on Columbus. We had to support the South Vietnamese who were coming up, so I was going to just swing on out west. The mission hadn't changed; we were still out there to try to find the enemy. So I had them move out by foot. I could move them out by air later if I had to. Albany was just a spot on the route; just pass through and on to Crooks.[10]

This was the concept as Colonel Brown, the 3d Brigade commander, understood it. Most of the comments by the company commanders and the battalion commander were significantly different.

Almost all of those men understood they were moving to an extraction, not to another phase of a search and destroy mission. Even a future Chief of Staff of the Army and the then 3d Brigade executive officer was confused about the exact mission and movement orders of 2-7 Cav:

> The proposal was for 2-7 to move over north and find a suitable LZ. I don't think there was even an Albany plotted on the map. Later, when I had to brief the press, it was clear to me that this thing could not have been a classic ambush, since the enemy did not know where we were going. Hell, nobody knew where this battalion was going.[11]

This confusion is seen most clearly in the words of the battalion commander:

> We really didn't know a goddamned thing, had no intelligence, when Tully [2-5 Battalion commander] and I left X-Ray. We had no idea what to expect out there. They told me to go to a place called Albany and establish an LZ; nobody said we would have to fight our way to that LZ, just go and establish it. There are other things that follow from this. There is the time pressure. They say, Get there and organize the LZ. So you plow through; you don't feel your way or creep along. So I just blundered ahead. "That is my objective, so let's go." We were on foot going toward Albany all morning. We had word we were to stop and hold for an hour or so while the B-52 strikes went in. We sat on our asses, then started again.[12]

Under this confusion and lack of understanding, the soldiers of 2-7 Cav marched from LZ X-Ray toward LZ Albany in the heat and humidity, with limited or no sleep over the previous twenty-four hours. The 2-5 Cav led out and fired artillery spotting rounds four hundred meters in front to adjust the supporting guns. Lieutenant Colonel McDade did not allow Captain Sugdinis to conduct this same type of recon by fire, to prevent the loss of surprise. The battalion moved with A Company in the lead. The company was in a wedge, with the attached reconnaissance platoon as the point element. D Company, the combat support company, followed with C Company, then the headquarters support personnel, and finally A/1-5. The battalion followed 2-5 Cav toward LZ Columbus for about 2,000 meters, then turned to the left (north) toward LZ Albany.

The battalion struggled through the thick foliage and fallen trees. The exhausted soldiers began to discard gear in an attempt to lighten their individual loads. As they neared the clearing, the reconnaissance platoon identified and captured two prisoners. These men claimed to be deserters, yet they carried new equipment and were apparently well fed. Later it was learned they were from an outpost, one of the members of which made it back to the battalion headquarters to inform them of the Americans' arrival. Lieutenant Colonel McDade came forward with his intelligence officer and an interpreter to question the prisoners. Eventually he called all of his company commanders forward.

The column had stopped completely, and many soldiers simply flopped onto their rucksacks as a sort of backrest. Soldiers lit cigarettes and began conversations, relaxing after the nearly four-hour march. Some of the men had been awake for sixty hours, and their exhaustion resulted in their lack of discipline.

A Company was in the lead and still inching forward toward Albany. The battalion command group and all of the company commanders were with them. D Company was spread out, yet there was little organization, because the mortars simply dropped their gear instead of emplacing it. C Company had set out flankers, but the majority were relaxing. Many of the headquarters element were forward with the battalion commander, so a gap of about thirty to forty meters had developed in the column. Trailing was A Company, 1-5 Cav. Captain Forrest saw many of the lounging soldiers as he moved forward with his radiotelephone operators (RTOs).

While all of the commanders were assembled, the lead platoon identified enemy moving toward them, and small-arms fire began. The fire rapidly built to high intensity, then a series of "whumps" were heard as mortar rounds were launched at the column. Almost simultaneously, the mortar rounds exploded up and down the unit, followed by waves of attacking NVA soldiers. This was what Lieutenant Colonel An saw as a natural continuation of the battle at LZ X-Ray. General Giap taught that they must always win the first battle, and the NVA commanders still saw this as the first battle.

The initial contact was at the head of the column, but as A Company defended, the NVA soldiers flowed around them like a wave around a rock and found the less-prepared units farther down the column. Eventually the entire column was engulfed.

All of the company commanders were with A Company. Many of them had also brought artillery forward observers, and some brought their first sergeants. Captain Forrest was the only one to return to his own company. His sprint of nearly six hundred meters brought him back to his unit, but both of his RTOs were killed. He rallied his men and formed a perimeter. Captain Forrest's company and the lead company were the only coherent defenses that existed in the entire column. Everywhere else the men fought as small groups or as individual soldiers.

Different stories relate that men would get up to move, following the directions of their platoon leaders, only to be cut down by automatic weapons fire from the direction they were heading. Others identified dozens of enemy forces tied up in trees, firing down on the Americans below. This gave them a significant advantage, because as soon as a soldier went to ground, his world became very small.

The battalion command group called for indirect fire against the attacking forces and air strikes. The brigade commander and his fire support officer were overhead, trying to understand the situation below:

Major Roger Bartholomew, commander of the aerial rocket artillery [ARA] helicopters, was in contact with Captain Tademy [brigade fire support officer] and flew a zigzag pattern over the forest trying to get a fix on the location of friendly troops so that his helicopters could support them. He had no luck. Captain Tademy had the artillery fire smoke rounds to try to register defensive fires. No luck there either. "It didn't help because everybody was so mixed up by then on the ground. We had tactical air, ARA, and artillery and still we couldn't do a damned thing. It was the most helpless, hopeless thing I ever witnessed."[13]

Some of the air strikes delivered napalm on both friend and foe alike. Some reported seeing burning Vietnamese in the trees and hearing the screams of Americans. Despite the gruesome losses, the napalm was keeping the enemy at a relative distance.

The picture was confusing at all levels. The accounts of the privates and specialists reveal a picture not unlike that of the battalion and brigade commander. No one had a grasp of the total picture. This was a result of the loss of leadership and the related communications caused by bringing the company commanders forward. It was also a result of so many of the subsequent company leadership being killed so early in the fight. After the first thirty minutes, there were few surviving platoon leaders and executive officers. The battalion commander described the confusion:

> In that first hour or so, the situation was so fluid that I was acting more as a platoon leader than a battalion commander. We were trying to secure a perimeter. I was trying to figure out what the hell was going on, myself. I don't think anybody in the battalion could have told you what the situation really was at that time. I can see where I might have left Tim Brown [3d BDE commander] in the dark about what was going on; I didn't really know myself until things quieted down. . . . I could have yelled and screamed that we were in a death trap, and all that crap. But I didn't know it was as bad as it was. I had no way of checking visually or physically, by getting out of that perimeter, so all I could do was hope to get back in touch. I wasn't going to scream that the sky was falling, especially in a situation where nobody could do anything about it anyway.[14]

Colonel Brown did order 1-5 Cav to send a company overland from LZ Columbus to link up with and support 2-7. He also ordered B/2-7 to move from Camp Holloway to LZ Albany.

Throughout the day, those in the middle of the column fought a pitched battle against both friend and foe. The following is an account from ABC News reporter Jack Smith, who was a specialist in C Company during the battle:

Within a span of perhaps twenty minutes everyone around me was dead or wounded, except me. You have to understand that in our area the elephant grass was chest-high; once you hit the dirt your world was about as big as a dining-room table. Your world was completely confined to that area and the six or seven men around you. At that point, we were isolated. Alpha Company was in the same shape. Then the North Vietnamese swept through. I believe they came between Alpha and our company and began to shoot people. We didn't know if the noise from five feet away, as they began to shoot people, was friendly or enemy. . . .

Often they [American machine-gun crews] were firing right into the muzzles of other American machine guns. People were screaming to stop the shooting. It began to have all the elements of a massacre. Nobody was in control because all the officers were to the front and our radio operators had fallen dead on their radio sets. . . .

The NVA were roaming at will shooting people, hurling hand grenades, and if they weren't doing it we were shooting each other. I moved away, napalm falling so close it was making the grass curl over my head. I went to another area and again I was the only man there who wasn't wounded. It terrified me. I was bandaging up a sergeant when all of a sudden some NVA jumped on top of us. I pretended to be dead; it was easy to do since I was covered with those people's blood. The North Vietnamese gunner started using me as a sandbag for his machine gun.

The only reason he didn't discover I was alive was that he was shaking more than I was. He couldn't have been much older than me, nineteen at the time. He started firing into our mortar platoon; our mortar platoon started firing grenades at him and his gun. I lay there thinking, If I stand up and say, "Fellows, don't shoot me," the NVA will shoot me. And if I lay still like this my own men will kill me. Grenades started exploding all around; I was wounded, the North Vietnamese on top of me was killed, that sergeant was killed. I moved to yet another position and this went on all afternoon. Everywhere I went I got wounded, but I didn't get killed. All the men around me were dead.[15]

B/1-5 linked up in the late afternoon with A/1-5; they formed a more solid perimeter and began to launch a series of counterattacks designed to rescue the wounded in between them and the command location. Later that evening, B/2-7 conducted an air assault into LZ Albany and linked up with A Company and the command group. Throughout the late afternoon and the night, helicopters landed in extremely challenging and dangerous circumstances to evacuate wounded personnel. Also during the night, the situation became even more confused for those between the two perimeters, and there were numerous incidents of the NVA soldiers shooting the wounded. Some individual U.S. soldiers were able to escape the battlefield, and they made it back to various U.S. units in the surrounding terrain.

The next morning the two perimeter units conducted the "mad minute"[16] and received no enemy response. They then began to move out and police the battlefield. This was the first time that the extent of the destruction became known. American soldiers also killed wounded enemy soldiers as they swept the battlefield; the emotion from the night and day of terror was released in a killing frenzy that a few individuals participated in. The tragedy of LZ Albany was the loss of humanity through the pressure of such personalized and isolated combat. By late afternoon, nearly all of the remaining wounded were evacuated. Some elements remained until 19 November to continue retrieving the dead and wounded, but the battle was now over.

Time Line[17]

Date	Time	Event
17 Nov 1965	0900	2-5 Cav moves from LZ X-Ray
	0910	2-7 Cav moves from LZ X-Ray
	1157	2-7 Cav captures two enemy prisoners
	1307	Recon platoon cleared to western edge of LZ Albany
	1315	Battle of LZ Albany begins
	1430	1-5 Cav alerted to assist 2/7
	1455	B/1-5 begins movement from LZ Columbus toward 2-7
	1600	B/2-7 begins preparations for air assault
	1630	B/1-5 links up with A/1-5 and other elements of 2-7
	1745	B/2-7 begins movement from Camp Holloway
	1845	B/2-7 assaults into LZ Albany and links up with A/2-7

Battlefield Leadership

The battle of LZ Albany was a very individual style of conflict, yet this represents one of the primary ways in which low-tech forces are going to try to fight and hope to win against a high-tech enemy. That is accomplished by the lower-tier force closing in so tight that the use of the overwhelming firepower becomes problematic and at times completely impossible, without risking a significant portion of its own force. This style is extremely evident in the decisionmaking and tactics of the NVA forces. It was further compounded by the critical decisions of the American forces.

The first critical decision was to walk out of LZ X-Ray rather than be airlifted out. This placed the two battalions at a significant risk from the outset. The forces were under continuous enemy observation and were outnumbered. There was a constant American assumption that the display of U.S. firepower was intimidation enough, and the NVA would cower in their holes until all the deployed forces were safely back at Pleiku. The arrogance manifest in such decisionmaking demonstrates a continual U.S. or any high-tech force weakness when dealing with low-tech forces.

The next decision that was crucial to the dissolution of 2-7 Cav was that of the battalion commander to summon all the company commanders forward when the prisoners were captured. This left all the companies without experienced leadership. Only the lieutenants remained to try to form some sort of coherent defense. Many made the attempt, but most were killed while trying to lead their platoons into a perimeter. The only company able to provide protection was A/1-5 Cav. This was because of the heroic charge by the company commander to return to his company, thus providing critical leadership. Though Captain Forrest refers to his decision to return more as instinct, it was another decision that proved crucial to the entire fight. This prevented the destruction of the vast majority of the battalion and provided an anchor for others to build on.

Significance

The battles in the Ia Drang valley had several major impacts on the war. This is a case where a series of engagements at the tactical level of war would impact the operational, theater, and grand strategy levels of war. The initial impact came as General Westmoreland received a briefing from the 3d Brigade commander, Colonel Brown, about the battles. Colonel Brown briefed almost exclusively on the success at LZ X-Ray and completely avoided the happenings at LZ Albany. This left the MACV commander with the false impression of how well this new style of war would work. This was the first major engagement between the U.S. Army and the NVA, and it was X-Ray, not Albany, that was being used as the basis for future tactics against the NVA:

[T]he U.S. too often lost, covered up or ignored the lessons of
the Ia Drang—that the North Vietnamese soldier was brave and
tough, that it would cost more American lives than anyone believed to defeat him and that it would be impossible to crush
the North Vietnamese Army so long as it could escape into
Cambodia. The first lesson came before the battle was over,
when a 400-man battalion was cut to pieces after it blundered
into an ambush. . . .[18]

The preeminence of American firepower was proven on the field
of battle, and the American army had achieved a loss ratio of more
than 11:1. The officers at MACV headquarters considered this sort
of casualty figure to be more than acceptable, and this drove the development of the attrition policy of fighting the war in Vietnam, because "the White House wanted a victory, not a lesson."[19]

Numbers of Soldiers Involved and Casualties

	American	NVA
Troops Engaged	450	800?
Casualties	285	503
Killed	155	503
Wounded	125	na
Missing	5	na
Percentage of Force Casualties	63%	63%

Sources: Harold G. Moore and Joseph L. Galloway, *We Were Soldiers Once . . . and Young: Ia Drang, the Battle that Changed the War
in Vietnam.* Joseph L. Galloway, "Vietnam Story," *U.S. News &
World Report,* 29 October 1990, 36–46.

Few people knew about or even studied the issues at LZ Albany,
and therefore no one grasped the lessons that the NVA were learning from the Ia Drang engagements. They learned that to defeat the
Americans they must negate their firepower advantage by closing

with the enemy in an individual style of warfare. This would prevent the danger from above and also negate the strength of the enemy's land-based firepower as well.

General Giap, the commander of the NVA and the victor of Dien Bien Phu, gave his assessment: "After the Ia Drang battle we concluded that we could fight and win against the cavalry troops. . . . We had a strategy of a people's war. You had tactics, and it takes very decisive tactics to win a strategic victory. You planned to use the cavalry tactics as your strategy to win the war. If we could defeat your tactics—your helicopters—then we could defeat your strategy."[20]

At the grand strategy level of war, these battles presented an almost completely different picture. The United States had not had losses anywhere near this severe prior to November 1965. The impact of nearly three hundred casualties was crucial in the policy-making arena.

Secretary of Defense Robert S. McNamara visited Vietnam following the battle and was initially caught completely off guard by the results and the recommendations for additional troops. His remarks following the completion of briefings in Vietnam demonstrated the realization of the open-ended nature of the war: "The decision of the Vietcong [and North Vietnamese Army] to stand and fight [at the recent battle of Ia Drang], recognizing the level of force we can bring to bear against them, expresses their determination to carry on the conflict that can lead to only one conclusion. It will be a long war."[21]

The greatest impact of the battle was felt in the homes of the families of these servicemen. Because of the limited casualties prior to these battles, the military in the United States was completely unprepared to deal with the effects of large casualties: "It was early in the war, and the Army had not yet formed the casualty-notification teams that later delivered and tried to soften the terrible news. The telegrams were simply handed over to taxi drivers to deliver. Some women collapsed at the sight of a cab pulling up outside; others huddled inside, refusing to answer the knock."[22]

The backlash from the hundreds of body bags was the first wave in the ocean of protesting that was to come. The Ia Drang valley battles almost immediately elevated Vietnam in the consciousness of every American.

Lessons Learned

All the lessons from the Ia Drang valley engagement at LZ Albany center on the concept of understanding the battlefield. One of the primary questions the U.S. Army's transition to an "Objective Force" is supposed to answer is the question: Where are my friends? The inability of any member of the 2-7 Cav to answer this question denied the benefits of technology.

Identification: At all levels of strategy, this represented a U.S. failure to identify the nature of the conflict and the techniques that the NVA were to use. The lack of understanding about the ideas and doctrine of the enemy existed despite all the information from the French about the same battlefield commanders. This left 2-7 Cav unprepared, because no one could illuminate the threat. All of the U.S. decisionmakers thought the battle was over; the NVA did not. The movements of the NVA regiments were completely undetected. Little to no attempt was made by units at any level to provide reconnaissance ahead of the moving column. This failure resulted in a surprise engagement and allowed the NVA commander the opportunity to grab the American forces by the belt and hold on. Only accurate intelligence and effective reconnaissance will give future commanders the time they need to prevent the enemy from closing with them.

Isolation: The inability of the technology of the U.S. military to effectively seal the Vietnamese border and deny the resupply of NVA regiments resulted in the challenges faced in the Ia Drang valley. Rather than facing units weary from one engagement at Plei Me, the elements of 3d Brigade, 1st Cavalry Division, fought units fresh from North Vietnam by way of the Ho Chi Minh trail. The NVA had complete freedom of maneuver. The forces engaged with 2-7 Cav were not reinforced because there were no forces available, not because they were denied.

Suppression: Only after the initial confusion was overcome were the Americans able to use their air support to deny the enemy opportunity to maneuver. Suppression can happen only when there is an appropriate amount of standoff.

Maneuver: Following the initial maneuver that brought 1-7 Cav into the area, the rest of the 3d Brigade fought the way infantry had for the previous twenty-five years. The 2-7 Cav was completely fixed in place. It was not moving until reinforcements arrived. Surprise denied the ability to maneuver.

Destruction: Failure of the battalion or brigade to accomplish effectively any of the preceding four elements ensured that 2-7 Cav would not be able to destroy the enemy. Fighting for survival from the beginning of the engagement until its sudden cessation denied any ability to gain the initiative and allowed only for the force to protect itself from total annihilation. Ultimately the failure of the United States at all levels to identify the tactics used by the NVA directly resulted in a failure to destroy the NVA in South Vietnam.

Conclusion

Landing Zone Albany is a classic view into the future of conflict—a tier-three/-four nation against the tier-two nation is one of the ways that cross-tier conflict is conducted. The lower-tier nation seeks to engage the higher-tier nation in severely restricted terrain, and close within the range of the high-casualty-producing weapons. This tactic completely negates the ability of the air- and land-delivered fire support firepower and forces an infantry-to-infantry struggle. Because of the very nature of light infantry combat, the better-trained, better-motivated soldiers will always prevail. All things being equal, motivation and energy will carry the battle. Motivation and energy are in large part a determination of timing. In this case, the NVA determined the time of the engagement and therefore were able to husband their strength and emotional energy, whereas the American forces were at the end of a long and mentally and physically arduous path.

The Objective Force goal of understanding the location of friends being one of the bedrock pieces of information was proven during this engagement. If Lieutenant Colonel McDade had known where his people were located, the U.S. Army could have used the massive firepower that waited in the air and on the ground. Proposed systems would allow future commanders to understand where their soldiers and vehicles are and therefore make it easier to designate the location of potential enemies.

The success of the lower-tier forces was completely discounted by the former success of the higher-tier forces in the battle at LZ X-Ray. The difference between the two battles defines the way a future lower-tier force can have success. In X-Ray, the higher-tier force was in a set defensive perimeter with interlocking fires. It had the ability to hold the attacking enemy at a distance that allowed for the use of massive amounts of fire support. In Albany, the higher-tier force was caught unsuspecting while in a loose column and completely unprepared for any sort of significant defense. The lower-tier force closed well within small-arms range and completely intermixed with the higher-tier force within minutes. This negated the firepower advantage.

Even with these two styles demonstrated, a critical issue was the lack of preparedness at the grand strategy level for the acceptance of so many casualties. Nearly three hundred casualties shocked the military casualty system and distressed a great many family members. Additionally, the political system was completely unprepared for either the reaction from military families or from the civilian population at large about the casualty figures, especially when the battle was characterized as a victory. This forced the military and civilian leaders to adopt a policy of attrition based on the idea that the U.S. Army would be able to force the NVA into more X-Ray sorts of battles. This was a faulty premise that never materialized, because the NVA learned the lessons of not fighting X-Rays but seeking to fight more Albany-style engagements. The result effectively wore down American resolve and public support, resulting eventually in a withdrawal from Vietnam.

Chapter Five

Battle Analysis: The Battle of Goose Green
Falkland Islands War, 27–29 May 1982

The battle of Goose Green from the 1982 Falkland Islands War was a cross-tier conflict between a tier-two nation (Great Britain) and a tier-three nation (Argentina) at the end of their respective power projection capabilities. The conflict started as an unexpected and unprepared-for contingency operation by the British military. The British had focused on combating the Soviet Union on a European battlefield. Much of the infantry in the Falklands was trained in mechanized combat and was familiar with fighting using armored personnel carriers (APCs). No such vehicles were deployed to the Falklands. Because of these reasons, this battle has significant relevance for the American military professional. Since 1990, the American military has deployed to dozens of locations around the world to resolve or fight conflicts, many of which were entirely unforeseen, and for which the units deployed had to rapidly prepare in an ad hoc fashion.

This is also a rapid time frame conflict—now termed a "burst" operation—which is similar to the preferred style of the post-Vietnam American military. The Falklands was the first of several of these operations by Western nations. The conflicts in Panama, Grenada, Desert Storm, Somalia, and Haiti are all uses of force that follow this intent. Similar to the speed of the modern conflict is the size. With the exception of Desert Storm, all modern conflicts feature primarily brigade-level and below engagements. In this battle analysis, the focus battalion is the 2d Battalion, the Parachute Regiment.

Geographical Setting

Location

The Islas Malvinas, or Falkland Islands, are a series of islands approximately four hundred miles east of the Argentinean coast and more than eight thousand miles south-southwest from the British Isles. The two most significant islands in the group are the West and East Falkland Islands. The capital of the Falkland Islands—Port Stanley, is on East Falkland Island. The vegetation is sparse—mostly grass, gorse, and a few other types of shrubbery. An east-west ridge, denoted as the Sussex Mountains, dominates the barren and rocky ground on East Falkland Island. These mountains, extending from the San Carlos settlement all the way to Port Stanley, were the site of the majority of the ground campaign as the British attacked Argentinean positions at locations including Mount Kent, Two Sisters, Tumbledown, and Wireless Ridge. The largest engagement of the ground campaign was the one conventional engagement that did not occur on this ridge system.

As a person walks south from the Sussex Mountains, East Falkland Island narrows to an isthmus about four hundred meters wide prior to opening back up into the southern portion of the island. This isthmus has two settlements, Darwin and Goose Green. Goose Green, which is several times larger than Darwin, has a population of approximately 115 persons.

Terrain/Vegetation

The isthmus is as barren and rugged as the rest of the islands, with the ground sloping down toward the sea from the center. The ridgelike center of the isthmus has two higher positions, one referred to as Darwin Hill and another, close to the settlement, called Boca House. Along the western shore the ground has a lip of about eighteen inches before descending to the beach. Just to the south of Goose Green is a grass airstrip used by the Argentineans to base propeller-driven Pucaras. South of this airstrip is more high ground. The ground is extremely broken, with steep ravines and bare granite rock in numerous places.

Weather

The weather throughout the majority of the battle was a hindrance for the British attack. The temperature throughout the campaign was below freezing, with freezing rain and snow. The peat bogs had a thin layer of ice, through which the heavily laden paratroopers would break, making each step a significant effort.[1] From late in the afternoon of 27 May until approximately midmorning on 28 May, there was an almost constant rain. This made movement difficult and life generally miserable for the soldiers trapped or pinned down in the open. In addition to rain there was fog on the morning of 28 May that prevented air support until mid- to late afternoon. There was also a fifty- to sixty-mile-per-hour wind blowing across the isthmus throughout much of the attack.[2] This served to further complicate the fire support situation. The weather delayed tactical air support, helicopter medical evacuation, and the infantry advance.

Units Involved

British Forces

The primary unit involved in this battle analysis is the 2d Battalion, the Parachute Regiment (commonly called the 2d Para). This unit drew some of its history from the battles in the streets of Arnhem during Operation Market Garden in World War II. Then–battalion commander John Frost refused to surrender to the SS panzer divisions and instead held the eastern edge of the Arnhem bridge until ordered to withdraw. In this vein, the 2d Para left England in hopes of not missing "the show" in the Falkland Islands.

The battalion was augmented with numerous other supporting arms. Many of these elements participated in the battle only in parts. For example, the 29th Field Battery, Royal Artillery, was not able to deploy in its entirety to support the attack because of logistics constraints. Only three guns could be moved by helicopter with the required ammunition. This shortage of supporting fires was to be overcome by the use of Sea Harriers and the frigate HMS *Arrow*. The guns from *Arrow* were roughly equivalent to an entire field artillery battery. The major drawback of the naval gunfire support was that the ship was to return to the relative safety of the Port Carlos anchorage by dawn. In addition to the shortage of supporting artillery, the battalion commander assessed that his men could not carry all of the battalion's mortars and accompanying base plates and ammunition, so he ordered that only two mortars be brought to support the attack.

The infantry component of the 2d Para that began the attack on Darwin and Goose Green was approximately 450 personnel.

Argentinean Forces

The Argentinean forces in and around Darwin and Goose Green numbered from 1,400 to 1,600 personnel. Many of these were transported in on the night of 27 May 1982 following the BBC broadcast of the imminent attack. The forces were augmented during the battle by personnel brought in on one Chinook and six Huey helicopters. Most of these personnel were not able to effectively enter the battle and were dispersed under artillery fire, to be captured in the days following the battle. The forces in Goose Green itself were a mixture of Argentinean air force, navy, and army. The air force personnel, approximately ninety, supported the air operations from the adjacent grass airstrip with Pucara bombers. These aircraft were used in defense of the positions, dropping high-explosive and napalm canisters, one of which was shot down during the engagement with a Blowpipe missile. In addition to the aircraft, there were several artillery pieces and antiaircraft guns used in a ground support role.

Key Leaders in the Battle

British Forces[3]

- Lt. Col. Herbert "H" Jones—commanding officer of the 2d Battalion, the Parachute Regiment. Joined the Devon and Dorset Regiment, then transferred to the paras in 1980. He was described by his XO as a person who "wouldn't suffer fools" and "a real leader." His attitude during an attack was that, at times, a small number of casualties now could save hundreds of casualties later.[4]

• Maj. Chris Keeble—executive officer of the 2d Battalion. He "[j]oined the Royal Anglians from Sandhurst in 1963, and transferred to the paras in 1971. He found them 'far more professional than most infantry units. In an ordinary infantry battalion, there is an undefined limit about what you can do. The philosophy of the Parachute Regiment is that there is nothing you cannot do. I find that very attractive. There are no limits.'"[5]

• Maj. Dair Farrar-Hockley—commander, A Company. Thirty-five-year-old infantryman with a passion for military service, and the son of the colonel commandant of the regiment.

• Maj. John Crosland—commander, B Company. Formerly served in the Special Air Service (SAS) and saw action in Dhofar.

Argentinean Forces

• Air Vice Commodore Wilson Pedroza—senior Argentine officer in Goose Green. Commander of the aviation personnel. In the late afternoon of 28 May, he agreed to a cease-fire for the night. Later his condition for surrender was that his airmen be allowed to do so with honor. He brought his airmen out and conducted a short ceremony with the Argentine national anthem; he saluted, then formally surrendered.

• Col. Italo Pioggi—senior Argentine ground force officer.

Grand and Theater Context

Grand Strategy

The strategic context of the battle of Goose Green involves the political fate of the Falkland Islands and the Anglo-American–Latin American relationships. The debate about who should have sovereignty extends back to the eighteenth century, yet this debate became more and more heated in the latter half of the twentieth century as Argentina sought to demonstrate its military and political abilities at the expense of a declining British Empire. The United States was torn between two major competing policies: support of NATO and the "special relationship" that had existed with Great

Britain since World War I, and general support of the Monroe Doctrine and assistance to another Western Hemisphere nation. These demands were reflected in the personalities of the major policymakers of the United States. Secretary of State Alexander Haig, a former Supreme Allied Commander, Europe, strongly favored the NATO and, therefore, British connections. His statements communicate the fact that if the United States were to condemn Britain, support Argentina, or even remain entirely neutral, a rift in the Atlantic Alliance would be apparent to the Soviets during the height of the American arms buildup.

The U.S. ambassador to the United Nations, Jeane Kirkpatrick, held the opposing viewpoint: that active support of Great Britain by America would set back American relations in Latin America by decades. Additionally, whether by coincidence or Argentine design, Ambassador Kirkpatrick was at a dinner at the Argentinean embassy the night Argentina launched its attack to seize the Falkland Islands. The United States walked a relative middle ground, though Americans did come out in open statements condemning the Argentine invasion and provided C^{4}ISR (command, control, communications, computers, intelligence, surveillance, reconnaissance) support to the British forces. It also provided logistical support, yet no troops, aircraft, or naval craft from the United States supported the action.

Theater Strategy

In many ways this was a struggle for logistics more so than arms. The distances were extremely daunting: nearly 8,000 miles—more than 3,750 to Ascension Island by air and more than 4,000 by sea—from where Vulcan bombers made the first strikes against the Argentine positions in the Falklands. The British needed to gain footholds in the region, from which they could conduct operations. This led to plans to regain South Georgia Island, a British possession south of the Falklands, also seized by the Argentineans. More importantly was the need to base aircraft and troops off the Falklands using aircraft carriers, both those manufactured as such and makeshift ones. Two containerships were used as carrier platforms for the vertical take-off and landing (VTOL) aircraft, the Sea Harrier, and helicopters. Finally, the overall goal: to retake the Falklands capital and force the capitulation of all Argentine forces on the islands.

Both nations fought at the limits of their power projection capability.[6] The British constantly struggled with getting combat power into the theater. One example is the manner in which bombing runs were conducted against the Port Stanley airfield. Vulcan bombers were stationed at Ascension Island to conduct raids against and possibly render the airfield inoperable. To get one bomber over the target required in-flight refueling on both the outbound and inbound legs, in addition to the fueler receiving in-flight refueling. Several of these missions did little more than demonstrate resolve, because virtually no significant damage was ever achieved against the runway. This mission was possible only one bomber at a time.

Throughout the fight the British naval battle group was under attack from the Argentine air force, losing six vessels. Numerous other ships were attacked and many had bombs hit, but for whatever reason many bombs did not explode. Much of the British success would have been far different had even one or two more bombs simply exploded on contact. In addition to the shipping losses and the Royal Air Force (RAF) difficulties, there were severe limitations on rotary-wing availability. This was due primarily to the sinking of the *Atlantic Conveyor*, a converted containership that was carrying approximately 50 percent of the task force rotary-wing assets and all but one of the heavy-lift helicopters.

These problems would directly impact the 2d Para attack. For example, the ship that carried much of the para's equipment had to be rapidly abandoned—with most of the heavy equipment remaining—after an unexploded Argentine bomb lodged in the bulkheads. This forced the soldiers to move without some of their warmest clothing in below-freezing temperatures. Additionally, the paras were ordered to begin the attack without an adequate stockpile of ammunition and under faulty ammunition predictions. The soldiers fired more than four times the expected small-arms ammunition and five times the expected artillery ammunition.[7]

The aviation, naval, logistics, and rotary-wing difficulties combined to take a former Great Power nation, one that figured strongly in the defense of Western Europe, and make it roughly equal to an emerging Latin American nation. This near equality made the ground campaign the pivotal focus. Only through physical eviction would the Argentine forces depart the Falklands.

Operational Context

"The fighting for the Falklands was more a contest between a British naval task force and land-based Argentine air forces than a struggle between armies."[8] Despite this truth, this chapter focuses on the ground campaign. The overall plan was to seize the capital, Port Stanley, and capture, kill, or force the retreat of the Argentine land forces.

This began with a series of special operations actions against enemy airfields and outposts. Following these actions was the preparation for and the actual landing at San Carlos. This task was accomplished against virtually no resistance. An SAS unit effectively destroyed the few Argentine troops in the area. The 3d Commando Brigade conducted the operations, taking control of the entire inlet and the surrounding high ground. The 2d Para was sent to the south to secure portions of the Sussex Mountains. The initial plan called for bypassing the enemy airfield and garrison at Goose Green and attacking overland toward the highlands surrounding Port Stanley. This plan was altered to ensure the protection of the force's southern flank and to gain an initial victory, demonstrating British resolve. The attack on Goose Green was initiated as both a political and a security event in support of the main-body forces. Additionally, the 2d Para was supposed to be employed in the attack, then withdrawn to support later operations by the 3d Commando Brigade. These operations included an overland movement to the east to pressure the forces in and around Port Stanley.

Technical Context

In general the British military had the most modern weapons and supplies, whereas the Argentine military was using Korean War–era equipment. An example of the disparity is the *General Belgrano,* an Argentine destroyer sunk by a British submarine. The *Belgrano* was originally a 1939 American warship that survived Pearl Harbor. The logistics problems for the British meant that much of their equipment did not arrive. Therefore, the Argentine soldiers were materially better prepared. Some accounts indicate that several British paras discarded their submachine guns in favor of the more powerful Argentine weapons, which had a longer range and greater muzzle velocity.[9] Because of the power-projection distance and the fact that this was not fought on a Cold War battlefield, the technology actually shifted to the lower-tier nation's favor.

Another example of the shift in technology was that of fire support, which proved critical in this battle. The British had a limited number of tubes (artillery and mortar) and ammunition. In fact, the mortars ran completely out of ammunition during the battle, and the artillery battery had to be replenished several times by helicopter. The HMS *Arrow* provided a significant amount of firepower throughout the early portion of the battle, but a mechanical malfunction and orders to return to the safety of the San Carlos anchorage removed this valuable asset relatively early in the fight. Weather prevented airpower from playing a large role, but aircraft were effective in the afternoon in destroying a 35mm antiaircraft battery being used against the attacking paras. This action provided a tremendous amount of freedom of maneuver.

Goose Green was essentially a classic light infantry struggle, where the weapons systems were not nearly as important as the hearts and dedication of the soldiers involved. The Argentine forces had a superiority in night vision equipment, infantry, artillery, and air support, and were defending a well-prepared trench line, yet in the end they lost to a force that they still outnumbered more than three to one at the time of the surrender.

Tactical Chronology

The battle for Goose Green began with the departure of the 2d Para from assembly areas in the vicinity of the Sussex Mountains south of the San Carlos anchorage. This was the second departure. The battalion had been ordered to conduct the same attack a few days prior but was recalled by the brigade commander. This time the battalion departed during the night of 26 May 1982 to move to its tactical assembly area, in the vicinity of a farm called Camilla Creek House. At this position the battalion was in a covered and concealed location, and it utilized the house and outbuildings for shelter the remainder of the night. These buildings became crucial, because the paras left much of their equipment, including rucksacks with sleeping bags, back at the Sussex assembly areas, and the cold, damp air meant that most of the soldiers shivered the night away as they attempted to sleep.

While they were in this position, the BBC broadcasted during morning international news that British forces were within five miles of Goose Green. The correspondents in London who were briefed by the defense ministry of the current operation generated this broadcast. The BBC correspondent who was accompanying the 2d Paras was caught completely off guard. Lieutenant Colonel H confronted the correspondent and threatened to sue the minister of defense and the BBC for manslaughter should any members of his battalion be killed. Following the broadcast, at least one more Argentine company reinforced the garrison during the late evening.

C Company was sent to conduct a reconnaissance and clear the route to the proposed line of departure. This resulted in the first intelligence that the battalion was facing more than one understrength battalion. A captured Land Rover, with its occupants, revealed that there were considerably more personnel around Goose Green. The battalion moved into positions during the late night and deployed with A Company on the left (east) and B Company on the right (west) as they attacked to the south. The attack began at about 0500. Both companies were halted with machine-gun fire from an Argentine trench line that spanned much of the isthmus. Most of the trench line did not incorporate significant reinforcing obstacles, which allowed the paras to successfully overcome the position once superior firepower was established. In some cases this proved difficult and took a considerable amount of time. It was against this initial trench line that the majority of the British casualties were taken.

A Company struggled against a series of bunkers with overhead cover and interlaced fields of fire. These halted the company after it rapidly seized its first two objectives and was close to entering the small settlement of Darwin. Lieutenant Colonel H came forward with A Company to assess the situation and directed that the bunkers be reduced. The paras used Milan antitank guided missiles and light antitank weapons to reduce the positions. Major Farrar-Hockley went forward with a small detachment to gain some advantage, but it was unsuccessful. As the men moved back, the A Company commander was informed that Lieutenant Colonel H had taken a small detail around the eastern shoreline to find a bypass. He and several others in his party were killed. Major Farrar-Hockley then called the battalion XO forward. Major Keeble took command just as the A Company paras had destroyed several of the machine-gun positions and were once again advancing.

B Company in the west was having little more success. In fact, the enemy had them completely halted. The Argentine positions were based off the Boca House farm. The building effectively anchored the position, and the limited vegetation allowed observation of all movement.

D Company had been directed to follow and support the two lead companies. They were busy cleaning up the positions that were bypassed during the predawn movement and collecting prisoners. Now they were directed to move along the western coastline and attack the Boca House from the flank and rear. This required the paras to crawl for approximately a thousand meters using an eighteen-inch lip where the beach and the land joined. This lip allowed them to pass the Argentine positions without being seen and to reduce the position from the west and south.

C Company had been sent to pass through A Company, which was now exhausted from the fighting, to seize the positions around Darwin Hill and occupy Darwin. A Company provided one platoon to C Company to assist in its attack. C Company ran into extremely difficult opposition at a landmark structure that was the settlement's schoolhouse. This was the last significant obstacle to surrounding Goose Green.

The building blocked the northern approaches and had been occupied by about fifty defenders. During the engagement, Pucara aircraft dropped napalm canisters, which narrowly missed British positions. One of the Pucaras was engaged and shot down by Blowpipe antiaircraft missiles. The attack was fierce, and a great deal of ordnance was expended. After significant weapons fire was placed on the structure, a white flag was seen. A young lieutenant went forward to accept the surrender. He and several others were shot. The paras then completely reduced the structure; in fact, the building exploded in a burst of flame, possibly after the ignition of some stored ammunition. There were no survivors from the schoolhouse. The XO would later state that the death of the lieutenant was probably unintentional, an act caused by the smoke and confusion.[10]

The battalion now converged on the positions around Goose Green from three directions—C Company from the north, D Company from the northwest, and B Company from the southwest—as it conducted a wide encirclement of the positions.

This encirclement could occur only after three Harriers destroyed a set of 35mm antiaircraft guns being used in the ground support role. During this period, several helicopters landed and disgorged approximately an infantry company's worth of Argentine soldiers south of Goose Green. Well-directed artillery fire was able to force those soldiers to move south and not link up with the garrison.

Once the garrison was completely surrounded, at approximately 1600, Major Keeble made radio contact with the Argentine garrison and coordinated a temporary cease-fire.[11] The XO then pulled the companies into an effective defensive position overwatching the town for the night. He developed a series of requirements for support of the battalion in the upcoming attack. These were predominantly fire support items. The mortars had completely run out of ammunition early in the day's battle, and they, plus additional tubes, were moved forward with more ammunition. The artillery pieces were also repositioned to support the morning attack.

On the morning of 29 May, Major Keeble sent forward two Argentine prisoners under a white flag with surrender terms. Within an hour, the garrison commander came out and negotiated for surrender. At 1000 hours the entire garrison marched out of Goose Green. There were ninety Argentine air force personnel and more than 1,200 Argentine army personnel. The 450-person battalion had fought and defeated a force of nearly 1,600 soldiers.

Time Line

Date	Time	Event
26 May 1982	2000	2d Para begins move from Sussex Mountains
27 May 1982	0300	2d Para arrives at Camilla Creek House
	0600	BBC broadcasts that British units are within five miles of Darwin
	1200	Argentine Land Rover captured
	1600	Lt. Col. H briefs officers of 2d Para on the mission
		Lt. Col. H briefs artillery gun position officer
	1800	C Company begins advance
	2200	Remainder of 2d Para begins advance
28 May 1982	0235	A Company crosses "start line" and becomes engaged 500 meters short of Burntside House
	0320	B Company begins to move and encounters a machine-gun position
	0530	A Company advances to its second objective
	0600	Lt. Col. H joins A Company and approves advance
	0630	A Company begins attack against Darwin Hill defenses
	0800	HMS *Arrow* forced to retire to San Carlos

Date	Time	Event
28 May 1982	0900	Battalion mortars run out of ammunition
	0930	Lt. Col. H and tactical air command (TAC) attack machine-gun position; Lt. Col. H killed
	1115	D Company attacks Boca House from flank and rear
	Dusk	Argentinean Chinook and six Hueys land in support of Goose Green
	1600	Radio contact made with Argentine garrison; temporary cease-fire agreed upon
29 May 1982	0600	Two Argentine prisoners sent into Goose Green to discuss surrender terms
	0830	Maj. Keeble and Air Vice Commodore Wilson Pedroza meet
	1000	Argentine garrison at Goose Green surrenders

Battlefield Leadership

The victory of a heavily outnumbered British force in the attack against an Argentine force with superior firepower in well-prepared defensive positions, including extremely proficient use of overhead cover, demonstrated one of the dominating concepts in future warfare: Highly trained, professional forces are the keystone of success on the battlefield. Despite the overwhelming odds in all forms, the British advanced and destroyed the effectiveness of the defense.

Three critical leadership events occurred during the course of the battle. The first was the death of the commanding officer. When a unit loses a commander, there is always a risk of significant combat degradation and possibly the complete loss of unit cohesion and fighting spirit. This almost always produces an immediate loss of initiative, then stagnation, and eventually defeat. None of these negative effects occurred. In fact, Major Keeble was able to oversee the complete victory and made several crucial decisions. This is a direct result of high-quality training and can be extrapolated to the strengths of most professional militaries. Units composed of professionals, from nations that invest money in training these soldiers, get a direct return in this sort of action. Contrast this with Argentine officers, most of whom never left the small settlements and did not appear with their soldiers in the field.

The second critical decision was D Company's passing around Boca House using the small lip between the land and the beach as a means of maneuver. The XO directed a short pause in the offense while D Company traveled nearly a thousand meters in a crawl to flank the positions. This completely unhinged the defensive system and opened the door to Goose Green.

The third important decision was really a combination of decisions: to surround Goose Green by bringing three companies from each of the available cardinal directions, then to send the prisoners forward with an opportunity for surrender. The final step was the manner in which the XO handled the surrender discussion. The Argentine air commander wanted to surrender with honor, march his people out, and have a small ceremony. Keeble consented to this, and the Argentines conducted a small ceremony with their flag and airmen once out of the settlement. This allowed for the tired paras to take captive many more than otherwise possible had Keeble been unwilling to accept any terms or conditions.

Significance

The battle of Goose Green provided a tremendous boost to British morale, both in theater and back at the home front. The fact that the British captured so many Argentines made the accomplishment that much more significant. One of the primary reasons for the battle was the nebulous "to demonstrate British resolve," and this was accomplished. Even though the war had many more engagements to follow, this set a tone and raised the confidence level of the attackers. The Argentines were competent fighters, but they were poorly led and organized. Time and again, these assertions were proven to be correct.

Aside from the morale and public-relations challenges, the Argentines suffered a major defeat. Specifically, they lost one of their airfields, forcing them to rely entirely on the Port Stanley field; in addition, more than 1,600 personnel were lost defending a position that did not directly help the main defense around the capital. These losses were not overcome.

Lessons Learned

There are many lessons to be derived from this battle from all aspects. Many of the most questionable decisions made by the British were forced on them by various logistics constraints and have importance for the U.S. military when contemplating the effect of deployment distances on soldiers at "the tip of the spear."

Identification: The location of the Argentine positions was identified early on in the British ground operations. There were some failings in the coordination between British Special Forces and the paras who conducted the attack in communicating the size of the enemy force. The ease of identification was due in part to the terrain. The isthmus upon which Goose Green is located is barren and offers almost no concealment. Additionally, the Argentine defenders opted to defend in a classic industrial-age defensive pattern. There was no attempt to fight in even a moderately unconventional manner.

Isolation: Failure of the British civilian leadership to maintain operational security allowed Goose Green to be reinforced prior to the fight, and a lack of sufficient antiaircraft weapons allowed for reinforcement during the battle. Only effective and rapid use of indirect fires denied the linkup of the reinforcing and defending elements. The terrain and the static nature of the Argentine defense also played a significant role in keeping the garrison isolated. At the theater strategy level, the islands were effectively isolated by British submarine forces and a fear of both parties of involving civilian shipping.

Suppression: This battle demonstrates the danger that higher-tech forces face when they are brought to the end of their deployment capability. The British forces went into battle without all of their organic mortars and field artillery, and with limited ammunition and limited time for naval gun support. All of this had the effect of delaying the successful conclusion of the battle.

The British soldiers' use of the existing indirect and direct fires effectively held the defenders in their positions. No significant repositioning occurred once the two lead British companies became engaged in the fight. Again, the method of defense also assisted in keeping the defenders relatively stationary.

Maneuver: D Company's crawling attack along the beach created maneuver space where there was none. This risky and ultimately successful use of maneuver was the turning point of the battle. Once D Company was behind the trench system, the Argentine forces had to withdraw into Goose Green, where they were rapidly placed under siege.

Destruction: Once the 2d Paras had Goose Green surrounded by ground maneuver and fire support systems, the futility of remaining in the town became evident. The high number of prisoners demonstrates that destruction does not always mean killing or destroying property; it can also mean the destruction of an opponent's will to fight.

Conclusion

Goose Green was a window to the future. A small conflict, far from home, short on logistic support, resulted in a typical clash of infantry along the World War II hedgerow or Korean mountains scenario. This is where the leadership of individuals—squad leaders on up the chain—was put to the test.

It is possible to envision that precision weapons could have destroyed the Argentine positions, but how would they have done so without risking the lives of more than a hundred civilians? Satellite imagery was used to pinpoint major naval targets, because this was primarily a navy war. The land battle was secondary in importance, so the high-tech C⁴ISR was targeted elsewhere. This was a classic cross-tier engagement at the edge of power projection capability, resulting in the common-denominator struggle—light infantry against light infantry. This is more clearly stated in the following quote:

> As Ibn Saud said of Lawrence of Arabia, technology is a double-edged sword. The reliance on technology brings the edge of triumph or disaster much closer. Victory can be swifter and cleaner, but as Norman Friedman noted, command and control systems can be countered and overloaded to invite equally swift disaster. An over-reliance on technology can invite disaster. In late 1972 when "The Computer" at Headquarters, 7th Air Force, Saigon, broke down for a few days, the air war over North Vietnam came to a halt. So dependent was the Air Force on its big computer that—in answer to the author's question at the time—the human brain and verbally transmitted orders to strike were deemed inadequate. The loss of the computer had paralyzed the headquarters. That is the problem with any infatuation—the heartbreak is so much the greater. . . . The Falklands, then, sustained the eternal supremacy of the human factor in war. . . .[12]

Neither military was truly prepared for this war in this place at this time. The more unprepared was also the most technologically advanced. British operations were thrown together in a hodgepodge effort.

The lack of logistics at the end of the rope is a critical notion as American forces plan and prepare for a war on terrorism in places that are atypical. A light infantry battalion requires little logistical support in comparison to a mechanized infantry or tank battalion. Fuel and ammunition alone require tremendous amounts of lift capacity and storage space, and they also require a great deal of security. The struggle discussed here is no different from myriad potential contingencies that American land forces could be asked to fight. Certainly the current policies will deploy forces in small numbers to wide-reaching parts of the globe, over issues and in places previously unconsidered. The leadership and training of the 2d Para should be the template of how to best deal with the worst possible scenario and still be overwhelmingly victorious.

Chapter Six

Battle Analysis: The Battle of 73 Easting
Operation Desert Storm, 26–27 February 1991

America's performance in its first battles rarely has been impressive. The Gulf War broke the mold. For once, America took the field with a team that was ready to play. And the result was the shortest, most successful, and in American lives least expensive military campaign in modern history.

— Paul Van Riper and Maj. Gen. Robert H. Scales, Jr.

The battle of 73 Easting, one of the most significant battles of the entire Operation Desert Storm, has been held up as one of the great examples of modern combat. The reality is that Operation Desert Storm is the exception rather than the rule. The previous chapters discuss three ways that a lower-tier force seeks to engage and defeat a higher-tier one. First, the lower-tier force seeks to overwhelm the higher-tier force with human wave attacks, trying to use its resource strength to negate technology; second, the lower-tier force attempts to close with the higher-tier force to intermingle the forces and negate the advantages of massive firepower; third, the higher-tier force is drawn to the extreme of its power projection capabilities to weaken the force logistically. These three techniques are not exclusive but may be used in conjunction with one another, and all are used with the concept of terrain in mind. A lower-tier force typically seeks victory by drawing the higher-tier force into unfavorable, usually severely restricted terrain, where the greater mobility and shock effect of the more technologically advanced force is muted. In this particular battle, a fourth technique is attempted: using conventional weaponry and fighting a conventional tank battle in an open desert environment. It appears that the Iraqis made assumptions that the severe casualties they could inflict by simply fighting a traditional battle would discourage the American forces to such a degree that they would give up. Instead of seeking to fight in severely restricted terrain, or even in the complex terrain of Kuwait City, the Iraqis fought the battle of 73 Easting in the open desert.

The battle of 73 Easting is an example of a way in which a lower-tier nation may seek to engage and defeat a higher-tier force and be completely overwhelmed. Most important, this battle is used to refute the sometimes-common misconception that Operation Desert Storm was a precursor for the future of conflict. It was an aberration; and though it deserves study and many lessons can be derived, it was not a prophetic vision of conflict.

The battle of 73 Easting derives its names from map coordinates. The Saudi and Iraqi deserts were so featureless that the American soldiers were forced, for the most part, to refer to locations by map coordinates alone. The map coordinates were determined by using global positioning system (GPS) devices, which allowed the American forces to know where they were at all times. Military maps have grid lines—not latitude or longitude but lines specifically designed for military navigation. This grid provided the references supported by the GPS. As soldiers traveled north, they crossed east-west grid lines called "northings." When the forces turned east, they crossed north-south grid lines called "eastings," because one drives across them going east. This battle was fought by elements of the 2d Armored Cavalry Regiment as it drove east into the Tawakalna Division, and it happened in the vicinity of the 73 north-south grid line, or "easting."

Geographical Setting

Location

Kuwait is a small emirate on the northwest corner of the Persian Gulf. It is bordered by Iraq to the north and west, Saudi Arabia to the south, and the Persian Gulf to the east. Southern Iraq and northwest Kuwait are similar. The most significant features are the cities. Kuwait City, along the Persian Gulf, is the largest city in Kuwait and the only major metropolitan area in the small nation. Basra, the major city in southern Iraq, is situated approximately midway between the confluence of the Tigris and Euphrates Rivers and the mouth of the river into the Persian Gulf. The Euphrates River is also one of the area's most dominant features. It runs from the confluence upstream in an easterly direction, then turns more to the north. The river was used by both the allies and Iraq as a major dividing line in the conflict.

The Wadi Al-Batin, also a dominant terrain feature dividing Iraq and Kuwait, is a steep-walled valley between ten and thirty meters deep and eight hundred to fifteen hundred meters across. It was along this terrain—on the Iraqi side of the wadi—that the Iraqi army based a significant portion of its defense with the Republican Guards Divisions. The battle of 73 Easting took place in a relatively shallow wadi to the northwest of Kuwait City and about twenty-five miles west of the Wadi Al-Batin. There is virtually no vegetation in southern Iraq, and what little exists is only sparse scrub brush. Although other than the Wadi Al-Batin the terrain looks flat and relatively featureless when viewed over a significant distance, the ground actually undulates. This gently rolling terrain was deceiving, and several specific engagements involved the terrain's deceptions.

Terrain/Vegetation

The battle was fought mostly around what is called an intervisibility (IV) line and a wadi. The wadi was where Ghost Troop fought against the withdrawing elements of the Iraqi army. Eagle Troop fought much of its portion of the battle around an IV line, which is a ridgeline or the crest of a rising terrain feature. The line essentially divides individuals on opposite sides, so a person on side A cannot see a person on side B. Only as the individuals get very close to the line can they see one another. The steepness of the terrain determines how close to the IV line a person must be to see a person on the other side. The IV lines during the fight at 73 Easting were very shallow, and as such provided the Tawakalna Division essentially a reverse-slope defense.

Weather

The weather throughout the majority of the battle was a hindrance for both forces. "Blowing sand and rain, along with dense smoke from burning oil wells, made visibility extremely poor. These conditions early in the ground operation improved the U.S. technical advantage in electro-optics. At the same time, it inhibited CAS [close air support]. . . . The bad weather at the beginning of the attack also threatened sustainability by making cross-country mobility difficult for wheeled logistics vehicles."[1]

Temperatures were relatively moderate, but there was rain falling prior to the battle, mist and fog during the battle, and battlefield obscurants. Additionally, just prior to the engagement a *shamal* (winter sandstorm) began. Visibility was reduced to less than half a mile. Despite poor visibility, thermal imaging devices on the tanks and Bradleys were capable of identifying targets out to approximately three thousand meters (nearly two miles). The Iraqis lacked similar systems and were forced to fight blind. The *shamal* negated American airpower, because all rotary-wing aircraft were grounded throughout its duration.

Units Involved

American Forces

The primary unit involved in this battle analysis was the 2d Armored Cavalry Regiment (ACR). The discussion of the regiment focuses on the specific actions of the 2d Squadron, particularly Ghost and Eagle Troops. The 2d ACR is one of the oldest American fighting units, drawing its history from the 2d Dragoons, which were organized at Jefferson Barracks, in Missouri, in 1836. The unit fought in numerous campaigns and battles and was, for the last four decades preceding the Gulf War, stationed in Germany as one of the border units.

The 2d ACR also participated in the large maneuvers called Return of Forces to Germany (REFORGER). These exercises were designed to replicate the movement of forces from the United States to Europe to defend Germany against attack. REFORGER involved tens of thousands of soldiers conducting operations over thousands of square miles of the German countryside. The exercises also tended to help subordinates improve skills for independent action and thinking. This institutional independence of thought would prove useful during the course of the battle in Iraq; troop commanders would make decisions that resulted in the destruction of entire brigades of Iraqi armor and infantry.

The 2d Squadron consisted of three ground cavalry troops (GCT). Each GCT had thirteen Bradley fighting vehicles (BFVs) and nine M1A1 tanks. The BFV is the equivalent of a light World War II tank except it can carry up to nine infantrymen in the back. It has a 25mm Bushmaster chain gun that can engage and destroy armored personnel carriers at distances in excess of 2,000 meters. The vehicle also has a tube-launched, optically tracked, wire-guided (TOW) missile system. The TOW missile is an antitank guided missile (ATGM) with a range of more than 3,500 meters. The M1A1 contains a 120mm main gun with the ability to destroy enemy tanks at ranges in excess of 3,000 meters. The significant difference between the two primary tank-killing systems, the TOW missile and the tank main gun, is velocity. A tank main gun round can travel the distance from muzzle to 3,000 meters in about two seconds, whereas it takes a TOW-2 missile approximately twelve seconds to cover the same distance.

The American army spent years developing a system that could be used on the European battlefield to provide the standoff range needed to cause attrition against the larger Soviet force without becoming decisively engaged. The Bradley and the M1 were the results of this development. They are both fast and lethal at extremely long ranges. An ACR squadron has a tank company in addition to its three GCTs. The tank company has fourteen M1A1s. The regimental squadron has forty-one tanks and thirty-nine BFVs in its subordinate troops. Additionally, the squadron has one firing battery of eight 155mm artillery pieces, and each troop has two mortar tubes as indirect fire support. The mortars and field artillery battery would prove crucial in conducting the battle.

In addition to the organic elements of the regiment, making it one of the most powerful organizations of its size, there were numerous attachments made after arrival in the Kuwaiti theater of operations. The augmentation was the 210th Field Artillery Brigade, 82d Engineer Battalion, 214th Military Police Company, 172d Chemical Company, 177th Personnel Services Company, and 2-1 Attack Aviation Battalion. These additions made the "Dragoon Battle Group" an organization of more than 8,000 soldiers.[2]

Iraqi Forces

The primary Iraqi forces involved at 73 Easting were from two divisions: the 12th Armored Division and the Tawakalna Division of the Iraqi Republican Guard. Both units were considered in the upper tiers of Iraqi training and capability. They possessed the most advanced tanks in the entire army and had the greatest levels of support throughout the campaign.

During the Iran-Iraq War in the 1980s, the Iraqis essentially retrained their entire force. The Iraqi army began the war without the ability to conduct combined-arms warfare at the battalion level. Combined-arms warfare is the synchronization of effects of multiple weapons systems, utilizing the strengths of each in concert to achieve victory. This requires a tremendous amount of training and practice. During the eight years of battle, the Iraqis pulled some of their top units out of contact with the enemy, reorganized them, and trained them to conduct this combined-arms warfare. The Republican Guards were then used as "the major assault force in each of the 1988 multi-corps offensive operations that reclaimed the Al-Faw peninsula, Fish Lake, and the Majnun Islands from the Iranians."[3] They formed the best units and they received the most training, developing the combined-arms skills at the battalion and brigade levels.

The Tawakalna Division, one of the Republican Guard divisions, was positioned to protect the western flank of Iraqi forces in Kuwait. It was also a theater-level reserve with a task of defeating any coalition penetrations toward Kuwait City. This meant that after the sack of Kuwait it was pulled back into southern Iraq to avoid the majority of the American firepower and, as the only force trained in combined-arms operations, to conduct counterattacks into any attacking coalition forces.

Despite the high status of the Republican Guards divisions, they were still suffering from the effects of the aerial bombardment. The destruction of bridges and the interdiction of supply columns by coalition airpower reduced the amount of support these soldiers received. Around the Rumelia oil fields, captured Iraqi soldiers were emaciated. They had been living on rice captured in Kuwait and a few tomatoes as their only sources of fresh fruit or vegetables.[4]

Key Leaders in the Battle

American Forces
- Col. Leonard D. Holder—commander of 2d ACR. Stoic, soft spoken, reserved, observant, the consummate thinker, he would make the difficult look easy. He provided enough guidance and direction in the planning process to allow for initiative and creativity in subordinates without upsetting the plan.[5] Prior to the invasion of Kuwait, Colonel Holder led his regiment on a series of training events that were to have a direct impact on the battles to come. In addition to the traditional gunneries that every mechanized unit conducts (the last of which the regiment conducted in August 1990 in Germany as the Iraqi army was invading Kuwait), he led his key subordinates on a staff ride to the Napoleonic battle of Koeniggraetz in Czechoslovakia to discuss meeting engagements. He also conducted a series of officer professional development courses that were to focus on mobile warfare. This supported the RE-FORGER missions fought during 1990, in which the regiment conducted an offensive covering force and coordinated for the passage of lines of the 1st Armored Division.[6]
- Lt. Col. Michael Kobbe—commander of 2d Squadron, 2d ACR.
- Maj. Steve Campbell—intelligence officer (S2), 2d ACR.
- Capt. H. R. McMaster—commander of Eagle Troop, 2d Squadron, 2d ACR.

- Capt. Joseph Sartiano—commander of Ghost Troop, 2d Squadron, 2d ACR.

Grand and Theater Context

Grand Strategy

The battle of 73 Easting is one of many engagements between forces in a battle of larger proportions. In some ways, this was the first post–Cold War war and also the first information-age war. Each of these new concepts of conflict brought separate dynamics.

The post–Cold War dynamic is best encapsulated in the words of American president George H. W. Bush when he discussed a "New World Order." This order was envisioned as a time and place where nations stood up against unacceptable aggressors and bonded together in a new sense of common outrage, without the constraints of Cold War alliances and entanglements. This was represented by the enormous diplomatic and political efforts to form the largest coalition in history. Nations from all over the globe supported the coalition with troops, supplies, food, fuel, and medical personnel. Some of the contributions were relatively insignificant, such as the mujahideen providing 300 soldiers to defend holy sites in Saudi Arabia. Others were extremely significant, such as the Egyptian, British, and French contingents.[7]

Prior to receiving overwhelming global support, the United States had to first convince the Saudi government of the importance of allowing U.S. forces onto Saudi soil. The normally closed kingdom was convinced only after a series of briefings to top Saudi officials, including King Fahd himself. The briefings, given by General Schwarzkopf and Secretary of Defense Richard Cheney, used the highest-quality satellite imagery to convince the king of the danger posed by the Iraqi army poised on his northern border.[8]

The satellite imagery was one aspect of the effect of technology, but the media also demonstrated what information warfare would look like. During Vietnam, the American public could watch the Tet Offensive during the evening news. During Desert Storm, they watched it like a violent soap opera. The level of communications technology allowed a significant increase in coverage. This had a direct impact on the negotiations, which seemed to occur over the fiber-optic cables of CNN more than across the diplomatic meeting table. President talked to president not over a hotline but over satellite news networks. The media role was not new or completely unexpected, but it was at a greater level than during any other conflict in history. The American people watched bombs fly through doors and barely miss a car on a bridge; they also watched and heard the initial attack on Baghdad through a microphone held out of a Baghdad hotel window. The media's influence had an impact at all levels of the conflict. Many military unit commanders received the first news of their impending deployment over television. Additionally, many of the commanders were able to watch the "commander in chief's news conference, and then watch as his [own] immediate superiors translate that news into military intent. . . ."[9] New, faster communications technology also was manifest on the battlefield. This aspect is addressed under "Technical Context."

The two dynamics of a "New World Order" and a greater level of information caused this war to be an aberration of sorts. The weakness of one of the superpowers in relation to the other, and the threat to much of the world's economy, was easy to see and identify, which translated into a large combination of nations against a lone attacker. Once the decision to use military force was made and agreed to by the entire coalition, it became clear that nothing short of victory was likely. Even with the overwhelming military capability, the nature of coalition warfare typically means that it would be a war of limited objectives. These objectives were identified in various UN resolutions and were challenged and tested by the government in Iraq right up to the last moments before the ground campaign began. After more than a month of the air war, the Iraqi and Soviet leadership agreed to an Iraqi pullout. The Iraqis stated that they would leave Kuwait "unconditionally," then went on to state conditions. This drew scathing remarks from the American leadership and an ultimatum that required Iraq to begin the withdrawal from Kuwait within twenty-four hours.[10] Less than seventy-two hours later, the U.S.-led coalition ground forces crossed into Kuwait.

Theater Strategy

General Colin Powell put it best when he stated that the strategy of the coalition in reference to the Iraqi army in Kuwait was, "We're going to cut it off, and then we're going to kill it."[11] The coalition that was amassed to accomplish this mission was enormous. It goes far beyond the scope of this chapter to even attempt to identify the elements involved. The coalition sought to achieve its success through a series of simple moves best identified in the following CINCCENT's (Commander in Chief Central Command) intent statement:

> We will offset the imbalance of ground combat power by using our strength against his weakness. Initially execute deception operations to focus his attention on defense and cause incorrect organization of forces. We will initially attack into the Iraqi homeland using air power to decapitate his leadership, command and control, and eliminate his ability to reinforce Iraqi forces in Kuwait and southern Iraq. We will then gain undisputed air superiority over Kuwait so that we can subsequently and selectively attack Iraqi ground forces with air power in order to reduce his combat power and destroy reinforcing units. Finally, we will fix Iraqi forces in place by feints and limited objective attacks followed by armored force penetration and exploitation to seize key lines of communication nodes, which will put us in a position to interdict resupply and remaining reinforcements from Iraq and eliminate forces in Kuwait.[12]

These moves were broken down into steps. First was to deny the Iraqi military the use of electronic and physical means to observe the coalition forces. The second was to deny Iraq president Saddam Hussein the use of strategic weapons storage, production, and manufacturing facilities. The third, accomplished almost simultaneously with the second, was to deny the Iraqi army an opportunity to resupply. The fourth was the systematic targeting and attrition of the ground forces in Iraq.

Each step was accomplished with the intent of forcing Saddam Hussein to capitulate. It was hoped that the air bombardment would be sufficient for victory, though the buildup of forces did not rely on an easy campaign. Despite the complete destruction or paralyzation of the Iraqi air force, the blinding of all electronic means of observation, the destruction of all bridges over the Euphrates River, the bombardment of many production and other major facilities (including utilities), and the thunderous bombing of the ground units, the Iraqi forces were still in Kuwait.

The naval forces completely sealed Iraq from any outside assistance being received over the water. The airpower kept most of Iraq's surviving aircraft on the ground or forced them to escape to Iran, a former enemy. Army aviation was used to destroy radar facilities to allow the initial attacks. The offshore Marine presence kept several divisions pinned along the coast to defend against a possible attack from the sea. Each of these portions of the service so effectively conducted their segments of the war as to completely defeat all but the ground forces.

Even with success on the sea and in the air, the Iraqis proved adept at confusing the aerial attackers. They used some of the oldest deception measures known. Diesel fires set following a bombing run on already-destroyed vehicles caused pilots to assess more kills each run than were really serviced. The following quote details these efforts, as related by an Iraqi battalion commander, Major Mohammed, of the Tawakalna Division of the Iraqi Republican Guard:

Mohammed's unit was the unhappy recipient of frequent runs by U.S. and coalition heavy bombers. He . . . was attacked an average of once every 10 hours for more than 35 consecutive days.

"We had 36 tanks when the bombing started, Jan. 17th. Before your attack yesterday [27 February 1991] we had lost only nine tanks to the attacks from the air," Mohammed said. "We discovered quickly that if we set fire to the tanks that had already been destroyed, the air crews would think they had hit us hard and would not come back for secondary runs."[13]

(All times are Saudi Arabian time)

Date	Event
17 Jan	0300: Operation Desert Storm begins with initiation of air campaign.
30–31 Jan	Battle of Khafji—Iraqis attack a northern Saudi town called Khafji. Saudi and Qatari troops counterattack and retake the town.
24 Feb	0400: ground phase of Operation Desert Storm begins.
	101st Airborne conducts largest air assault in history toward Euphrates River.
25 Feb	Scud missile strikes American barracks in Al Khobar; 29 killed, largest single wartime casualties of the conflict.
26 Feb	Coalition forces make direct fire contact with Republican Guard.
27 Feb	Pres. Bush halts campaign after 100 hours.

Source: Gwen Flanders, ed., "Operation Desert Storm: A Day by Day Account," *USA Today*, 8 March 1991, 11E.

One of the major fears of the coalition was the potential use of chemical agents by Iraq. There has been a great deal of debate about whether or not the authority to use weapons was delegated to the field commanders, or even if chemical munitions were in theater.[14] Regardless of the debate, the fear of chemical use was foremost in the minds of military and political leaders. This led to the focus on SCUD missile launchers and attacks on all known chemical weapon manufacturing and storage facilities.

Each of the services provided a significant amount of destructive firepower to the attack on Saddam Hussein's army, yet they still needed to be forcibly ejected from Kuwait by a comparable ground force. This was possible after the completion of the deployment of the U.S. VII Corps. This heavy armored corps was moved to Southwest Asia from Germany to provide offensive muscle to the coalition. Once the corps was in place, the coalition could begin the attack.

The corps could not get into place, however, until the Iraqi government became blind—by the loss of reconnaissance assets—to what was happening along its border with Saudi Arabia.

Operational Context

The ground component of Operation Desert Storm was the largest armored force since World War II. This was also the first time since the Korean War that an army headquarters commanded an American army in the field. The two corps controlled by the U.S. Third Army represented the majority of the U.S. ground combat power. Fully eight divisions were engaged from the army. The XVIII Airborne Corps, which was the first to arrive, had been moved latest to a position on the extreme western flank of the army. This corps featured only one armored or mechanized division, plus an armored cavalry regiment. It also had control of the French division in theater. The VII Corps from Germany had the majority of the armor and mechanized equipment. It boasted four armor or mechanized divisions along with an armored cavalry regiment, and was the largest armored corps in history.[15] VII Corps was placed between XVIII Airborne Corps to the west and the Marine and coalition corps to the east with the expectation of defeating the Iraqi Republican Guard. To the east of this corps was one of two joint forces, followed by a U.S. Marine Corps force and another joint element. These three forces were tasked with the responsibility of securing the country of Kuwait with a focus on the Wadi Al-Batin in the west and Kuwait City in the east.

The stated goals of the ground attack were:[16]

- To complete the envelopment with a U.S. corps-sized armored force positioned west of the Republican Guards Forces Command (RGFC) and a U.S. corps armored force positioned south of the RGFC. A combined Egyptian, Syrian, Saudi, Nigerian, and Kuwaiti armored force would be positioned on the north-south LOCs [lines of communications] in Kuwait.
- Draw Iraq's reserve forces away from the main attack with deception, feints, and two supporting attacks.

• The U.S. supporting attack was to defend the right flank of the main attack from a counterattack by the tactical reserves, draw forces away from the main attack, and block LOCs.

• The main attack was to bypass forces and attack west of the Kuwait border, occupying a position west of the RGFC to prevent successful counterattack by Iraq's strategic reserve, and attack the RGFC.

• Conduct psychological operations (PSYOP) to degrade Iraqi morale.

• Use Special Operations Forces (SOF) for deception, direct action, and surveillance.

• Use electronic warfare to disrupt Iraqi communications from corps to brigade after this first supporting attack began, and from corps to General Headquarters before the western supporting attack began.

The overall plan called for a feint up the Wadi Al-Batin by the army reserve, the 1st Cavalry Division. This was intended to pull some of the Iraqi reserves down toward the border. Following this feint, the three elements in the east would attack against the center of the Iraqi defenses. This was also designed to force the commitment of the Republican Guard and other reserve elements into Kuwait in an attempt to stop the coalition advance. Following this expected movement, VII Corps would begin breaching the defensive berms along the border and attack along the Kuwaiti-Iraqi border to the north, then, just short of the northern border of Kuwait, turn east into the heart of the Republican Guard. Farther to the west, the XVIII Airborne Corps would conduct a screening operation of the army's left flank with the French division and attack to the north with the air assault and armor elements toward the Euphrates River valley. Once in the vicinity of the Euphrates, the mechanized division would turn east and attack to prevent the withdrawal of escaping Iraqi forces.

The attack began much better than expected, which caused General Schwarzkopf to move up the attacks of VII and XVIII Corps by nearly twenty-four hours. Although this caused some problems, the forces were able to begin the attack.

VII Corps led with the 2d ACR, which performed an offensive cover mission. The ACR was to protect the main body of the corps, find the Republican Guard, and pass the heavy divisions through to complete the destruction. The conduct of this mission went nearly flawlessly; the regiment destroyed several outposts and minor elements of the 12th Armored Division and the Tawakalna Division of the Republican Guard as the 2d ACR received the orders to turn east. Much of the theater-level detailed intelligence information was being received from the JSTARS aircraft, which tracked ground targets.[17] The plan was—as JSTARS fed the information down to the theater- and corps-level commanders—to continue to push the regiment's aircraft out ahead for early warning and attrition of the enemy with indirect fires. This plan was soon altered, because a *shamal* became so strong as to force all aircraft in the corps to remain grounded for the duration of the storm.

The regiment then continued its movement with some concern over the movement of the 1st British Armored Division. VII Corps sent out a fragmentary order (FRAGO) at about 0200 on the tactical email system that changed 2d ACR's orientation to due east. The 2d ACR called the 1st British Armored Division in reference to the FRAGO, but the British unit did not receive the message. The regimental headquarters informed their subordinate headquarters, with emphasis on keeping 1st Squadron informed; it was the right flank unit of the regiment. This passing of radio traffic kept all units informed and allowed 1st Squadron to stop a potential fratricide.

The British had crossed the 2d ACR boundary and were being observed by elements of 1st Squadron, 2d ACR, as they engaged a company of Iraqi armor in the 1st Squadron zone. Once this situation was cleared, the regiment began to make contact initially with stationary forces, then with the retreating elements of the 12th Armored and Tawakalna Divisions. It is likely that these units were conducting local repositioning. As they did so, they were hit in the flank and forced to withdraw through elements of 2d Squadron, 2d ACR. Throughout the movement, 2d ACR was essentially conducting a movement to contact. The enemy location was not defined beyond a five-kilometer by three-kilometer division symbol on the regimental commander's battle map. The regiment was looking for contact with T-72s. Once the squadrons reported contact with T-72s, the commander and staff knew they had found the Tawakalna Division. This is where the tactical portion begins.

Technical Context

Despite the fact that the Iraqi army represented the most sophisticated antagonist of the five battles studied, the difference in technology was nearly the greatest. Only the battle in Somalia represented a more significant difference in technological capability. The 2d ACR brought with it some of the most advanced equipment in war. The M1A1 main battle tank represented nearly twenty years of American automotive and ballistics development. It combined speed, firepower, and crew protection in a manner that no other tank of the time equaled. Despite the performance it would demonstrate during the battle, the M1 was one of the most criticized tanks in the world for the feared maintenance problems associated with a turbine engine in a desert environment. The Bradley infantry or cavalry fighting vehicles were equally criticized. Despite the criticism, the operational readiness rate for Bradleys was more than 90 percent, and one particular armor brigade conducted the entire offensive operation without losing a single vehicle to maintenance.[18] The M1A1 fleet was equally impressive, and the 3d Armored Division did not lose a single one of its 350 tanks to maintenance.[19] The regiment also possessed the Apache attack helicopter, which had numerous advanced avionics and targeting packages. The assets represented by the regiment were truly overwhelming.

It was not the vehicles themselves that represented the technological advantages. Instead, it was the small gadgets carried by soldiers or within the vehicles that were the breakthrough. The 2d ACR conducted a series of compass courses to train and improve mounted navigation in the relatively featureless desert prior to the attack, but received the global positioning system (GPS) receivers only a matter of weeks before the attack began. The ability of the coalition force to maneuver anywhere it wanted to across an essentially featureless plain was provided by these small receivers. Nearly all companies and many platoon leaders possessed them. The Iraqis were completely unprepared for this; they frequently established defenses oriented along roads. The Tawakalna Division, for example, used a major (two-lane, hard-surface) pipeline road around which to organize its defense. The second significant advantage was thermal sights. The 2d ACR troopers had the ability to fight at night and in limited visibility as no army had before them. The desert conditions only added to this advantage, because the ground cooled rapidly, allowing the warm vehicles to stand out in more significant contrast. There were numerous anecdotes during the course of the war of Iraqi tank commanders being unaware of the approaching coalition forces, then an explosion of a neighboring vehicle would cause a turret to fly into the air.[20] This provided a significant psychological as well as technological edge. The *shamal* reduced the Iraqis' already limited night vision capability to approximately 800 meters rather than the 2,400 to 3,000 meters of the American systems. Once again, the Iraqis were completely unaware of their opponents' capabilities.

In addition to the technology at the vehicle or platoon level, there was a tremendous advantage at the division and corps level. The corps commanders received periodic updates from assets such as JS-TARS, unmanned aerial vehicles, and satellite imagery. These assets functioned with little interference from terrain or vegetation. Only Iraqi deception efforts provided any confusion, and this was limited.

Despite the perception of perfect understanding, this first information-age war still presented the commander with some challenges. The passage of lines of VII Corps through 2d ACR was a challenge because of the ever-present "fog of war." The regiment was in contact for more than four hours before the regimental commander was even aware of it. The challenge of fighting and reporting simultaneously was a technical problem that occurred in this battle as well as many previous ones. The 2d ACR skillfully navigated, using the assets from space, into a position of advantage so tremendous that a completely unaware industrial-age army had no chance to achieve any measure of victory.

Tactical Chronology

The battle of 73 Easting was essentially one engagement in a very large movement to contact. Colonel Holder described his mission to "[m]ake contact, hold and develop the situation so the corps commander could exploit the gaps."[21] During the latter half of the movement, the regiment was ordered to turn east and continue the attack toward the Iraqi-Kuwaiti border. As the regiment turned east, it began to control movement by the use of grid lines.

On 25 February the regiment had met and defeated a brigade of the 12th Armored Division in defensive positions; the corps commander had directed them to continue and fix the Republican Guards elements to the east and be prepared to pass the 1st Infantry Division forward.[22] Colonel Holder clarified the mission: "My orders were to destroy all enemy armor and artillery, but bypass infantry. We didn't involve ourselves in unimportant fights. We concentrated on the objective, which was the Republican Guard."[23] The bypassing of unimportant units began as the regiment "aimed for a gap between the Iraqi 26th Infantry Division and the 46th Infantry Division to its west . . ."[24] right after it crossed the initial line of departure. The regiment continued to move through the rest of the day and into the night, allowing the 3d Armored Division to come abreast on its left (north). By 0900 on the morning of 26 February, the weather had become poor; a sandstorm moved into the area and grounded the aviation support from the regimental air squadron. Continuing to the east, the corps commander again visited the regimental command post and reiterated previous guidance. The 2d ACR moved with three squadrons abreast, and in the late afternoon, at approximately 1500, it passed the new line of departure given the change in orientation to the east. Seven hours later, it was passing the 1st Infantry Division after it had fought and defeated elements of two divisions.[25]

The 2d Squadron conducted the movement to contact in a squadron box formation, with two troops forward and two troops back. The forward troops from 2d Squadron were Eagle and Ghost Troops, Eagle on the right (south) and Ghost on the left (north).

The southernmost troop of 3d Squadron was Iron Troop. It also became embroiled in the engagement, and the three troops combined to destroy more than a brigade's worth of equipment. Typically a ground cavalry troop moves with scouts (in Bradleys) in front, to identify the enemy location and disposition, and tanks behind, to react to enemy contact without being initially engaged.

In the late afternoon, the *shamal* turned the sky almost completely dark. The two forward troops continued to move. Several minor engagements throughout the afternoon involved the security forces of the Republican Guard and the 12th Armored Division. The regiment received satellite and other imagery approximately fourteen hours previous to the contact. It knew the location of a large armored force, probably the Tawakalna Division, and its disposition.[26] These minor engagements were typically against a few tanks or armored personnel carriers. Each engagement lasted only a few moments.

Even though these were short engagements, they signaled contact with the larger force, and the regimental commander made the recommendation to VII Corps of passing the follow-on divisions at the 70 Easting. During the engagement to follow, the Iraqi crews were caught completely unaware. Regardless of the lack of warning, the Iraqi gunners stubbornly began returning fire, aiming at the muzzle flashes of the American tanks through the sand of the *shamal*. Judging distance is difficult in a flat desert, and the Iraqis had zeroed (bore sighted) their tanks at a standard range of 1,800 meters. The Americans had begun the engagement at 2,400 meters, so the initial Iraqi rounds fell short. The Americans continued the attack while charging forward. This caused more Iraqi gunnery problems as they adjusted for the short rounds and subsequently fired over the tops of the advancing Americans.[27]

Eagle Troop continued to move in a traditional cavalry formation, with the scouts forward and the tanks in the trail. Captain H. R. McMaster, Eagle Troop commander, ordered the tanks forward shortly after he received word to pass the 1st Infantry Division at the 70 Easting. The tanks rolled faster to come even with the Bradley mounted scouts. Captain McMaster came over a small IV line and was immediately well within range of several Iraqi tanks (T-72s). He gave the fire command to his gunner and directed the tank platoons to come forward with his tank. Once all nine tanks crested the berm, they opened fire, destroying nine targets nearly simultaneously. The Iraqi tanks did not respond. McMaster ordered his troop forward, informing the squadron that the 70 Easting was right in the middle of the Iraqi assembly area it was attacking. The troop was given permission to move to the 73 Easting. In the course of the battle, thirty tanks, sixteen BMPs (Soviet-made infantry fighting vehicles), and thirty-nine trucks were destroyed with direct fire. Once through the brigade assembly area, the troop established defensive positions.[28]

Field artillery assets played an important role in protecting the squadron from defeat as the units supporting the battle fired "[m]ore than 2,000 howitzer rounds and 12 MLRS rockets spewed 130,000 bomblets on the frontline Iraqis and targets beyond the range of direct fire weapons. When a company of T-72s threatened to overrun 3rd Platoon of G Troop, howitzers fired an immediate suppression mission that stopped the Iraqis cold."[29] Artillerymen would later fire in support of the battle of 73 Easting against targets identified only by aerial photographs and destroy more than a company of armored vehicles and various other Iraqi vehicles and fortifications.[30]

Ghost Troop, to the north, began the engagement in a similar manner to Eagle's with the exception of the commander's changing formation prior to contact and pushing his tanks forward based on reports of contact from the south.[31] They set defensive positions as well, but elements of the Tawakalna and 12th Armored Divisions kept trying to push through them in hopes of escaping the deadly attack of the coalition forces. Major Campbell later stated that the two Iraqi elements had become entangled and "were trying to retreat through the same narrow piece of terrain."[32] One artillery sergeant stated that he saw "tanks coming over the hill like there's no tomorrow. . . . They were fighting for their lives, trying to get out."[33] During the course of the battle, the use of indirect fire was crucial in the destruction of enemy equipment as the artillerymen directed "720 howitzer rounds." This was essential in ensuring the survival of Ghost Troop elements.[34] Unlike Eagle Troop, they did not do this without loss of their own. The troop suffered several casualties, including one death. The troop struggled to defend against repeated attack, at times forcing the commander to reposition tanks to support the more vulnerable Bradleys, yet they repelled every attempt, until the enemy was completely exhausted and unable to send any more against the troop.

It has been reported that the "defending Iraqi commander later remarked that after losing 2 of his 39 T-72s in five weeks of air attack, the 2d Cavalry had annihilated his entire command in fewer than six minutes. . . ."[35] Ghost Troop was credited with destroying the "equivalent of an Iraqi brigade" during the night.[36]

Following the successful defense of Ghost Troop and the effective engagements of the entire regiment, the corps commander was able to send the 1st Infantry Division forward. The elements of the regiment would finish the war as the corps reserve in a much quieter situation. The other battles with the Republican Guard were to be fought by the division tank and mechanized infantry battalions.

Time Line[37]

Date	Time	Event
20 Dec 90		Entire regiment in the desert
mid-Jan 91		Regiment replaces M3s with new M2A2s
11–13 Jan 91		Command post exercise held to develop regimental command and control
17 Jan 91		Air war begins
23 Feb 91	1330	210th Field Artillery Brigade opens fire for nine minutes
	1339	2d ACR begins attack into Iraq
	1530	20 kilometers into Iraq
24 Feb 91	1400	2d ACR soldiers don chemical protective equipment
	1730	2d Squadron elements clear Objective Merrell
25 Feb 91	0640	2d ACR resumes attack numerous engagements against single vehicles to battalions. No significant issues posed by Iraqi elements.
	1600	Lt. Gen. Franks arrives at regimental

Date	Time	Event
		headquarters and gives guidance to Col. Holder
26 Feb 91	0205	Elements of the regiment receive rocket artillery fire while in nighttime positions. Some losses are incurred.
	0330	Regiment receives fragmentary order to change the movement direction to due east Ghost Troop destroys two BMPs; Eagle Troop destroys remaining BMP. Tawakalna Division has lost its security.
	0600	2d ACR turns due east
	0730	4th Squadron (Aviation) engaged by tank fire from T-72s
	0845	2d Squadron halts to allow following divisions to stage for the passage
	0900	*Shamal* in the area; flight operations halted
	1200	Multiple small contacts with security forces
	1600	Eagle Troop engages a small village with Iraqi armor present
	1607	Eagle Troop engages and destroys nine tanks, then continues the attack as more enemy positions are identified. By 1630 it has halted just east of 73 Easting and consolidates after destroying numerous Iraqi equipment.
	1620	Ghost Troop encounters T-72s and BMPs. They engage and destroy the vehicles. More vehicles appear as the Tawakalna Division attacks them.
	1800	1st Infantry Division coordinates passage of lines. Ghost Troop still in heavy contact.
	2200	Battle subsides
	2230	1st Infantry Division begins passage of lines

Battlefield Leadership

The 2d Squadron destroyed Iraqi elements at least three times its size over the course of this quickly fought battle. For Eagle Troop, the battle lasted twenty-five minutes or less. The rapid defeat of the Iraqi forces was accomplished through the development of subordinate leaders during training. The philosophy of the regiment was to train in peacetime the way it planned to fight in war. This essentially meant espousing and fostering the ability of junior officers to make important decisions during maneuver training. It was this sort of philosophy that allowed Captain McMaster the opportunity and confidence to attack the Iraqi assembly area and inform his higher headquarters during execution, rather than asking and waiting for instructions. Rapid decisionmaking made the success of the battle possible.

In the engagements there were two important decisions: the Eagle Troop commander's decision to attack and the Ghost Troop commander's decision about when and where to defend.

The first decision resulted in the destruction of a significant amount of Iraqi equipment. This was possible when the commander identified the fact that the Iraqi tanks were not returning fire. Capitalizing on this confusion saved American lives, because the Iraqis were completely unprepared and disoriented.

The second decision was that of Ghost Troop to defend in the wadi. This meant they sat astride the escape route of a significant portion of a division. A terrain decision, made by a captain, resulted in the destruction of a colonel's command.

Significance

The battle of 73 Easting enabled VII Corps to transition from the movement to contact into the pursuit phase of the operation. The success of the regiment is summed up in these words:

In four hours Holder's three cavalry troops had fired three hundred TOWs and tank rounds, plus seven thousand cannon and machine gun rounds. More than two hundred Iraqi armored and wheeled vehicles were destroyed. Nearly all of one Tawakalna brigade and elements of the 12th Armored Division had been obliterated. Because troops on the regimental right had encountered no T-72s, Holder was able to ensure Franks that the cavalry had found a gap in the enemy defenses to the south. Into that breach the corps commander could now steer the Big Red One. . . .[38]

The battle of 73 Easting also demonstrated the ability of small-unit commanders to succeed on a modern battlefield and the importance of ground power in demonstrating dominance.

The Iraqi units involved had been subjected to hundreds of hours of bombings, yet they were still viable, highly motivated combat forces. These units would never have left Kuwait without the American army's forcing them to leave.

Because of the success of American forces in these engagements, many have extrapolated this victory as leading toward a trend of future conflict. Some have used this success to espouse the need to "retain our [American] technological edge out into the future . . . [and] to be ready for the next Desert Storm–like contingency that comes along."[39] The technological advantage held during Desert Storm was critical to the ease of the victory and was especially critical for the survival of the 2d ACR during the battle of 73 Easting. The main significance of the battle of 73 Easting—and, even more, the entire operation—was best stated by the commander of the 24th Infantry Division: "[The] legacy is two million free Kuwaiti citizens and an enduring message to both free and oppressed people throughout the world. . . . There is hope; freedom is never without cost, and Americans will fight and die for our principles."[40]

Less than a day after the battle ended, U.S. president George H. W. Bush made the following statement: "Kuwait is liberated. Iraq's army is defeated. Our military objectives are met. . . . I am pleased to announce that at midnight tonight, [27 February 1991] Eastern Standard Time, exactly 100 hours since ground operations commenced and six weeks since the start of Operation Desert Storm, all United States and coalition forces will suspend offensive combat operations."[41]

Lessons Learned

The lessons learned from this battle focus on how they may be used in the future rather than simply on what went right or what went wrong. It is a foregone conclusion that, from this enormous defeat, Saddam Hussein learned a great deal about how to fight and win against the West.

Identification: The ability of the coalition force to clearly see the enemy was truly a combat multiplier. Never before had a field commander enjoyed such an informational dominance over his opponent. Despite this knowledge, the information still had difficulty getting down to the lower levels in the command chain. There are currently programs to provide technology that will pass on this sort of information to all units. Even with this technology, it must be remembered that the Iraqi army defended in an industrial-age manner in terrain devoid of significant cover or concealment. Because of this, the world learned the foolishness of attempting any similar sort of operation in the future.

Isolation: Within the scope of this battle the enemy was not isolated, but at the operational strategy level, the Iraqi army was completely isolated from any outside support. This denied any effective logistics efforts and completely limited resupply to tactical units. The effect on soldier morale was a direct contributor to the large numbers of prisoners of war. It was this isolation in logistics, maneuver support, and information that allowed the Iraqi units to be caught off guard, then blunder into the engagement areas of the 2d Squadron, 2d ACR.

Suppression: The air war, though not conclusive, completely denied the freedom of maneuver to the Iraqi army. The only relief came with the *shamal* in that it denied the attack aviation support.

Maneuver: This was a tremendously successful though simple maneuver that resulted in the attack of an assailable enemy flank.

Destruction: Success of the first four elements in this list led to the complete destruction of the enemy force by a smaller attacking one.

Conclusion

The battle of 73 Easting is at the edge of the information age. Some of the equipment, such as JSTARS and GPS, are at the heart of the revolution in military affairs. Even with these gadgets, the situational awareness and digital communications had not been fielded. The army of today is as different from the army of Desert Storm as that army was from the one in Vietnam. Yet there is still much to be seen of the future. When a higher-tier force engages a lower one in terrain that is essentially neutral with little to no cover and concealment, technology can operate without constraints. This brings the full weight of precision munitions and the arsenal of a superpower against the lower-tier power and will almost always result in higher-tier victory.

Desert Storm, and particularly this battle, demonstrates the dominance of higher-tier firepower. The Iraqi soldiers seldom saw or heard what killed them, and few ever saw or heard what killed their companion vehicles. This was a result of the use of advanced optics over the archaic passive sights used by the Iraqis.

Even though this was a cross-tier fight, most nations have learned from this type of tactic when fighting higher-tier forces. Few leaders will engage a higher-tier force in open terrain with time to prepare. If anything, there is more to learn from the Iraqis than from the American victory. When a similar scenario was conducted during the 1998 Army After Next Spring Wargame, the individuals playing the Iraq-like nation attacked rapidly to seize the urban environments and established prepared urban defenses by the time the American forces arrived in theater. This forced the Americans to deploy from extended distances rather than into prepared Saudi airfields and ports. It also forced the Americans into urban rather than open-terrain battles. Future foes, to include Saddam Hussein, will follow the second example rather than Saddam's own mistakes of 1990–91.

Chapter Seven

Battle Analysis: The Battle of Mogadishu
Operation Restore Hope, 3–4 October 1993

Yes, the Russians were militarily incompetent in Chechnya. On the other hand, they had no choice but to use armored vehicles in city streets—like all advanced armies, they lacked the infantry strength to reduce the city building by building. . . . [O]ur soldiers found themselves in deadly combat in Mogadishu under conditions that begged for armor. Apart from the political considerations that denied our troops the tools they needed to overwhelm their opponents, the military itself was guilty of relying on traditional approaches to urban operations that are no longer feasible when domestic elites panic in the face of casualties (friendly or enemy).

—Ralph Peters

The battle of Mogadishu is a recent example of a tier-four nation attempting to defeat the intent of the United States. During the battle, warlords and civilians who armed themselves fought elements of the American army within the maze of streets of the Somalia capital. This pitched battle demonstrated the fifth of the methods that lower-tier nations use against higher-tier nations: drawing the higher-tier force into an urban or a complex terrain environment. Somalia also presents further evidence of the first method of mass human wave attacks in a tier-four fashion.

Unlike the previous four battles, this one was fought in an environment often referred to as an operation other than war (OOTW) or security and stability operation (SASO). The soldiers did not necessarily expect a warlike environment, which makes this battle one of the most intriguing. This battle's context creates a possible scenario for future operations conducted in an OOTW or a SASO environment.

The battle of Mogadishu was a case where the American army achieved a significant tactical victory but was defeated on the grand strategy level. The eventual withdrawal of forces from Somalia was precipitated by the events discussed in this chapter. Some people have classified this battle as a watershed in American national security policy, that the lack of willingness to endure casualties in pursuit of an accepted policy demonstrated by the immediate cessation of offensive engagements was an indicator of future events. Certainly many who watched the event—and few leaders around the world did not—understood the pain threshold of the American political and military leadership.

The battle of Mogadishu was precipitated by the events of the previous ten months. The reasons for the American deployment, and the changing mission of the remaining American personnel following the withdrawal of the majority of the American contingent, are critical to understanding why the operation was initiated as part of a stated humanitarian relief mission.

Geographical Setting

Location

Somalia is the "horn of Africa." Neighbored by Ethiopia to the north and Kenya to the west, Somalia is slightly smaller than the state of Texas. The nation itself had been ruled by Muhammad Siad Barre, a military dictator, since 1969. After the collapse of the Soviet Union and the Cold War that sent millions of dollars of aid into the region, the nation began to crumble. The decline became precipitous until President Barre fled Mogadishu for the Kenyan border. The tribal clans that forced this development continued their fighting to gain the critical power of the nation—the ability to print money and run up debt on the national account.[1] This civil war eventually reduced the nation to a group of warlords with hired guns.

The civil war led to a complete disintegration of national-level support. The chaos that resulted was further compounded by a severe famine throughout the region. Publicizing the effects of the famine brought a significant outpouring of financial and food aid. Much of the early aid sent into the country by the United States was delivered through airfields in Kenya to prevent entanglements in the more populated and chaotic urban areas. Later, the aid flowed into and through Mogadishu.

Mogadishu is Somalia's capital and the most modern of the nation's cities. During the initial U.S. occupation and into the UN occupation, the entering forces established a major dividing line, called the Green Line, that marked clan borders. The U.S. forces were located near the ocean on the southern edge of Mogadishu at the airport, allowing for easy resupply and support from shipboard personnel. Other UN supporting nations were divided around the city at various locations. The Pakistanis, for example, were located at a sports stadium in the northeastern portion of the city.

Terrain/Vegetation

Mogadishu had little vegetation, and almost none of military significance. The only vegetation that did have an impact on the battle was a few trees that grew at random throughout the city. These were often used to provide cover from the withering fire. Most of the terrain was dominated by what could be classified in military terms as existing manmade obstacles: specifically, buildings. Most of the buildings were constructed of cement blocks or mud bricks; some had walled courtyards. The high-walled courtyards, combined with very narrow, poorly maintained roads, created a sort of urban maze. Poor urban planning and lack of civic support structures (such as refuse removal) added to the mazelike nature of the streets, causing much frustration for American commanders. The difficulty navigating and directing the movement of rescue columns caused the greatest delays and allowed the Somalis the opportunity to mount a difficult defense.

Weather

Tropical heat with little humidity made the battlefield an uncomfortable place. Most American soldiers elected not to take canteens of water, because they expected the mission to be over within one to two hours. The dry climate meant that helicopter rotor wash created a brownout[2] every time the aircraft got close to the ground.

Units Involved

American Forces

The units involved were divided into three basic subdivisions. The first was called Task Force (TF) Ranger, actually a combination of U.S. Army Rangers and the Special Operations Forces Detachment–Delta (Delta Force). Task Force Ranger included the soldiers tasked with the original mission. They had a group of forces to air assault in, and a ground convoy designated to exfiltrate with TF Ranger personnel and the hostages. This was a combination of the most highly trained light infantry in the world. Rangers are soldiers who volunteer for demanding additional training to become part of a storied unit. The Rangers are typically young, between twenty and twenty-three years of age. Delta Force is typically older, averaging close to thirty years of age. To become a member of the secretive Delta Force requires passing a special selection course, undergoing detailed psychological evaluations, and spending hundreds of hours honing individual and team skills.

The second group was the UN-designated quick reaction force (QRF), which consisted of 2d Battalion, 14th Infantry, from the 10th Mountain Division. This force was divided into three companies. The first company out, C Company, was the quick reaction company. It was tasked to be able to move from the U.S. compound within thirty minutes. Additional companies were to be ready to move within an hour.[3] The American forces had no armored vehicles in country, which forced coordination with the UN commander to gain support from the Pakistani or Malaysian contingents.

The third American unit was the air assets in country. Many aircraft were sent from TF 160—the Nightstalkers. This is the U.S. Army's Special Operations Aviation Regiment. The pilots of this unit spend hundreds of flying hours training to fly in the most demanding environments. This type of flying requires significant training with the supported ground unit. Task Force 160 is designated to support elements such as TF Ranger on a regular basis. The aviation assets in country were of two particular types: the AH-6 (Littlebird) and the MH-60 (Blackhawk). The Littlebird could carry two personnel in addition to the pilot and copilot, or it could carry a minigun and ammunition. The Blackhawk carried up to twelve fully loaded soldiers. Both aircraft were equipped with six-barrel miniguns, designed to fire thousands of rounds a minute either automatically or manually with the addition of door-gunners. Other aviation assets also existed in country, most coming from elements of the 10th Mountain Division's Aviation Brigade. During the course of the engagement, the Littlebirds supported the Delta Force and TF Ranger personnel. Additionally, several of the Littlebirds and Blackhawks had Delta Force snipers on board to help support the operation.

To reach the ground from the aircraft in the narrow streets, the soldiers would utilize a technique called fast-roping. The crew chiefs of the aircraft would swing out two three-inch-diameter nylon ropes, one on either side of the aircraft; then the soldiers would slide down the ropes like children at a playground sliding down a pole. This was a practiced and rehearsed skill. Many of the soldiers involved might have had this sort of training close to a hundred times. The aircraft was most vulnerable as it hovered to allow the fast-roping. It was then that the crews showed the greatest level of discipline and courage. A premature departure would cause either death or serious injury to those who had yet to depart the rope.

The soldiers designated as ground convoy support were supported with less technically advanced equipment. They had hardtop high-mobility multiwheeled vehicles (HMMWVs) and open-bed, five-ton trucks. The HMMWVs had some armor protection, but only against the smallest-caliber weapons being used. The five-tons had no protection whatsoever. The soldiers traditionally placed sandbags in the interior of the vehicles to protect themselves from small-arms fire and ordnance fragments.

Somali Forces

The Somali people in Mogadishu normally associated themselves with their tribal group or clan. The Habr Gidr clan, of Somali clan leader Mohammed Aidid, was centered in the market region of the city, where TF Ranger was to strike. In this area there were thousands who possessed some form of infantry weapon: handguns, grenades, rifles, machine guns. This clan and others who lived in the area would be the primary attackers.

Over the previous six years of civil war, the Somali clans had broken into innumerable sets of warlords. Some of the warlords might have only ten to twenty men at their command. Men usually belonged to these warring clans, though many women became involved as well. These small war bands coalesced into a larger force, like fish in a school, which instinctively reacted to the invading Americans. There was no central control or effort to control the fight. In many cases it was simply an enraged mob taking out its anger against the Americans.[4]

In addition to the war bands that claimed allegiance to a clan, there were groups of freelance fighters, who worked for the highest-paying employer. These people were referred to as technos because they always rode in their vehicles, called technicals. In many cases the technicals were trucks, Land Rovers, or other vehicles with large-caliber weapons mounted to the frame. This group also became involved in the attack on the American personnel and vehicles.[5]

Key Leaders in the Battle

American Forces[6]
- Maj. Gen. William F. Garrison—commander of TF Ranger. During the Vietnam War he helped create the infamous Phoenix project. He has spent the majority of his career in special operations.
- Lt. Col. Gary Harrell—mission commander. He monitored and controlled the entire mission from a command and control Blackhawk.
- Lt. Col. Danny McKnight—commander of the TF Ranger ground convoy.
- Lt. Col. Bill David—commander of 10th Mountain Division's quick reaction force.
- CWO3 Cliff Wolcott—TF 160 MH-60 pilot. Flew Super 61, a Blackhawk, shot down by a Somali-fired rocket-propelled

grenade (RPG). He was killed on impact, which crumpled the airframe around his body. Extricating him from the crash site required a tremendous effort, including vehicles and chains from the rescue column to pull the aircraft away from his body.
• CWO3 Michael Durrant—TF 160 MH-60 pilot. Flew Super 64, a Blackhawk, shot down by a Somali-fired RPG. Captured by the Somali militia and kept alive as a bargaining tool.
• MSgt. Gary Gordon—Delta Force commando. A sniper on Super 62 who volunteered to jump out of the aircraft to help defend the crew of Super 64. Killed in action and later awarded the Congressional Medal of Honor.
• Sfc. Randy Shughart—Delta Force commando. A sniper on Super 62 who volunteered to jump out of the aircraft to help defend the crew of Super 64. Killed in action and later awarded the Congressional Medal of Honor.

Somali Forces[7]
• Mohammed Farrah Aidid—leader of the Habr Gidr clan. Designated by Major General Garrison and others as the primary block to UN initiatives in Somalia. This designation was given because of an attack directed against Pakistani peacekeepers that killed fifty people. Later it was suspected that Aidid directed a remote mine attack against an American convoy, killing several American soldiers.
• Yousef Dahir Mo'Alim—Somali militia leader from Habr Gidr clan. Led a small group of his militia to Chief Durrant's helicopter. He found Durrant and was the primary person responsible for keeping him alive during the initial rage of the mob.
• Abdullah Hassan—Aidid's propaganda minister. Known as "Firimbi," he personally cared for Durrant.

Grand and Theater Context

In late November and early December 1992, it became clear that the situation in Somalia was not going to improve. Numerous aid organizations had been threatened, and thousands of tons of foodstuffs sat rotting on the docks in Mogadishu. Only after paying the technos could a convoy hope to reach the inland regions that were the most affected. Images of this lawless environment and the starvation of thousands gripped Americans.

The New World Order that was supposed to be ushered in with the overwhelming success of Desert Storm, rapidly followed by the collapse of the Soviet Union, created a sense of euphoria regarding the power of the United States. President George H. W. Bush announced that troops were being sent to assist in the famine in Somalia. The scenes over the next several weeks were somewhat humorous, as Marine reconnaissance units and SEALs were greeted with dozens of reporters and bright white television lights in the middle of the night.[8] The landing came unopposed, and the American forces rapidly began to spread into Mogadishu. The city was eventually secured and food began to be transported. The sight of heavily armed American soldiers and marines flying the American flag gave the technos pause and made possible the saving of thousands of lives. Despite the success, the "U.S. military was going into Somalia knowing nothing about Somalia."[9]

The initial success was followed by a relatively rapid withdrawal of much of the initial force. By March 1993, the United States turned over the responsibility for providing stability to Somalia to the UN. The UN then sought to extend the mission from one of feeding starving civilians to building the national infrastructure. Nation building was critical if Somalia would ever return to being a nation rather than a warlord-ravaged desert. With the UN came Pakistani, Malaysian, and Saudi soldiers, who took over the role of escorting food convoys and enforcing peace in the city.

Before the Americans left, the euphoric welcome of the Somalis had turned to feelings of distrust. The soldiers had begun to confiscate weapons. Soldiers bursting into homes and violating the Somalis' privacy led to a disenchanted view of the UN occupation. The majority of Americans left before the anger began to grow too far. Now the UN soldiers started to bear the brunt of the vented hostility.[10]

Operational Context

The hostility grew when the UN declared that Aidid and his clan were the stumbling block in the peace process. The taking of sides against the most powerful warlord in Somalia was the turning point in the entire UN mission. The Somali militia now stepped up its attacks. They were no longer sniping or mortar attacks but ambushes of armed UN convoys and remote detonations of explosives.

The attacks culminated in the deaths of twenty-four Pakistani peacekeepers in a daylight ambush, which got the attention of the American national leadership. The attack on the Pakistanis was answered with an American helicopter attack on one of the primary Habr Gidr headquarters. The rocket and missile attack killed and wounded dozens. More importantly, it alienated the vast majority of Somalis, regardless of clan. The use of what was seen as excessive force created a backlash against the entire mission. The next attack was a command-detonated mine that targeted an American relief column, killing several American soldiers. The pleas for a capability to seize and arrest Somali warlord Aidid were now answered.

Task Force Ranger prepared to be sent to Somalia. An advance team moved into the area to determine the possibility of capturing Aidid. It was reported as likely. Permission for the deployment was approved.[11] The elements of Delta, Ranger, and TF 160 arrived in country and began to train for the missions. The first several attacks proved frustratingly ineffective. Then in early September, TF Ranger arrested two top clan officials. In early October, the possibility of a large arrest appeared. Task Force Ranger did not have much time, so it rapidly put together an operation to capture nearly two dozen clan leaders.

Technical Context

Task Force Ranger was, without question, the most highly trained group of light infantry in the world. Despite this, their technological advantage was rather limited once on the ground. The mission was estimated to last one hour or less, with the extreme of three hours, taking place in the midafternoon. Soldiers elected to leave behind extra water and their night vision devices.[12] When night fell, the single best technology edge at the soldier level was sitting at the Mogadishu airport.

The soldiers of TF Ranger were transported by extremely capable and modern aircraft into the target area. The support from the air throughout the battle was critical to the survival of the force on the ground. This was the most significant high-tech advantage. The next advantage was the use of radio communication. Every Delta member of the assault had a headset microphone, allowing for communication with all other members of the team throughout the operation.

The Rangers and the QRF did not always enjoy communications free of difficulty. Several times, elements entered communication dead zones, where no communication could get out. This resulted in elements of the original chalks (a designation of troops, cargo, or equipment that constitutes a complete aircraft load) and the relief columns getting separated, then pinned down without the ability to inform anyone of the situation. Despite the problems, the American forces still had a tremendous advantage in communications.

At times, this advantage proved to be part of the problems. As the tenacity of the battle increased and casualties mounted, a great deal of confusion was broadcast. The emotionless communications practiced in training failed to appear in combat. This also caused difficulties when guiding the relief columns from the air. A navy aircraft was using high-resolution television to broadcast a live picture back to the headquarters at the airport.[13] Rather than allow the aircraft to communicate directly with the relief column, all transmissions were relayed through the command post. This meant delays in execution. For example, the pilots would direct the convoy to turn right, but by the time the convoy received the transmission from the command post, it had turned down the wrong street. This resulted in the original convoy failing to link up after more than an hour of attempts, despite only a three-block original separation.[14]

The Somalis used weapons that were thirty years old; AK-47s, M16s, and RPG-7s were common among the militia members. These are some of the most prolific small-arms weapons ever produced and could have come directly off a Hollywood production of a Vietnam War movie. However, regardless of the age of the equipment, bullets still pierce human flesh.

Tactical Chronology[15]

The battle began during the late afternoon of 3 October. Delta received word on the location of a secret meeting that was to involve numerous high-ranking members of Aidid's clan, which was the prime target. The plan involved Delta roping onto the top of a multistory building where the meeting was to take place. Rangers would also rope in and secure the corners of the block, one chalk at each corner. As soon as Delta had the prisoners, the entire group was to be exfiltrated by the ground convoy of Ranger HMMWVs and five-ton trucks. The entire operation would be finished and the soldiers back at the airport in less than an hour.

It did not work out that way. Delta's operation went smoothly. The men entered the building, surprised the meeting, and were using handcuffs to secure the prisoners within only a few minutes. Nothing else, however, was going right. Chalk four was misplaced in the initial rope. It was a block out of position. Additionally, one of the members of the chalk had missed the rope on exiting the aircraft and plummeted to the ground seventy feet below. He had severe injuries. The ground convoy supplied three vehicles to evacuate the seriously wounded person. They began a harrowing ride through the city. Already roadblocks were being hastily erected and mobs were forming. The three vehicles made it back with several other members wounded. They immediately turned around and prepared to rejoin their comrades still back at the target building.

Chalk four never linked up with its original position. The Somali militia leaders rallied their forces as soon as the helicopters began their thrumming over the market area. The gunfire was greater than any of the soldiers had seen before in the city. The Rangers were already fighting for their lives. Early on, an RPG hit the Super 61 helicopter piloted by Chief Wolcott; it went down about three blocks from the target. Most of the crew was killed on impact, but the crew chiefs survived. Within a few minutes, elements of the Ranger security force were running through the city to link up and defend the downed helicopter. In addition to the Rangers making their way through the city streets, an air force search and rescue team was roped into the crash site. This was the only such team supporting the operation. The team had medical and security personnel who helped to secure the wreckage and treat the wounded. After assessing the casualties, the medics noted that Chief Wolcott was trapped in his seat by the crumpled engine compartment. This would prove important, because precious hours would be spent trying to free the trapped pilot.

The downing of Super 61 brought Chief Michael Durrant's Super 64 into the fray as he entered a rotation over the city. The rotation was a pattern that each helicopter flew over a designated sector, to be able to effectively use the supporting weapons aboard and allow the mission to be accomplished. Super 64 had been in its pattern for only a few moments when it was hit by an RPG. Although the damage to the tail section was serious, the pilot tried to bring the helicopter back to the airfield. He had gone less than a mile when the remainder of the tail section fell off; the pilot was forced to contend with a spinning aircraft plummeting to the earth. He was able to fight the controls and land the aircraft without losing a crew member; however, all the crew members were hurt. There was no available rescue team, and the Rangers were still a long way away. The pilot of one of the circling helicopters, which had three Delta snipers on board, called to the command post and requested permission to off-load two of the snipers to provide additional security. It was agreed, and Randy Shughart and Gary Gordon jumped into the alleyway. They worked with the aircrew to defend against the growing mob. It was not long before the increasing hail of bullets would claim the lives of all the crew except Michael Durrant.

One of the militia leaders, Yousef Dahir Mo'Alim, arrived at the scene and found Chief Durrant, with his ammunition expended, leaning against a tree. The angry mob was tearing at the bodies of the other men, and the militia leader realized the importance of keeping this one alive. He had his small band protect the pilot as the men began to move him away from the angry masses. As they carried him, a technical with a larger machine gun came up and the technos demanded the pilot. Mo'Alim had no choice but to turn over Durrant. The technos sold Durrant to Aidid's clan, where he was cared for by Aidid's propaganda minister, Abdullah Hassan.

The battle around the first crash site was growing. The three-block area between the crash and the target was filled with gunfire. The Delta commandos placed the prisoners in the five-ton trucks, and the ground convoy was directed to move to the first crash site, then the second. The remainder of the Rangers fought their way to the first site on foot. Most made it within a block of the site, but intense gunfire kept all the personnel from establishing a unified position. The experience of those on foot was dramatically different from those in the convoy.

Lieutenant Colonel Danny McKnight received his driving directions from the surveillance aircraft flying overhead. Real-time television footage was being transmitted back to the command post, and guidance was relayed to McKnight. The crew in the aircraft gave directions to take the next right and so on, only to see the convoy miss the turn and take the turn down a later street. The delay in relaying the messages caused a series of bad turns, which would have been comical had lives not hung in the balance. The convoy was receiving more and more wounded as it proceeded. A distance of three blocks, which should have taken less than fifteen minutes, now had the convoy winding through the maze of streets for more than an hour. Finally the casualties were so high that McKnight made the decision to return to base without linking up. It was already becoming dark; Task Force Ranger had been fighting for several hours.

Even after the decision was made, numerous more were wounded as they fought their way out. As they reached the halfway mark to the headquarters, they linked up with the first evacuation convoy returning to assist with the rest of the mission. The two convoys fought their way back to the command post. Many vehicles were so badly shot up that trucks were needed to push the broken HMMWVs. At times, McKnight's convoy had come within a block of the downed aircraft, but the location never was effectively communicated to the frustrated group.

The QRF had already been dispatched and was likewise fighting a pitched battle with little forward movement. The Somalis had chosen not to strongly contest the aircraft moving into the city, because they realized that any force deployed could not get out by air. So the militia members began erecting roadblocks immediately upon recognizing an American attack. The hastily created barriers were, in some cases, lit on fire to provide additional deterrence. The QRF could not penetrate the roadblocks. The HMMWVs and unprotected trucks were not sufficient muscle against the storm of bullets being placed against them.

Another rescue column was being formed using available UN forces. A company of Malaysian APCs and four Pakistani tanks were placed under the control of Lieutenant Colonel David, the 10th Mountain Division battalion commander. David also had a company of his own battalion and Ranger and Delta elements from the previous convoys. This time the convoy would use armored muscle to break through.

The major deterrents to getting the element moving were not the Somalis but the UN bureaucracy and old-fashioned language barriers. The Malaysian officers spoke English, but the individual vehicle commanders did not. The Americans related their needs, but the translation took time. The Malaysian APCs were needed, but the infantrymen were not. Lieutenant Colonel David wanted to dismount the Malaysian infantry and replace them with his own soldiers. This finally happened, and the column was formed. Another difficulty was the role of the Pakistani armor. The platoon leader indicated that he was not supposed to lead the column. Finally, a compromise was reached, and the tanks provided protection about halfway, then waited for the column to return.

The column moved through the city streets, fighting for every intersection. It was slow moving, because the infantry dismounted to clear an intersection, then remounted as the convoy passed. The delay produced more casualties, but still there was progress. At one point some of the APCs took a wrong turn. No one could reach them on the radio to tell them to stop, and once the American platoon leader inside realized what had happened, he could not get back. He had entered a radio dead zone, making communication impossible. This part of the convoy would have to fight its own way out the following morning.

The relief column fought its way to the first crash site and was able to relieve the elements there. The wounded were loaded onto the APCs. The body of Chief Wolcott was still trapped in his downed Super 61 helicopter. It required hooking chains to the airframe, and vehicles pulling the frame apart, before the pilot's body could be removed. The column had split to send elements to both crash sites. At the second site they found nothing; all the bodies had been removed. Now came the fight out. The column was receiving a significant amount of fire, especially whenever it reached an intersection. The men fought to get to the soccer stadium, which served as a UN compound; it was much closer than the American position.

Once the men reached the stadium, it became apparent what had occurred: eighteen dead and seventy-seven wounded. It was estimated that the Somali dead were approximately five hundred and the wounded in excess of a thousand.

The battle was not truly over until Michael Durrant was returned to American control. This followed the images of the dead crew of Super 64 being dragged through the streets of Mogadishu.

Time Line

Date	Time	Event
4 May 1993		Majority of U.S. contingent withdraws and turns control over to the UN force
5 Jun 1993		Attack on Pakistani peacekeepers by Habr Gidr clan; 24 Pakistanis killed
12 Jul 1993		U.S. helicopter gunship attack on the Abdi house, killing dozens of Habr Gidr clan leaders

Date	Time	Event
Aug 1993		Remote-control mines kill American soldiers on multiple occasions
30 Aug 1993		TF Ranger, including a squadron of Delta Force, operational in country
21 Sep 1993		Successful capture of Osman Otto, Aidid's banker and munitions supplier
3 Oct 1993	1532	Helicopters take off from U.S. compound at Mogadishu airport
	1543	Littlebirds make first gun run over target to clear the way for Blackhawks following
	1545	Raid begins
		First casualty; Ranger falls 70 feet from helicopter
		Prisoners taken and loaded on trucks
		Super 61 shot down by RPG
		Super 64 hit by RPG; it limps away, then crashes into city
	2030	10th Mountain Division battalion arrives at airport for mission
	2100	QRF links up with UN forces at New Port
	2145	Rescue column ready to move
	2200	Rescue column begins movement from New Port
4 Oct 1993	0030	Lead elements of rescue column link up with TF Ranger
	0330	All casualties loaded onto APCs
	0600	Pilot's body recovered; rescue column begins movement out
8 Oct 1993		Robert Oakley meets with Habr Gidr clan leaders to demand release of Michael Durrant; he is released hours after Ambassador Oakley departs country

Battlefield Leadership

The elements of this operation supporting the American and UN efforts inflicted casualties at an almost 30:1 ratio. This is staggering and could have occurred only through the discipline of the American soldiers and the power of the air support they received. Unlike the battle in Desert Storm, this was not a short engagement, but a drawn-out and costly one. The success that did occur was entirely reliant on thousands of hours of training conducted by the various elements. It is possible that if this battle had involved elements of a regular infantry unit, the entire command might have been destroyed during the operation. It was the highly trained and disciplined operators of Delta and the Rangers that allowed them to survive in the maelstrom. The medical treatment was especially critical to the saving of lives, despite the horrible conditions.

One of the most important decisions impacting the battle was one made by the secretary of defense weeks before the battle began. Secretary Les Aspin decided to deny a request for infantry fighting vehicles and an AC-130 gunship to support the operation.[16] Sending such high-visibility equipment into a peacekeeping mission was considered politically damaging. This decision, when it was revealed before the U.S. Congress, resulted in the resignation of the secretary.

As for the battle itself, three major decisions determined its outcome. The decision to evacuate one person early on, separate from the rest of the convoy, dissipated the combat power of the element and prevented a massing of vehicles that might have been useful during the major exfiltration. The second decision was the use of surveillance aircraft messages relayed through the command post on the same frequency as the first 10th Mountain Division rescue column. Trying to direct two separate columns, both under fire, was problematic. It would have been much faster to have the column charge straight down the three blocks. The third decision was that of waiting to fully assemble the final rescue column. Combining all the available power was critical to the mission's eventual success, even though delays with UN companion nations were exasperating and did cost American lives.

Significance

Whether or not the battle of Mogadishu is a watershed is left to the individual reader's perspective and the reactions of the various administrations to follow. Still, it did have a dramatic impact on a change in American policy immediately following the battle. Though no one officially offered an exchange of prisoners, shortly after Michael Durrant was released, the captured Somali leaders were also released. The entire reason for the raid was given back.

During hearings before the U.S. Congress, the debate became heated. No one likes a loss, and that was how this battle was viewed. Despite the overwhelming loss ratio, which clearly demonstrated the superiority of American infantry training and support, Congress demanded the pullout of all American support in Mogadishu within six months. The fact that this battle was considered a loss demonstrated the casualty-sensitive nature of the American political leadership. Many polls indicated support for retaliation for the losses inflicted, but the political leadership decided to pull out. Colin Powell sums up the political reaction with this statement: "Americans were horrified by the sight of a dead U.S. soldier being dragged through the streets of Mogadishu. We had been drawn into this place by television images; now we were being repelled by them."[17]

Much of the casualty sensitivity was driven by confusion over the purpose of the losses. Many accused the United States of giving a blank check to the UN to support nation building. Criticism of the UN was the primary rallying cry, with the abuse of the concept of "mission creep" coming in a close second. *Mission creep* is a term coined by congresspersons in reference to the slow evolution of the American role in Somalia. It started out as a humanitarian mission to provide food to starving tens of thousands; then it became a police mission to secure the streets of the capital by confiscating weapons from the warring factions. Next came the singling out of a particular faction as obstructionist. Finally, there were attempts to arrest members of the "outlaw" clan and force a peaceful settlement. The changing nature of the overall mission and the U.S. role in it created the greater part of the vehemence and has created a backlash against the changing of any mission once it is initiated.

The other significant outcome was the compression of the levels of strategy. This entire battle was fought at the tactical—and, in reality, the technical—strategy levels; however, it had direct impact on the grand strategy level. This is not a new phenomenon. Small engagements in times of general peace always have greater impact. The bombing of the Khobar Towers in Saudi Arabia, the bombing of a German discotheque, and the shooting down of an Iranian airliner over the Persian Gulf all had high-level impact because they were the "only show in town." Such is the case in this instance. Even so, the addition of the increased media coverage does provide increased impact. No cameras were with young Lt. George S. Patton, Jr. when he gunned down one of Pancho Villa's own lieutenants in a movielike gunfight on the Mexican border in 1913. What would have been the impact if cameras had recorded it? Few military events will happen in the future without extensive media coverage. This brings the importance of clear and intelligent policy further to the forefront.

Lessons Learned

It is most interesting to note that what Saddam Hussein wanted and failed to do, Mohammed Farrah Aidid accomplished: He caused so many casualties that he forced an American withdrawal.

Identification: The struggle with fighting a mob is the difficulty in defining and locating the enemy. This hampered those associated with TF Ranger. Once the enemy was identified and located, they were rapidly apprehended. The additional challenge was understanding the mind-set of the average Somali. It was apparent that the senior American officials were unaware of the anger and hatred that existed among the men on the street. All of this conspired to create a large, angry population that was willing to make tremendous sacrifices to destroy the American forces when they came out of their sanctuary at the airport.

Isolation: Not understanding the enemy situation made it problematic to isolate any portion of the battlefield. The fact that those fighting the American soldiers were willing to use their civilian nature as a cloak to mask their intent made it that much more difficult for the American force to clearly delineate between friend and foe. The use of unarmed women and children further clouded the identification of combatants. Another issue was the nature of the terrain. The complex, poorly maintained buildings and streets made infiltration much easier against the helicopter gunships. All of the gray area denied the soldiers on the ground the ability to effectively protect any area of the battlefield and prevent repositioning.

Suppression: As indicated in the previous section, the presence of too many elements made suppression nearly impossible. The complex terrain and lack of precise yet overwhelming firepower denied the ability to focus fires on a single group or avenue long enough to clear that avenue of enemy forces. Additionally, so many Somali citizens were willing to risk their lives for the possibility of defeating the Rangers that they continued to flood into the area well beyond nightfall.

Maneuver: The use of helicopters to provide significant firepower saved the ground troops. It was this technological advantage that provided any semblance of maneuver. The fact that the soldiers on the ground would not depart from the downed aircraft sites and leave the dead or wounded, combined with the overwhelming press of enemy, denied any possibility of ground maneuver.

Destruction: The ratio of dead between the American and Somali forces was nearly 30:1. This is staggering considering the harrowing ordeal that TF Rangers went through. It is also surprising that so many Somalis continued to attack despite the withering fire. It can be argued effectively that TF Ranger did destroy its opponent at the technical and tactical levels. It can be equally argued that the Somalis destroyed their opponent at the theater and grand strategy levels. The Americans would withdraw because the military and political leadership would not stomach what was seen as unacceptable losses for limited benefit.

Conclusion

The battle of Mogadishu is the first major urban engagement in the information age. The Revolution in Military Affairs (RMA) began just as this battle was being fought. This was warfare's first use of sophisticated imagery and real-time visual and communication links. Commanders and staff watched the units as each heard their requests. The lessons from this engagement have to be considered in the context of its geostrategic environment. This was not a small battle in a larger war. It was a small battle in an operation other than war (OOTW) or security and stability operation (SASO). The OOTW nature of the engagement caused political decisions that impacted on equipment and rules of engagement. It is quite possible that if this battle had occurred as part of a larger war, there would have been fewer casualties, because heavier vehicles would have been available. It is also probable that this battle would then be held up as a hallmark for urban combat and the way it should be done. The loss ratio indicated overwhelming success.

It is the contention of this entire book that these battles will more likely be fought in exactly this fashion in the future, and that complex terrain conflict in the scope of larger conflict will be the exception. The rule will be complex terrain engagements in OOTW/SASO situations or in the war on terrorism, which may or may not be part of a larger battle. This rule makes the lessons of this battle that much more important. Restrictive rules of engagement (ROE) in an attempt to limit destruction and death is a morally good concept. As forces of a nation that strives to be morally correct, soldiers must expect to have conflicting ROE.

The very nature of OOTW/SASO also means that a change in mission and purpose is likely. At the outset in any OOTW/SASO, there is the importance of stabilization, and this changes to a resolution. Depending on the exact type of OOTW/SASO, there may be a number of steps in between. These two lessons always apply, whether it is fighting forest fires, assisting hurricane victims, feeding starving children, or vaccinating thousands of at-risk civilians. Once the political leadership understands this, it must effectively communicate the purpose of each phase of the proposed operation. For example, in the case of Somalia, the American people needed to understand as early as possible that the task and purpose of the first phase was to protect the distribution of food to prevent starvation and allow for a greater level of security within the populace. The second phase was to create a national stability that would allow the development and training of the institutions essential for national existence and survival. If this stability were to require the armed suppression of subversive elements, then this should also be stated up front. Once the American people and political leaders understand the reasons behind the action, they tend to support it. This is not an endorsement of the management of the conflict in Somalia, but simply an example of how to frame the conflict and express that to the American people. Nebulous reasoning will not be supported in the stark reality of death and destruction.

Chapter Eight
Battle Analysis: Summary

The historical case studies demonstrate techniques that nations have already used against more technologically advanced opponents. Each was followed with lessons. As America prepares to fight a war on terrorism as well as continue to defend and promote its national interests, some general lessons in each of the categories can be drawn from the battles just discussed.

Identification: To identify an opponent, it is first necessary to understand that opponent.

- In Korea, the U.S. intelligence community thought that the Chinese Communist forces (CCF) would fight much as any of the other industrialized nations of the world fought. Instead they fought with an emphasis on pitting their strengths (infantry and terrain) against the UN force's weakness (road bound).

- In Vietnam, the U.S. commanders felt that the NVA would be overwhelmed by the demonstration of firepower and recognize their demise. This denied the nationalistic commitment and the patience demonstrated by many of these same opponents against the French a decade earlier.

- In the Falklands and in Iraq, the lower-tier nation fought the higher tier using the same tactics. In each case, the lower-tier force was defeated.

- In Somalia, failure to understand the anger of the populace and the willingness to sacrifice their own lives resulted in a response that nearly overwhelmed any possible defense.

• In the future, it is likely that the opponents of the United States will not fight a war with which we are familiar but will instead seek to fight us on their own terms. The terrorist attacks of 11 September 2001 demonstrate just this sort of approach. The attacks of computer viruses, poison gas, and biological weapons are possibilities. Saddam Hussein has taught the world much about how not to fight the United States.

Isolation: The isolation of an opponent is possible only when the opponent's location is known and his limits are defined.

• In Korea, the United States did not truly understand the nature of the CCF intervention. This failure was despite the efforts of reconnaissance aircraft and bombers to prevent just such an occurrence. The ability of the lower-tier opponent to use unexpected crossing points and totally unexpected areas of concentration meant that preventing outside support was impossible.

• In Vietnam, failure to understand the means of resupply and the amount of supplies necessary created a gap between the intelligence and maneuver communities. Most assumed that Vietnamese soldiers consumed supplies in amounts similar to those of Western forces, without truly understanding the cultural differences. Attacking supply lines of the NVA was not even remotely similar to attacking supply lines of a Western force.

• In the Falklands and Iraq, the military cultural, organizational, and doctrinal situations of the opponent countries were roughly similar. This allowed for a greater understanding and a more effective targeting of support structures. The result in both cases was fighting a lower-tier opponent who was cut off from outside support.

• In Somalia, the fact that the lower-tier force included the majority of the civilian population and that the military was not an organized structure of subordinate units provided an opponent to the United States for which commanders and the support structure were unprepared. Additionally, there were no assets in theater for the higher-tier force that could provide the necessary fire support to truly isolate a portion of the battlefield.

• Future opponents will likely be of a different cultural mold than that of the major industrialized militaries. They will use the methods described in the preceding chapters as well as different mind-sets about victory, mission, purpose, and objective. This will make it difficult for the United States to identify and then effectively deny outside support. The U.S. leaders and planners need to understand what form that support may take and what means may be used to get it to the opponent.

Suppression: Freedom of movement is determined not by transportation but by strategy.

• In Korea, the lower-tier force utilized terrain undesirable to the higher-tier force and also used a strategy of turning movement and roadblock because it perceived a weakness in the higher-tier force. Once the strategy was set, the movement was ensured.

• In Vietnam, the strategy was to deny movement of both forces by the lower-tier force closing with the higher-tier force.

• In the Falklands and in Iraq, the lower-tier nations fought static prepared defenses. Even the reserves of the Republican Guard remained relatively static throughout the air campaign. This ensured the higher-tier force a simple suppression target.

• In Somalia, a strategy of chaos and swarming mass attacks of humanity that were to overwhelm the higher-tier opponent was used to tremendous effect. Even the extremely high casualty rates among the lower-tier force were not a deterrent. The higher-tier force did not possess any weapon that would have provided the shock necessary to suppress the mass of the lower-tier opponent.

• Opponents of U.S. interests will not provide an obvious target in future conflict. Targets will either be so dis-

persed as to be insignificant or will be so completely en-
meshed with the civilian populace and infrastructure as to
prevent effective targeting.

Maneuver: To gain a position of advantage, it is essential to understand the opponents' perceived strengths and weaknesses.

• In Korea, the CCF clearly understood the U.S. weakness—road-bound equipment. The United States did not
gain an understanding of the CCF weakness until after they
had retreated south of the thirty-eighth parallel. Then the
inability of the lower-tier force to supply itself and maintain
tempo in the attack became clear and was exploited.

• In Vietnam, the NVA targeted the United States' patience at the theater and grand strategy level.

• In the Falklands and Iraq, the higher-tier force faced
an opponent that fought in a conventional manner; therefore, the understanding of advantage was more obvious.
Terrain objectives that provided better fields of fire and prevented logistical support were sought.

• In Somalia, the understanding of the Somali warlords
was to inflict harm on U.S. and UN forces and create a political pain level sufficient to force a withdrawal.

• Terrorists already see that our symbols, our financial
markets, our information infrastructure, and our mass media have been and will continue to be targets as they are
identified as U.S. weaknesses. The ability of the U.S. military, particularly the navy and air force's ability to dominate
in their respective spheres of influence, is clearly seen as a
strength and will therefore not be targeted in direct conventional attack unless there is no other option.

Destruction: The destruction of will is the challenge of the future. Physical property in lower-tier nations, especially tier-three
and -four nations, borders on the irrelevant.

• In Korea, the lower-tier nation surprised the U.S. force
and created a mental victory long before it achieved a physical one.

• In Vietnam, the ability of the NVA to destroy the mental will of the U.S. political leadership and prevent its own

military force from suffering destruction at the other four levels of strategy directly resulted in the American withdrawal. In the specific battle in question, the NVA forced 2-7 Cav into a siege mentality as its perceived helplessness denied a greater level of reaction.

- In the Falklands, the use of effective maneuver mentally destroyed an enemy that was still superior in personnel.

- In Iraq, complete physical destruction of the lower-tier force's equipment and personnel resulted in unconditional surrender.

- In Somalia, the Somali reaction to the U.S. prisoner seizures was so vehement that the resulting destruction of personnel and equipment destroyed the will of the senior military and political leadership.

- In the future, it is likely that opponents of the United States will continue to focus on destroying the will of the nation rather than any physical destruction. Most, if not all, future opponents of the United States recognize the futility of fighting an attrition war that focuses on material destruction. In the current war on terrorism, terrorist organizations will fight a war of attrition focused on the will of the nation, seeing the current patriotic fervor as temporary.

Cultural changes in how opponents of the United States seek to engage in conflict are the real challenge for military and national security professionals to understand. In the Falkland Islands and the Gulf War, the lower-tier nations used methods of waging war that were similar to those used by higher-tier nations. In the other three examples, each of the lower-tier opponents sought methods that differed from the military culture of the higher-tier nation. The manner in which the lower-tier commanders understood the conflict was as foreign to the higher-tier commanders as the languages each combatant spoke. It is most important to understand the ideas of the opponent, then the technology.

Chapter Nine

The Future of Warfare: Trends Affecting the Ground Commander

Cycles of change in warfare are particularly difficult to comprehend and even more difficult to anticipate because, unlike endeavors in finance, medicine, or law, active experience in war is, thankfully, infrequent. Because warfare is not frequently practiced, soldiers must rely on the laboratory of past experiences to gain vicarious experience in war.
—Maj. Gen. Robert H. Scales, Jr.

Lessons from the historical examples are now applied with an understanding of the potential of future technological and cultural developments. The discussion is on techniques existing today or those that are just over the horizon for the potential adversary of the United States.

Much that has been written on future warfare focuses on technological possibilities and how these technologies can be used to benefit the military. A significant amount of the material discusses the potential benefit of this new technology to decrease the size of combat units, flatten the military hierarchy, and achieve information dominance. In fact, the sad truth is that many of the predictions and possibilities will probably never reach fruition. Additionally, there is a considerable danger in the path that follows what can be done rather than what should be or needs to be done.

Former U.S. Marine Corps commandant Gen. Charles C. Krulak gave his vision of the future by describing the events of Roman defeat on the Germanic border:

In 9 A.D., a Roman proconsul by the name of Quintilius Varus led three Roman legions across the inner Germanic border. Their mission was to put down a rebellion that was taking place in a Germanic tribe headed by a guy by the name of Armenius.

This was the second time that Varus had done this. Three years prior, he crossed the same border, attacked the same tribe and decimated them—sending more than 20,000 men, women and children back to Rome as slaves. Here he was crossing again. He came in three columns and at the head of each column was the famous Roman eagle, signifying the power of Rome.

On a hot August morning, at a place called Teutoburger Forest, where the city of Menden is currently located, the Romans and the Germans came together. But as the sun was setting at the end of that day, Varus was fighting a desperate rear-guard action, having been torn to pieces. And as he was driving toward the border a day or so away he had his head down and he could be heard saying over and over again, *Ne Cras! Ne Cras!* Which stands for, Not Like Yesterday.[1]

Whoever the U.S. enemy is, it is certain that they will employ a wide variety of actions to bring the United States down to their level. Most of these actions have been outlined in the previous chapters. In addition to the eight basic methods, there will be discrete variations and numerous new twists on the old themes. Beyond these original trends is a plethora of techniques that future adversaries will seek to use to unseat the United States from pursuing interests unpopular with the opponent. These techniques tend to target the United States at the theater and grand strategy levels of warfare. The reason for this is simple: Potential adversaries understand that they cannot successfully challenge the U.S. military at the operational or tactical levels of war and win conclusively. The North Vietnamese strategy during the entire Vietnam War is indicative of this philosophical strategy. Other nations will follow the North Vietnamese paradigm, using techniques that have historical proof of success and some that are new to the information age.

The techniques focused on in the rest of this chapter are as follows:

- use of civilians
- sophisticated political posturing
- weapons of mass destruction
- space operations
- information operations

other advanced technologies:

- harmonics
- imaging
- nonlethal

This is not an all-inclusive shopping list of capabilities but are some examples of ways that minor players on the world scene can become major. Intertwined among and alongside all of these is the manipulation of the media, which will play a significant role in most of these discussions.

Future Ground Combat

Initially, the overarching ideas of future ground combat need to be expressed. These ideas are captured in two major themes: knowledge and speed.[2] The trends boil down to a drive for information dominance, which is the ability to control the information war through imagery and other forms of intelligence, and a desire to reestablish the offense as the dominant form of warfare by creating a form of operational maneuver through the use of forces that can self-deploy from extended distances.

Information Dominance: Knowledge

It is accepted that the force that knows the locations of friendly and enemy elements and understands the intents and objectives of the adversary can use this information to tremendous advantage by applying force only to the area that denies the enemy force their objective. This understanding of the entire scope of the battlefield allows the commander to be economical with the size of force necessary. It creates the possibility of operational-level ambushes.

For example, if an enemy force of division size were to conduct an attack toward a major port city and a minor attack against the nation's capital, the commander with information dominance could place a small force to protect the capital while he sent a larger, more concentrated force to stop the attack against the port by attacking in an unlikely location and at an unexpected time. This scenario negates the need for numerical parity but allows for an economy of force structure. Major General Scales states that "[t]he coin of the realm in 2020 . . . is not going to be heft, weight, killing power. It's going to be knowledge."[3]

The ability to see the battlefield, whether with physical, electronic, or intuitive eyes, has been prized by all the greatest military commanders. The promise of information dominance is the ability to return a commander to the days of Hannibal and Scipio Africanus, when they could survey the entire battlefield with their own eyes and make decisions based on this firsthand knowledge. This is the greatest aspect of the current RMA. The benefit of having the complete vision of the battlefield in "real time" is relatively obvious. The concerns are not as obvious.

The primary difficulty is that the opposing force may have similar technology as well. The specifics of this are addressed in later sections. If the opposing commander has a similar view of the battlefield, the entire ambush philosophy becomes impossible and the military struggle returns to one of attrition. So a major component of this dominance is a denial of similar capabilities and assets to the enemy force.

Operational Maneuver: Speed

Currently the U.S. Army is conducting a transformation from a legacy force to an objective force. This objective force is targeted decades out, but the concepts that are to be integrated into this force have been thought through during a series of war games and utilizing several different battle labs. Each of these has produced conceptual thinking and determined the capabilities necessary to meet the concepts.

The basic concept is to move toward an organization that can achieve surprise at levels above tactical strategy. Either operational or theater strategy surprise is extremely difficult, because it requires the ability of an organization to appear and conduct battle in an unexpected location or at an unexpected time. Currently the weight and lift capacity of the ground and air components of the U.S. military do not allow this possibility. Many futurists have suggested a concept called air mechanization. In its base form it is the concept of a flying tank that can fight on the ground. The evolution has a great deal more detail. The concept started in the early 1930s with the Soviet military, and many futurists in and out of the U.S. military have considered similar concepts. This evolved through air-dropped vehicles to the idea of air assaulting the vehicles into the critical location. The concept of air assault is worthy of comment.

Between the Korean and Vietnam Wars, the use of the helicopter was viewed as a significant way to change the nature of warfare: a change designed to take ground conflict into the third dimension and attack the enemy by vertical envelopment rather than the traditional ground-bound approach. This was developed and tested and eventually fielded as an entire division in late 1964, becoming the 1st Air Cavalry Division. The concept was tested in combat situations during the Vietnam War and proved to be remarkably successful. The Americans enjoyed a level of mobility that completely confused and at times disoriented their enemy, who were used to fighting the French forces' more conventional tactics. Despite the initial success, the attrition nature of the conflict was not the ideal showcase for bold maneuver, and difficulty in identifying the enemy created a tremendous degree of frustration with all methods. After the Vietnam War, the 1st Cavalry went through a series of changes resulting in the only remaining air assault division, the 101st Infantry Division (Air Assault). This division enjoyed continued work on the concepts, and it refined the air assault tactics to one that featured the killing power of the attack helicopter battalions. During Operation Desert Storm, the division successfully demonstrated the strengths of attack aviation and played a critical role in threatening the Iraqi higher command.

Air mechanization is different from air assault in that the primary payload delivered consists of mechanized vehicles, not simply light infantry. Several specifics are discussed in professional journals,[4] but the real development of this theory was played out in the Army After Next Wargames.

To conduct maneuver at the operational strategy level requires the ability to deploy, then attack into theater from a range greater than five hundred kilometers. This range provides a tremendous ability to simply appear on the battlefield, causing the adversary to have to protect many areas simultaneously and allowing the higher-tier force the luxury of selecting targets and attacking in rapid ambushes. This would also require revolutions in logistics to develop better and more economical power sources that would allow extended self-sustainment.[5]

This is a very brief overview but should be sufficient for understanding the implications of the following concepts. The critical points are the self-deploying, self-sustaining, entirely mechanized (read few infantry), and integrated with legacy (Force XXI) units. The drive for speed and knowledge is summed up as follows:

> The secret of German success [in World War II] was the ability to take a small part of the force—10 percent, 10 divisions of 114 divisions, and equip such that it could break free of the railhead, dash to operational distances of about 100-115 miles, seize an objective and hold on long enough for follow-on forces to secure the victory. . . . That's all we seek to do. The only difference is we seek to do it by an order of magnitude, because the force that was effective in 1939 at 20 miles an hour, in 2025 is going to have to move at about 200 miles an hour.[6]

The U.S. Army currently is moving toward the vision above by means of the transformation previously mentioned. The current term for the new force is the Intermediate Brigade Combat Team, or IBCT. This lacks the air mechanization application, because the technology clearly does not exist to create such capability. The new design and movement from heavy armored vehicles to lighter, more deployable vehicles show the commitment to a greater level of deployability and thereby a movement toward operational maneuver. The well-publicized investment by the U.S. Army in information technology speaks volumes about the commitment to information.

Speed and knowledge can be mitigated and even defeated as the following tactics are employed.

Use of Civilians

The use of civilians for military gain is certainly not new. Jewish historian Josephus tells of a particularly effective use by the Tenth Legion of the Roman Empire as they assaulted Jewish Zealots at Masada in A.D. 70. The Zealots had started another of many rebellions against Rome and had been able to seize the isolated and well-designed fortress of Masada. This fortress was built by King Herod on top of a plateau overlooking the Dead Sea. The plateau was accessible only by narrow mountain trails that ascended the steep and sometimes sheer cliffs. The Zealots occupied the fortress and were able to effectively deny the narrow paths to the Romans. The legion commander established a plan to capture the fortress by building a ramp from the valley floor to the fortress walls using Jewish slaves. By the time the ramp was completed (it took three years), the Zealots—who had initially conducted daily snipings of the ramp workers—refused to kill their fellow Jews. Severely outnumbered, the Zealots committed mass suicide rather than surrender.

The use of civilians in this nearly 2,000-year-old example has been and will be duplicated again and again. There are two major reasons for the repeated use of civilians. One is the fact that they are where the battles are taking place. This will only increase in the future as cities grow even larger and the population continues to explode. The second reason is that there is an innate weakness for higher-tier soldiers seeing death or harm done to an innocent. These two combine to make the use of civilians a very low-risk, high-profit area.

The primary reason for this ability to use civilians effectively is the availability of instantaneous media coverage. "We interrupt your regularly scheduled programming for this breaking news . . ." This has become so commonplace that most adversaries count on the support of the media. They certainly have learned from the juvenile exploitation of the media used by Saddam Hussein. His patting a young boy on the head and the use of Western hostages were so poorly handled by the Iraqi public relations personnel that this enraged rather than pacified the world. Few leaders will make the same mistakes in the future.

The images of 11 September 2001 have been burned into the minds of all Americans and most of the world. This use of civilians as part of the guided missile was unique and one that others will seek to duplicate. The American response to the terrorist attacks will certainly involve civilians. Images of bombing and fearful women and children mourning for lost loved ones will fill television screens as the retaliation continues. Civilian casualties are a reality of war.

What impact will these images have on the world's psyche? How about American public opinion? Currently there is a great deal of anger and frustration; but after time heals the wounds, will Americans accept the loss of innocent lives in the pursuit of any policy? It is certain that Western reporters will seek to be part of such events, and equally certain that the American people will be interested in the miniseries sort of life that the very real human beings will represent. This humanization would create a very real psychological dilemma. How can we be killing these people? What kind of leaders do we have?

This is why the role of propaganda is so critical to the ability of a government to generate popular support for any type of military adventure. Even the worst Nazi concentration camp guard had human qualities that a sophisticated public relations agent could use to generate sympathy and support.

The previous example is a method of using civilians to support military aims in the future. The most common future use of civilians will be the exploitation of the urban sprawl that every nation will have. The Iraqis did this well during Operation Desert Storm. They placed antiaircraft weapons in mosques, on top of hotels, and next to hospitals and schools to avoid targeting by American aircraft. They also placed civilians in the top floor of a command bunker, then played on this to effectively end the air campaign against Baghdad once the bunker was targeted. The success of this action was a clear signal to any future aggressor.

Not only will the use of urban areas be duplicated, it will be expanded upon; lower-tier nations expect to use the urban terrain to their advantage.

American people have an advanced sensitivity to death and destruction during war. This poses an interesting dichotomy. We sit by and effectively ignore the thousands who are brutally murdered every year in our nation's own streets—more than 19,000 in 1996 alone—and we allow our children to play graphically violent video games and consume billions of dollars' worth of television and cinematic violence as if it were part of our inherent psychological design.[7] However, we refuse to allow our nation in pursuit of established and tacitly approved goals to kill civilians in another nation. It is precisely this conundrum that all future adversaries will play on to completely divide American opinion and paralyze political decisionmakers.

This sensitivity extends to the loss of soldiers' lives as well. This is not to somehow advocate the loss of human life or to minimize the seriousness of the decision that risks human lives; however, are there no longer values or ideals that are prized above human life? Between 3 and 4 October 1993, the U.S. Army lost eighteen lives in an action in Mogadishu, Somalia. This represented seven one-hundred millionths (0.00000007) of the population. Over that same two-day period of time, 134 people were murdered within the borders of the United States.[8] This represents fifty-three one-hundred millionths (0.00000053) of the population. As a society, we ignore the second statistic because it represents a very small segment of the population; however, the first statistic changed American foreign policy and effectively cemented as a priority an unstated policy to avoid casualties.

Sophisticated Political Posturing

The political savvy of most emerging world dictators is less than impressive. Typically they gain their position through direct means and are equally direct in their means of dealing with crises. This proves problematic when attempting to achieve a national goal involving the use of force or a goal that is outside the internationally recognized borders of their nation. Saddam Hussein is the most recent in this pantheon of personalities. He presented a bellicose persona and made demands that were entirely ludicrous and clearly unsupportable by the world community. These negative actions resulted in his inability to generate sufficient positive world opinion. Saddam had the typically arrogant, dictatorial attitude that he did not need world opinion to get what he wanted. On the other hand, the Kuwaiti emir hired a New York public relations firm to present his case to the American people and the world.

Saddam Hussein failed to realize that any significant effort to garner the support of world opinion would effectively deny the ability to form a coalition of the size the United States built to fight Iraq. Nations such as China need only the smallest reason to break from the U.S. lead. Once a nation gets a break in the UN Security Council, it has achieved a significant break in world solidarity. Saddam failed to accomplish this in 1990, but he has done a much better job since the conclusion of Operation Desert Storm, and the world community has remained divided. The very nature of nations and of national self-interest fights the notion of world unity. Each nation wants to assert its political and physical independence. As long as there is no overshadowing danger to force unity, the idea of coalitions along the Desert Storm model are not likely to happen. The coalition formed for the war against terrorism is just such an exception. Even as an exception, what will happen after the al-Qaida organization is eliminated and the United States identifies the next opponent? Will Iran, Syria, North Korea, or any of their remote allies continue in a coalition? What is terrorism to one nation may be freedom fighters to another.

In reality this is like the use of civilians. The rapid expansion of media abilities as well as their expected expansion in the next quarter century will allow world leaders to take their case directly to the people of any information-age nation. No longer will policy statements take hours or days but will instead be issued in minutes over television. This allows a speed of action that will almost immediately overwhelm the powers of traditional diplomacy.

American political aims and purposes around the world are so widespread and diverse that they defy simple logic. The American people understand and agree with simply stated national security goals and policies but do not appreciate or support murky, complicated, or legalistic explanations. Future world leaders will seek to exploit this critical national weakness as they become more media savvy.

Weapons of Mass Destruction

Despite the military nature of weapons of mass destruction, their most effective target is not against the military of the adversary nation but against the will of the people within that nation. Weapons of mass destruction typically fall into one of three categories: nuclear, chemical, or biological. Nuclear weapons are the most well known in the United States because of this nation's use of them at the close of World War II. Chemical weapons are next on the list. They were used extensively during World War I and therefore are somewhat understood. The wide variety of chemical agents includes nerve gases, burning and blistering powders, and aerosol sprays. These have been used most extensively and recently by terrorist organizations in Japan: for example, the Sarin gas attack against the Tokyo subway system. Biological weapons are probably the least understood. Biological weapons are diseases, viruses, and bacteria that are used for a military or political purpose. The poisoning of a nation or city's water supply to generate a widespread cholera or dysentery epidemic would be a relatively simple yet difficult to prove case of biological warfare. The spreading of hemorrhagic fever, or Ebola, is a more complicated yet more devastating example. Each of these types of weapons has its uses, which are discussed in turn.

Nuclear Weapons

Nuclear weapons are by far the most expensive and infrastructure-intensive of the three weapons. The critical piece is the fissionable material. This requires a high-grade reactor facility, which is easy to spot and costly to build and operate. It is nearly impossible for most nations to do so without going outside their nation for additional technical support. This makes the production very visible and opens the host nation to international condemnation and sanction. This is usually deterrent enough.

The use of these weapons is also somewhat problematic. They are not extremely accurate, because they do not have to be; yet their inherent lack of accuracy leads to a nonmilitary use. The idea of destroying large military formations is not realistic. Modern militaries disperse to such an extent that the use of a nuclear device would have limited military impact. Essentially these are the world's most powerful weapons of terror. The target is the will of the people. The only example is the American use of these devices against Japan. They were analogous to the firebombing of Tokyo and Dresden. The political effect was greater because the blow was delivered with a single device that was awesome to those not directly affected.

Nuclear weapons are reserved for the most extreme circumstances. It is clear from the Cold War that major nuclear powers will not use these devices against one another or against allies of major nuclear powers. Nuclear war between the United States and the USSR would have resulted in destruction of so much of the population of the two combatants as to make the concept of victory a ludicrous statistical anomaly. The megatonnage represented by the superpowers had the capacity to destroy nearly the entire planet. Minor nuclear powers, however, will undoubtedly consider use and will probably conduct forms of limited nuclear war within the next half century.

Despite the obvious destructive power represented by these weapons, they possess a much greater potential for electronic destruction. In a world so dominated by electronic equipment, computers, and gadgets, the electromagnetic pulse (EMP) created by a nuclear device possesses a greater danger now than ever before. Every nuclear detonation creates an EMP wave that precedes the shock wave and destroys every operating piece of nonhardened electrical equipment: radios, televisions, computers, telephones. The EMP functions much like a bolt of lightning generating a power surge; if a piece of equipment is turned on, the circuitry is completely destroyed. The EMP effects expand even more the higher the weapon is detonated. Here is an example: a minimal nuclear device detonated dozens of miles above Omaha, Nebraska, would degrade and potentially destroy all electronic devices from Denver (Colorado) to Columbus (Ohio) to Dallas (Texas) to Bismarck (North Dakota).[9] A nuclear device does not have to physically destroy things to have a mass destructive impact. Currently nations are seeking to develop nonnuclear EMP weapons. These can generate the EMP without the dangers of nuclear fallout and radiation.

As these weapons proliferate to other nations, the overwhelming political constraints do not exist. India and Pakistan may eventually develop arsenals of several dozen weapons. Each of these weapons would probably be less than a megaton in capacity. This could be construed as a potentially winnable nuclear scenario. Preemptive nuclear strikes against storage and delivery facilities, followed by attacks on major population and governmental centers, would effectively deny retaliation and paralyze the nation, allowing the seizure of key border areas that are under dispute. Between the United States and the USSR this scenario was never possible, because there was no possibility of destroying enough of the enemy's weapons to deny significant retaliation. Nations with fewer weapons could be enticed by the seemingly quick victory presented by these weapons.

The Indo-Pakistani disputes are the most noteworthy in this regard. On 11 May 1998, the Indian government detonated three nuclear devices with a total yield of approximately 30 kilotons, or 30,000 tons of TNT. This was the first test from a nondeclared nuclear state since India conducted a similar test in 1974. Many speculate that these detonations were to test a nuclear warhead to be placed on a soon-to-be-fielded ballistic missile. It is certain that other nations will follow this lead.[10]

Nuclear weapons are the (current) ultimate weapon. It is foolish for the five declared nuclear powers[11] to think that all the other nations will have the self-restraint that they themselves did not possess. Why should they? The changing nature of the world political climate does not foster trust and stability; therefore, nations will desire to protect themselves in the best way they can—which, for some, will include a nuclear arsenal.

Chemical Weapons

Chemical weapons are the cheapest weapon of mass destruction to develop and employ. The means of developing these weapons is not much different than the development of chemical fertilizer, some processed foods, and pharmaceuticals. Almost every industrialized nation has the infrastructure and raw materials to develop these weapons. They are nearly impossible to prevent, track, or target because of how widespread the production capabilities are. This is critical to understanding the proliferation of these weapons. They will be part of every major future conflict.

Like the nuclear device, these weapons have little impact against military targets. Military personnel are trained to work in protective clothing and practice occupying the correct protective posture. The military also has the means to decontaminate equipment rapidly. Chemical munitions are best used against fixed sites to deny unfettered access to stored equipment or to delay troop deployments by forcing them to decontaminate equipment prior to its use.

In all probability, these weapons will be used against civilian populations where their terror can be demonstrated with the greatest force. Saddam Hussein did this to members of the Iraqi Kurdish minority in 1988 in the city of Halabja. Here a mixture of mustard gas (blister agent) and sarin, tabun, and VX (nerve agents) was employed, killing "at least 5,000 people . . . immediately."[12] Several years ago a British geneticist traveled to this city to witness the long-term devastation. She described the impact in terms of increase in cancer, birth defects, and emotional and neurological damage. The results are horrifying and not much different from those within a few kilometers of ground zero at Hiroshima or Nagasaki.[13] It is precisely these effects that make these weapons effective as terrorist weapons. Unlike a nuclear blast, the immediate effectiveness of the weapon can last as long as forty-eight to even ninety-six hours, depending on weather conditions. This combined with the potential downwind hazards and long-term effects make this truly a weapon of mass destruction.

Many nations have or are developing these weapons. International treaties call for a ban on developing and stockpiling chemical munitions, yet the reality is that few emerging nations with visions of extraterritorial expansion will deny themselves the one weapon of mass destruction they can afford. Regardless of whether or not nations seek possession of these weapons, various organizations will. The incidents in Japan in the late 1990s demonstrated that it did not require the resources of a state to produce, store, and use these weapons. It must be expected that these weapons will continue to exist and be employed on the future battlefield.

Biological Weapons
Weapons using viruses or bacteria as a means of incapacitating the adversary are called biological. These are some of the least understood and least publicized. Prior to the anthrax scares during the Fall of 2001, few of the general populace had any idea how biological weapons could have any effect.

Biological weapons create a chain reaction, more so than either nuclear or chemical weapons. Nuclear and chemical weapons cause difficulties over generations with genetic mutations and cancer, but biological weapons can be spread from one infected person to another. The destructive capacity of these weapons cannot be measured just by the number of people hit at ground zero, or even those targeted by the downwind hazard, which can be extremely large, but also by those who receive the disease from an infected carrier.

The most recent biological weapon in the news is anthrax. This is a disease that until recently was attributed to sheep and those who raise them. The inhalation form of the disease is extremely deadly, killing nearly 99 percent of those infected. The viability of this virus is also of significant concern. Like nuclear and chemical weapons, there is a downwind hazard, but for anthrax the hazard is more than ten times greater. For example, one kilogram of aerosol-delivered anthrax released by a truck spraying along the Capitol Mall in Washington, D.C., would reportedly infect a very small percentage of healthy adult males living in Philadelphia, Pennsylvania, within ten hours. Of that percentage, 99 percent would be dead within forty-eight hours following infection.

The difficulty is in preventing these substances from being created and distributed. The equipment that incubates and grows anthrax is rather common and could be conducted in a place no larger than the average garage. Anthrax is also difficult to identify. A nuclear blast is tracked and known almost instantly anywhere in the world. A biological "warhead" could be placed in a major city's drinking water source and the impact might not be realized for days. This makes this sort of weapon very desirable for terrorists and fanatical groups attempting to make their political, religious, or economic point.

Space Operations

The 1997 Army After Next Spring Wargame featured a series of engagements in space to destroy or degrade satellite capability. This was escalatory in nature and was viewed as necessary by the Red nation to maintain its survival. The attack on space-based assets was conducted with nuclear devices detonated in the atmosphere. Detonations destroyed constellations of satellites and denied the U.S. Army the global positioning and imaging capabilities upon which it had come to rely. More on that aspect later, because the most interesting impact could not be played within the constraints of the game. That impact was on the commercial communications architecture. It was projected that this assault had the impact of sending the world back to a 1950s-era setting.[14]

The potential impact of war in space has become most critical with the exploding commercialization of space. In 1997, for the first time commercial space launches outnumbered military launches, and market revenue from commercial satellite data sales increased more than seven times from 1995 to 2000.[15]

It was expected in the early 1990s that thirty years in the future the United States would have a 9:1 advantage over any peer competitor in satellite imaging capability. The explosion in commercial systems has dramatically altered this assessment. The first commercial imaging satellite with intelligence quality capability was launched in December 1997, with more planned in the future.[16] These commercial satellites will narrow the United States' advantage to at best 4:1. This dramatic drop has created a reality that any major military movement will be observed. A recent example is the INDOSAT program in India. This is an Indian-operated reconnaissance satellite capability that is available on the commercial market. The American army recently purchased information from this service. The imagery proved to be very accurate and reliable. This same information could have been purchased by any nation with the appropriate funds.[17] There will no longer be the ability to avoid detection without conducting some sort of electronic interference or offensive space operations.

The term *offensive space operations* means actual combat in space. Unlike the *Star Wars* movies, this combat would be between remote devices or between ground-based or air-based platforms. For example, if a satellite is identified as hostile, or a nation wants to remove a particular satellite's capabilities from an adversary's menu of options, the following actions could be taken:

• Another satellite is designated to conduct a kinetic kill. This means there would be satellites in orbit with the fuel and ability to maneuver to destroy another satellite by simply running into it. These kinetic kill vehicles would be very expensive and not easily replaced. They are command controlled. A variation of this is a satellite with projectiles that can disable or destroy another satellite. This is still a kinetic kill.

• A ground-based laser is used to "dazzle" or "blind" the designated satellite. Ground-based lasers can also be configured to destroy satellites; however, this requires significantly more power and greater accuracy of targeting. The dazzling/blinding involves targeting the satellite's imaging capabilities and placing laser light on it for either a temporary or permanent effect. Dazzling is temporary in nature; blinding is significant permanent degradation of the capability. This requires no launch capability and can be regenerated faster than the other options, with physical control of the facility throughout. This was tested in 1997 using a thirty-watt tracking laser, which proved to be enough to disrupt satellite operations. "[I]t is estimated that 20 to 30 nations have access to this level of technology. . . ."[18] This is the safest and potentially the cheapest way to conduct offensive operations. Most nations concerned with American space capabilities will probably seek this option.

• An airborne laser is similar to the ground-based system but instead is mounted in an airframe. The prototype system the U.S. military is testing is mounted in a Boeing 747 airframe. This option is very flexible and controlled, and the laser does not need to be as powerful, because the jet aircraft flies above the majority of the atmosphere's thickness. This is a more expensive option, and probably only a handful of nations will ever seek it.

• Aircraft-delivered projectiles to target and destroy satellites is the most tested and the oldest method. In the case of the United States, an F-15 flies toward the satellite, then launches an antisatellite missile once it reaches a predetermined position and altitude. The concept is not much different from that of any antiaircraft missile. This provides a great deal of control and is significantly cheaper than the other options.[19]

These operations would be conducted against an imaging satellite. Actions against a global positioning system or communications satellite may be similar, or the adversary nation may choose to focus electronic interference and jam the signal. This is not simple but is much cheaper and involves fewer escalatory risks than any of the previous options.

As things stand, there are no real international agreements about escalation of conflict in space. Currently the Department of Defense sends 90 to 95 percent of its telecommunications over commercial networks, which are available only in the case of international consensus. If the United States were to unilaterally enter an internationally unpopular conflict, it is possible that the satellite communications could be denied.[20]

Is it an act of war for a nation to destroy a satellite from another nation? Is it an act of war for a nation to detonate a nuclear warhead over its own territory if the effects of that weapon are felt beyond its borders? How far above a nation does national territory extend? These are questions that were moot to American and Russian policymakers for most of a half century, because nobody else had significant assets in space. This is changing as more and more international firms place assets into orbit. What is the recourse of targeting these third-party assets? There are many questions and few answers.

Much of this section is on offensive space operations, because space assets are almost by definition lightly protected. There are no armor-plated satellites. A toothpick or marble could do significant damage if it struck in the right place at the right velocity. This means that offense becomes the best defense. If a satellite is targeted, then retaliation is to be expected, because these assets are so expensive and vulnerable. No nation can afford to have its space systems reduced in a series of minor incidents. A policy of massive retaliation is almost inevitable, as no nation or organization can afford to replace its web of systems within the span of conflict.

The powerful impact of satellites on information dominance, which is a keystone of American doctrine and will soon become so for other nations as well, makes them critical assets and, therefore, means that international war will extend into space. Adversaries of the United States cannot afford to allow America to have uncontested control of all space information.

Information Operations

Information operations (IO) seem to be growing in tremendous leaps and bounds without any "political or spatial boundaries, making what constitutes 'acts of war' ambiguous."[21] These operations range from computer hacking to the planting of logic bombs and viruses. They can be everything from dropping leaflets to rerouting electronic mail to generating the collapse of a national exchange. The potential in this area is vast, yet the nature of it is so foreign to most military members that its potential is just now being tapped. The U.S. Army defines these operations as "continuous military operations within the military information environment that enable, enhance and protect the friendly force's ability to collect, process and act on information to achieve an advantage across the full range of military operations; IO includes interacting with the global information environment and exploiting or denying an adversary's information and decision capabilities."[22]

Though the impact of a collapse of a stock exchange is relatively obvious, and the positive military benefit of disabling a nation's air traffic control is clear, the more minute benefits are not completely realized.

Current uses of information operations are witnessed in Bosnia, where "[c]ivil affairs soldiers operate across the countryside interacting with local figures. As the unit political advisors talk to village and county leaders, they also reinforce the information campaign through the thrust of their work in local communities and in their interaction with key officials."[23]

The ability to dominate this spectrum is inherent in the concept of information dominance, which is a key building block of U.S. Army doctrine. What if the United States did not achieve complete information dominance? Imagine the United States with its fully digitized Force XXI divisions rolling across the open terrain into battle, as many envision, and each vehicle commander is observing his or her force on a small screen inside the vehicle. It shows the entire friendly scene with every level of command, and the icons move across the digital terrain. These soldiers have been taught to trust these icons, and most were raised on computer and video games. As they watch the icons march, the adversary makes an effective uplink through a commercial communications satellite and interrupts the digital traffic. The vehicle commanders still see their icons, but now reports of enemy contact begin to be transmitted across the screen and red icons appear. These red icons begin to march toward the blue, and blue icons begin to disappear. The vehicle commander looks outside his vehicle into the dark, dust-filled sky and sees nothing. The commander returns to the screen and sees that most of the blue forces are gone. He then begins to withdraw, and others seeing his movement or the same computer feed do likewise. Possibly an entire unit is now moving in the opposite direction, in fear, from a nonexistent enemy force. This may not last long—maybe only a few minutes—but this may be long enough for the existing enemy to exploit the confusion and effectively disrupt the attack. This information attack introduces an entirely new era of shock to the battlefield.[24]

This open-terrain scenario is somewhat easy to refute, because the vehicle commander can probably visually confirm or deny the actions depicted on the screen, but what about operations conducted in restricted or even complex terrain? These areas do not allow for easy confirmation and therefore have an inherent confusion built in, without the aid of information operations. It has been suggested that the increase in information combined with the paralyzing effect of "information overload" may actually increase the "fog of war" rather than clarify combat decisionmaking.[25]

I have not even touched the surface of these sorts of operations, and the technical nature of them goes far beyond my understanding; however, they will have an impact on the battlefields of tomorrow. Some people go so far as to suggest that the battlefields of tomorrow may be entirely in cyberspace. Cyberwarriors attack and defend vital communications and financial and transportation nodes without the need for bullets and armor. This, however, is certain to trigger those who possess the bullets to find and destroy the offending creators of the viruses and bombs. The level of competition and confusion this area creates is enormous. How can you find the perpetrators if they are conducting these operations for a multinational crime syndicate or cartel? How do you use weapons against one person sitting in a garage within your nation's own borders but conducting attacks for another nation or foreign economic competitor?

These questions can cause a person's head to hurt. It is certain that the possibilities will continue to increase, but the reality is that full-scale information operations are decades, maybe even generations away. In the meantime, they will be used to augment an adversary's military muscle, especially with the U.S. military becoming dependent on computer gadgets and all that they do. Successful information operations are "predicated on the right person receiving the right information in the right place at the right time."[26]

Other Advanced Technologies

"Other advanced technologies" is an extremely nebulous title, and purposely so. No one knows how fascinating or bizarre the future weapons or tools may be. They may not technically be weapons. Several of the most interesting and potentially terrifying are direct from the pages and celluloid of science-fiction books and films. Recent articles have documented the unfulfilled predictions of past generations; however, many of these same concepts continue to resurface, and in fact can become critical weapons generations after they were first scoffed at.[27]

Harmonics

Imagine walking through a hostile city, directing subordinate soldiers to search the adjoining alleyways, when a heavy feeling grips your throat. You cannot speak, and it is becoming difficult to breathe. After a few moments you collapse to your knees, and you notice other members of your unit doing the same. As your eyes begin to close and you start to lose consciousness, you see enemy soldiers running toward you. That is the last you know.

There are tones or harmonies that are pleasing. Everyone enjoys certain chords of music when they are played. There are those that are just as unpleasant, and the body reacts to these. It is possible to target specific areas of the body with harmonic waves and cause that portion of the body to cease functioning or impede its normal function. In this case, the throat and chest cavity are targeted and forced to constrict, resulting in unconsciousness and possible brain asphyxia. This is a technically nonlethal technology that has implications far beyond this relatively calm use.

In the book *War in 2020,* Ralph Peters describes a weapon that uses harmonics to destroy synaptic pathways and essentially render a person completely unable to control bodily functions. Although not dead, the individual is rendered a vegetable permanently. The concept of harmonics is still dominated by theory; however, the theories are not all that comforting.

Imaging

Complex terrain requires tremendous manpower. Every room in a building must be cleared before the building is considered clear. Multiroom buildings require dozens of people. What if there were a device that allowed military commanders to see through the walls, like X-ray vision, to identify where the enemy forces were located within the building? Just like the benefits of information dominance in the open plains, this knowledge would limit the need to be everywhere. A unit could clear a single room rather than every room. The reduction in required manpower is obvious.

The difficulty is the development of this technology. How does the military gain a *Star Trek*–like technology to either sense human forms and their locations through solid walls or actually see through those structures? The possibility of this technology is certain to require tremendous resources in development and fielding, but the basic technologies already exist. Without this imaging capability, the fight in the city is doomed to remain a manpower black hole.

Nonlethal

This is a benign term that could include everything from handcuffs and zip-ties to harmonic destruction of neural pathways. These controversial technologies are creating concern in nations within the NATO alliance. Some pose possible breaches of the already existing chemical and biological weapons treaties.[28] This particular discussion focuses more toward those technologies being developed or considered to assist the complex-terrain battle.

As the force moves through a city, it encounters a sewer grate, which is removed and a superhardening foam is injected into the opening to seal the potential avenue of approach and deny the adversary unfettered access to movement through the sewer system. Small, unmanned aerial vehicles (UAV), most about the size of a model airplane, zip along looking into windows and scanning for snipers. These UAVs then use an aerosol to render the identified individual unconscious. The soldiers walk the street with their grenade launchers filled with sponge grenades, designed to knock a person down without permanent damage, and sticky webbing, a concept made popular by Marvel Comics' Spiderman.

Consider a truck similar to an insecticide truck that travels through neighborhoods today. Instead of killing bugs with its cloud of smoke, this truck targets human emotions. The gas is designed to make crowd control easier, because it causes individuals to lose the will to fight. Some of these possibilities are right now being fielded; others may be decades away.

In understanding the capabilities and the "gee-whiz" nature of these weapons, it is important to realize that "[t]here can be no guarantees that nonlethal weapons will result in no casualties. Great care should be taken to ensure that . . . policy-makers do not have unrealistic expectations. . . ."[29]

Conclusion

The future of warfare is truly a mystery. The interpretations demonstrated in this chapter show only several of an infinite number of possible avenues. Understanding the military culture of the opponent as well as speed and information dominance is critical to the American military culture and the American popular culture. The American people are a gadget and low-casualty people. The terrorist events of 11 September 2001 changed the political/military landscape. Until then, no recent American politicians or senior officers presented the idea of protracted conflict. In fact, they discussed conflict in terms of short duration and low casualties as definitions of success, as noted in previous chapters. Even in the current war on terrorism, many political leaders and news media personalities are impatient for victory after only a few months.

It is clear that nations seeking to either directly challenge or at least disregard the interests of the United States will enhance their possibility of victory by moving away from open terrain. The units of the future that are being discussed in military circles will dominate unrestricted and restricted terrain combat; there is little doubt. However, severely restricted and complex terrain will so degrade current and projected technologies that these types of terrain will provide the niche that low-tech nations seek.

The level of firepower and the speed that is proposed are certain to allow the United States to maintain the edge in maneuver warfare. The objective force proposed, however, does not possess the same advantages in the severely restricted terrain of a Vietnam or Korea or the complex terrain of the urban sprawl. In fact, the very capabilities that make the objective force so attractive in open terrain make them less attractive in complex terrain. Speed is almost entirely irrelevant when the opposition is secure in buildings. The deadly zone, which is the distance a force must travel while receiving direct or indirect fire to reach its objective, will increase in unrestricted terrain to tens of kilometers. In the urban sprawl, this deadly zone will remain the same as it has for decades—one building to the next. The M1 Garand (basic infantry weapon) from World War II is as effective as the most advanced infantry rifle in complex terrain. It is precisely for this reason that adversaries will draw the United States into the cities. The U.S. Army will not fight in the cities because that is where the money, road junctions, or people are, as some have suggested; it will fight in the cities because that is where the enemy is.[30] And enemies of the United States will be there because that is where the United States is the most vulnerable.

National security and military planners cannot expect that future adversaries will have a similar view toward the sacredness of human life. In fact, the opposite view is certain to be more likely. The lower-tier nations of the world will use their large populations to generate their military force and to provide civilian shields. Some of these people may serve both roles simultaneously. Civilians translate into political trouble spots for most democratic leaderships. This advanced understanding by potential adversary governments will further muddy the waters. Few future conflicts will be as clear as Saddam Hussein made Operation Desert Storm. Most leaders with plans for extraterritorial expansion will effectively divide the UN security council—and attempt to paralyze the members of the UN security council who oppose them—by sending confusing signals and demonstrating reasonable demands mixed with unacceptable ones. Confusion in modern war will allow them the time to seize the critical urban terrain within the desired territory prior to U.S. reaction, which in turn will cause greater political paralysis.

All of the political maneuvering combined with the undesirable terrain becomes further complicated by the threat and almost certain use of weapons of mass destruction. These weapons are sure to be targeted on troop concentrations, but terrorists can be expected to use them within the borders of the United States. Electromagnetic pulse warheads along with computer viruses and logic bombs can be combined to disable our networks and computer capability, and lasers and possible nuclear warheads can wound or kill our satellites.

The bleakness of this scenario is that most of these attacks do not require a Russian- or Chinese-sized opponent. The variety of other technological weaponry will be purchased "off the shelf" from technologically advanced nations who have few, if any, scruples about arm sales.

Some analysts and pundits may suggest that this scenario is too bleak, because no nation can handle the retaliation that the United States could bring. This is a probable analysis, but the possibility of a nation with an exploding population, poor food distribution, and a failing economy means that American rationality cannot be the measure used. Does it hurt a blind person if the lights are turned out? This is what the lower-tier adversary strives for—the lights out and all stumbling blindly in the dark. Now the advantage is to the blind.

Until several of the crucial technologies discussed are actually developed and fielded, the paradigm of manpower-intensive urban warfare will remain. Soldiers have to see through or into the buildings and be able to effectively deter, or control in a large-scale fashion, the masses of people who will either join the fight or at least impede our progress. Once these capabilities are present, the future force can be a lean, fast-moving ground element.

The future of warfare is dominated by possibilities without assurance. If the imaging, harmonic, and other nonlethal technologies can be fielded, the nature of warfare within the complex-terrain environment can in fact be changed. But until they can, the very nature of this sort of conflict will not be different. Many soldiers will need to personally place themselves at risk, and casualties will be common.

Conclusions

Summary

This project began with one fundamental question: What challenges will future ground commanders face in armed conflict and how does the United States prepare for them?

The first portion of this question is answered throughout the book: primarily that, as the only tier-one nation, the United States will face opponents who are technologically less advanced and will therefore seek nontraditional means to defeat the aims and goals of the United States. Each of the five battle analyses addressed a different method that a lower-tier nation might use. None of the methods was exclusive; most combined elements of the others. The dominant characteristic is the reliance on humans to make up for a lack of technology. Whether it was the attacks of the Chinese or North Vietnamese in the mountains and jungles of Asia, or the roadblocks of the Somalis, masses of humanity were used to overwhelm the firepower, close with the higher-tier force, and thwart the designs of the higher-tier elements. Even in the Falkland Islands, the Argentineans used more people than the British. Yet they failed to gain a decisive advantage, because they were in a passive defense. The Iraqis failed to capitalize on their superior numbers because they either remained stationary or blundered about blindly in the open terrain.

It must be noted that, in all but the Korean War example, the higher-tier force came out with a technical and tactical victory. Even at LZ Albany, the 2-7 Cav inflicted far more losses on the NVA than they received. It is the greater sensibility about casualties that causes the perception of defeat even when a numeric victory is achieved. The most stark example is that of the battle of Mogadishu, in which the United States killed the Somalis at an almost 30:1 ratio, and it was the Americans who withdrew. This sensibility is quite possibly the American grand strategic center of gravity.

The answer to the second portion of the question is both simple and complicated. The simple answer, as seen through all of the battle analyses, is that the nature of warfare at the tactical level changes very little. The experiences of the infantrymen in Mogadishu in 1993 were not much different from those of the Marines in the city of Hue in 1968, twenty-five years earlier. These experiences were again not considerably different from those experienced by infantrymen in Stalingrad in 1943, fifty years previously. The most significant difference was the airborne command post and imaging that the forces in Mogadishu utilized. The high-technology equipment was of little practical use, because the convoys still got lost, people were still confused, and the enemy was everywhere. It is the nature of war at the lowest level to be a brutal, confusing, infantry struggle.

The conflict of the future is certain to be conducted within the borders of nations. The international precedents set by the UN resolutions at the end of the Gulf War and during the conflicts in Bosnia-Herzegovina and Kosovo expanded the role of the international community to being able to conduct military operations within the borders of a sovereign state when conditions are deemed a threat to international peace. The possibilities of these precedents are staggering. If the financial problems of Indonesia were declared a threat to international peace, would American troops be sent in to stabilize the economy? The future of conflict will see many such interventions done with the authority of the UN. The lower-tier nations that are declared threats to international peace and are then compelled to accept international military forces will react negatively to the intervention. This reaction could come in any form, from civil disobedience to the outright armed defiance of the Somali people.

The information-age conflict is certain to be fought in the cities or urban sprawl. The lower-tier nations will seek to pull any high-tier nation into a long, dirty war. The cost of modern warfare will drive the high-tier nation to seek rapid, surgical, decisive engagements. The opposing views of success in war are fundamental to the ability of a lower-tier power to succeed. The North Vietnamese and mujahideen had the patience to wait out the larger nations on the grand strategy level. Sun Tzu's statement that "there has never been a protracted war which benefited a country" is true only from a wealthy nation's perspective. Protracted conflict is the seed for victory that all low-tier nations seek to plant. If a nation has nothing, then a long conflict risks nothing to gain victory.

American means of dealing with this "dirty" urban warfare are crucial to military and political success. Suggestions of siege warfare have been made by military futurists. Even when made as off-handed ideas, these are dangerous. Americans do not have the stomach for siege warfare. The economic embargo against Iraq following the successful completion of Operation Desert Storm has caused more than a few to realize the worthlessness of trying to force change by inducing suffering onto the citizenry ruled by a dictator. How will a siege be any different? Can American political will outlast the scenes of thousands starving to death? The other typically American solution is to use overwhelming technology to defeat the forces in a city. The technology to image through buildings, to have robot soldiers, or to use thought-altering sounds or chemicals does not exist. And it does not appear that these technologies will exist within the next quarter century. Until technologies are developed and can be used effectively, the idea of a clean technological solution is no more realistic than America's laying siege to Tehran, Mogadishu, or Pyongyang.[1]

The ground combat commanders in the first quarter of the twenty-first century will see war much like that of their predecessors. They will experience conflicts in cities and the associated urban sprawl by an adversary who will use tactics ranging from terrorist strikes to organized raids and ambushes to cause attrition to the American force in an attempt to break the American national will. They will seek no large engagements but numerous minor ones where they can pit their under-equipped force against a squad, platoon, or logistics elements.

The ground combat commanders must be able to react to this style of warfare in a politically sensible manner. They will need a sound knowledge of international relations and the political objectives. The amount of time spent as diplomat and spokesman will require that subordinates fully understand the mission and intent and can execute it in a relatively autonomous fashion. The political sensitivity will also be seen as the commanders serve as local administrators and environmental protectors. The nature of the conflicts—within a nation's borders rather than defending or attacking across borders—will further politicize the commanders' responsibilities. A lack of clarity of the situation—stability and security operations are typically confusing to the American populace—will result in limited public support for the operation and will create an environment for rapid change given a perceived significant defeat.

All of the political and administrative issues aside, when the firing starts, the ground combat commanders will not be much different from Lt. Col. Harold Moore or Lt. Col. George Armstrong Custer, who rode into battle with little information and were denied personal reconnaissance information by the terrain—in this case the urban sprawl. Both of these historic commanders had to make decisions on the move, with little knowledge and with even less useful assistance from higher echelons. The ability of the commander to assess the situation and react intuitively will make the difference in the battles of the future. Custer chose wrong, following his brash assumptions to defeat; Moore was correct, leading his force to victory.

Recommendations

In this environment, how can the American military commander weave through the jumble of issues to reach a desirable objective? Success in conflict begins years ahead. Virtually every commander linked the success of Operation Desert Storm to the developments started after the end of the Vietnam War to retrain and develop the American military. The U.S. Army fighting in Desert Storm was a product of reforms begun in 1975. The successes on the battlefields of 2025 will have their roots in the decisions made today.

Many lessons learned, and conclusions, have been stated throughout this book. The remainder of this chapter addresses the most important recommendations for the future success of the U.S. military. These recommendations are divided into three categories—force structure, leader development, and training—and include the pattern of identification, isolation, suppression, maneuver, and destruction. Most of the ideas discussed following are not new. Many great combat veterans have commented on similar concepts.

Force Structure

The intent of these recommendations is not to advocate a size or specific dimension of a unit within the force structure. The recommendation here is for a style rather than a shape.

Identification: The first and most important element is to design a force that allows U.S. ground commanders to understand the enemy and truly see the battlefield. This can come, in part, through technology, but it needs to begin with people. The U.S. Army has reduced the number of reconnaissance soldiers in a battalion from thirty to eighteen since 1998. This is a 40 percent reduction in the number of people who can provide direct observation, information, and analysis of the battlefield. In urban terrain this decision will be fatal. The Intermediate Brigade Combat Team (IBCT) has an entire reconnaissance and surveillance squadron, but this devotion to human intelligence must be expanded throughout the force.

Isolation: Strength comes not through numbers of vehicles but through adherence to Nathan Bedford Forrest's dictum to "get thar the fustest with the mostest." Force projection is more critical than force structure. This alone means that the U.S. Army needs to willingly take a seat farther back in the U.S. Department of Defense funding bus. The U.S. Air Force, the U.S. Navy, and the associated marine corps provide rapid combat power forward. The sustained presence of the army is important, and even essential, to achieving victory in every conflict; however, the need for large numbers of the high-cost, high-technology, high-weight systems should be over. Only through the ability to project force can the ground force hope to isolate a theater.

Suppression: The ability to suppress an opponent in severely restricted and complex terrain requires more systems on the ground and less reliance on distant firepower. Heavy artillery is of negligible use in the urban environment. Currently the discussions of future organizations always talk about greater engagement ranges and larger areas of operations. This greater dispersion is completely moot in the urban sprawl. The production of hypervelocity tank-killing missiles has almost no application within the confines of an urban environment. In what urban environment is there a five-kilometer line of sight?[2]

The army has altered and reshaped the primary structure of its units numerous times. Each time it is in search of the best way to utilize the available technology and defeat the identified threat. With this in mind, the movement to the Force XXI division removed fourteen tanks and Bradleys per battalion from its armor and mechanized infantry units.

The decision to reduce combat potential in hopes of creating a more deployable division is in direct opposition to what I call the "street corner" theory. If it is agreed that it takes one tank or Bradley and ten soldiers to effectively defend or secure one street corner, then a Desert Storm U.S. division with 522 such vehicles could secure no more than 522 street corners. That same division under Force XXI can guard only 405 such corners. This is a reduction of more than 20 percent. Greater engagement ranges of the M1A2 or the M3A3 and a better understanding of locations of these vehicles are moot within an urban battlefield. Rarely will someone shoot a tank farther than a thousand meters in any city, certainly not in the typical poorly designed and crowded cities of the developing world. The location issue is of lesser value in the city, because the relatively static vehicles require little effort to control.

These expensive (nearly $6 million for the M1A2) pieces of equipment are very vulnerable to top-attack systems fired from rooftops, and bottom-attack mines under manhole covers or buried in dirt roads or potholes. The vulnerability and potential cost create the danger of national will questions.

Inexpensive, low-technology units must be developed to allow for the manpower-intensive conflicts that will dominate the military landscape of the early decades of this century. The American soldier, with a significant load of technology, will be ill equipped to fight in the slums and run-down shanty sprawls of the cities of today or tomorrow. Heavy tanks and artillery provide little help with their multimillion-dollar price tags when a few hundred-dollar grenades launched by disposable launchers can destroy them. These losses will be intolerable to the budget and consequently to the American people. Soldiers must be equipped with high-quality, low-cost equipment and be augmented by the high-technology C⁴ISR gadgetry that can assist them in reaching objectives. Sixty-eight-ton $6 million tanks have no place in the narrow city streets surrounded by run-down buildings that crumble from a touch. A lighter, cheaper, more agile vehicle is needed, one that provides the firepower to reduce structures and open ingress-egress routes for the infantry at very close distances. This vehicle must also have the protection to allow for the evacuation of wounded under cover from small-arms fire.

The vehicle is an assault gun/transport. The term *tank* has developed a connotation of a tank killer, and this is not the intent. Tank battles do not occur in the city; even if they did, agility is much more crucial to success than heavy armor.

Maneuver: In the previous section I recommended a capability that is typically considered part of maneuver; however, in the ground combat of the future, bold maneuver will probably happen only from the air. Complex and severely restricted terrain significantly limit ground maneuver, yet aviation does not suffer from the same limitations. Aircraft, with their advanced optics and long-range precision targeting regardless of terrain, provide a greater level of survivability.

Destruction: The force encouraged by the Army After Next Wargames and the focus of the army transformation is a crucial part of the future landscape of war. Its deterrent capability and possibility of dominant maneuver in unrestricted and restricted terrain is essential. However, this development will force future adversaries into severely restricted and complex terrain to negate the advantages of the high-tier force. Once that is done, the United States needs combat power that is capable and financially expendable enough to then force the adversary out of the difficult terrain or defeat him where he is. This adds another level of capability without the attendant costs. The force of the future envisioned by the army is a combination of the future battle force combined with legacy Force XXI divisions. To this must be added a "Force 1944" element.

This "Force 1944" has a Sherman tank equivalent. Inexpensive, multi-role, rapidly deployable but with added agility (agility is not synonymous with speed)—all are criteria that should be used in designing the assault gun. Simple additions should also be ensured: multiple ammunition types, to allow for the variety of missions desired; communications on the outside, to allow for direct coordination between infantry and crew members; a compartment that can protect injured personnel; and a water pump that can be transformed into a water cannon for crowd control or decontamination. Some of these capabilities existed on previous American tanks. These are not new ideas, but they are needed.

No desire exists to revive the technology of the 1940s; however, the concept of affordable multifunction equipment must be brought back to allow the American military to enforce the policies of the U.S. government without bankrupting the nation in the process. It has been suggested that "[i]nfantry will rise in importance in the next century because of its ability to hide from and sneak through high-tech barriers. . . . [These infantry soldiers] will want hardware that is dependable, sustainable, cheap, and expendable, not sophisticated, complex, and costly."[3]

To achieve the necessary destruction of will or materiel, the ground force must have significant numbers of highly trained infantry.

Whether or not anyone will publicly admit it, the United States is the world's police force, and the neighborhood is getting messier. Future missions will not be any easier or less demanding than those of the present. It is relatively plain that the confused state of future engagements will result in more deployments, more commitments, and the need for more forces. The impact on a budget that cannot support the current structure is obvious. Only a lower-technology, and thereby less-expensive, force can be sufficient to accomplish the missions and support the budgetary constraints.

Leader Development

It was not the rifles or the Harriers or the HMS *Arrow* that were victorious at Goose Green. It was the leadership of Lieutenant Colonel Jones and Major Keeble. The battalion- and company-level leaders throughout the five case studies were the critical link to success. The decision of Captain McMaster to advance to the next intervisibility line, which resulted in the defeat of a brigade of the Tawakalna Division, and the decision by a lieutenant to throw rocks and tins of food to allow his unit to withdraw on Hill 219 were what brought the survivors home and resulted in success or defeat. The battalion- and company-level leaders are the individuals who must be trained at the highest levels.

The development of junior and middle-level leaders in a military organization is the responsibility of all members of the officer corps. The type of warfare envisioned for the 2025 time frame is expected to demand a great deal more of the soldiers fighting. These soldiers "will require higher levels of mental agility and psychological resilience" and will experience more "physical and emotional stress" as they "fight in a degree of isolation far more psychologically demanding than in past wars."[4]

The military as a whole and the ground components specifically need to ensure that the leaders of the future are trained to understand the opponent in all the possibilities. The failure of leaders past and present to identify the enemy has been primarily because those same leaders did not understand the enemy they were looking for. The understanding of ideas, organization, doctrine, and capabilities is essential to achieving victory. This must be instilled from the entry-level leadership courses to the highest levels of training. Only then will the leadership be able to effectively conduct the identification, isolation, suppression, maneuver, and destruction necessary to achieve victory.

The July 1997 Army After Next (AAN) Project report states the need for a change in leadership development: "Blue's tactical success depended to a great extent on his ability to execute decentralized operations. His strategic and tactical speed would have required an exceptional degree of mental agility and psychological resilience. We believe that the development of these qualities by 2025 will require nothing less than a cultural change within the Army that embraces a philosophy of decentralized action based upon a high degree of professional trust and confidence between leaders and led."[5]

This is significant, considering the current mental philosophy of leadership within the U.S. military. This is a place where units typically have formations to tell people to go home, where mountains of regulations exist to tell a soldier how to dress, how to behave, how to punish. The U.S. military is one of the world's largest bureaucracies with an ever-increasing level of oversight and directive.[6]

The development of junior-level initiative begins with training at the home station and continues through major exercises. This is the pattern that Colonel Holder followed that allowed him to maneuver so effectively during Desert Storm. He trained his officers through classes, terrain walks, staff rides, and large maneuvers to take initiative within the plan to accomplish their designated purposes. The mentorship and dedication required for this sort of development is not as obvious in today's army. Fear of failure and missed promotions infects the minds of many middle and senior leaders. The development of managers rather than warrior-leaders is dominant in the army schools. The focus on detailed plans and monitoring criteria and following synchronization matrices embeds a custom of detail and management rather than an emphasis on the ability to execute under stressful conditions. There are commanders and senior leaders who emphasize these traits and qualities and, more importantly, reward them when demonstrated. This must expand to most of the leaders rather than some. It must evolve to a "cultural change" at all levels. Intelligent, well-executed risk brings the greatest victories.

Training

The pattern of identification, isolation, suppression, maneuver, and destruction is not difficult, but it requires rapid decisionmaking, action, and ultimately culmination. To do all of this requires significant repetition for an individual and even more for an organization. The larger the organization, the more repetition is necessary.

Add to this the multifunction nature of equipment, which, in turn, requires the training of multifunction soldiers and most especially leaders. The critical difference between equipment and manpower is expense. Unlike the idea of having affordable equipment that can be expended, the leaders of tomorrow's force are not expendable and must have the greatest possible level of training. This training requires expenditures of money, but in the end the training will more than make up for a reduced technology capability in the equipment. General George S. Patton Jr. often remarked that a pint of sweat during training saves a gallon of blood in combat. This should be the mantra of the future.

Virtual training and the overwhelming use of simulations are driven by the expense of training with modern equipment. The tanks, infantry fighting vehicles, and helicopters of today are prohibitively expensive to maneuver; therefore, computer-generated training is devised. The benefits are remarkable. Soldiers can experience the battlefield with limited expense and no danger. Scenarios can be run and rerun to allow for a focus on specific objectives. Despite the benefits of simulation, however, it is simply a simulation. Units that are considered the best trained and disciplined are consistently those that spend the most on live training. The soldiers of the Special Operations Forces expend thousands of rounds of ammunition developing good shooters. The same concept needs to apply in all aspects of training. Only proper practice of the fundamental skills improves those skills. Simulation training is a great asset, to a point. Once beyond that point, all it really does is prepare soldiers for fighting simulations. The sad truth is that most units do not reach the point at which simulation becomes less beneficial.

An example of dependence on technology is that of land navigation. Numerous soldiers, after serving in line units for several years, lose the skill of navigation with map and compass, because they are so reliant on the global positioning system (GPS). The handheld devices are so prevalent in the units that nearly all leaders have them. The use of satellite technology to maneuver has removed the criticality of basic land navigation. Many times a leader has needed assistance to navigate once the GPS receiver has become inoperative. The primary reason for the lost skills is time. It requires precious training time to maintain and improve land navigation skills. Training to understand and use the technology also requires a considerable amount of time. Under the current operational tempo, commanders cannot do both. This dilemma has resulted in the loss of emphasis on basic skills in favor of technology training.

The importance of technology must not be played down. Technology is an important and possibly even crucial part of the U.S. military dominance. What must be struck is a balance. Soldiers must have not simply a firm grasp of basic soldier skills but a mastery of those skills, as well as a mastery of the technology that allows for the information dominance and speed of future maneuver warfare. A division of forces between Force 1944 and the high-technology force would allow soldiers to focus training more effectively. This comes only with the availability of training, and this—as with most issues—means having time and sufficient financial backing.

Conclusion

Meeting the recommendations and changing the course of American military thought at the grand strategy level requires fundamental changes in how the world and national security are seen in each form of power, and in understanding the impact of the media.

Economic Power:
 • Recognize that information-age military equipment is prohibitively expensive.

• Provide the force with equipment that requires such technology (command and control equipment, intelligence equipment, et cetera) or equipment that provides "leap ahead" opportunities (M1A2 SEP), and do not provide evolutionary systems (M1A2).

• Determine capabilities required and structure the force to meet those capabilities; do not purchase wants. Do we really require numerous Force XXI divisions, or will a few augmented with Force 1944 divisions be adequate?

Diplomatic Power:

• All-out war is a thing of the past. Any future conflict will be limited and will require very few casualties. The force must protect itself from severe losses yet be able to rapidly achieve the objectives for which it was deployed.

• A clear, attainable objective is critical to mission success. Coalition warfare—ideally, habitual coalitions—is the primary means of achieving success.

Military Power:

• Wars that involve the United States are limited to conventional and unconventional forms of combat, but not nuclear. Tactical success does not translate directly to strategic victory. Conflict requires objectives at all levels of strategy to provide for the proper translation of success from one level to the next.

• Deployability is the critical function of combat power. Smaller, more deployable forces, which can provide firepower and protection once on the ground, are the most desired systems.

• Most conflicts will be in complex terrain, which requires coordinated, rehearsed, manpower-intensive forces.

Media:

• With media present in the conflict zone, the levels of strategy are compressed. A soldier at a checkpoint who shoots at a civilian will require reaction from the national leadership.

• The nightly news will determine the future deployment of combat forces as much as the threat to the national interests of the parent nation.

Along with the change to the vision of the world, the U.S. military's ground forces must make a commitment of time, dollars, and professional style. The commitment needs to be based on a firm understanding of the real future of armed conflict. The vision of more World War IIs and the army expanding to encompass numerous millions of conscripts is not realistic; neither is the vision of a grand sweeping maneuver against another armored force across wide-open plains. These may happen in small degrees, but the future is full of short attempts to end conflict by the United States, frustrated by the desire to prolong the conflict by the lower-tier nation.

The conflicts of the future will not be repeats of past conflicts any more than history ever repeats itself. However, there will be variations on a theme. The theme is similar to Vietnam, and possibly some aspects of Korea, Somalia, and maybe the Falkland Islands, with conflicts looking like Panama, Lebanon, Grenada, and many others. The next twenty years will be full of instability and chaos. They will also be full of possibility and promise, but these must be seized and expanded upon. This can be done with the creation of the lighter, less expensive, and better-trained force envisioned here. This force could be used more efficiently to engage the world and demonstrate U.S. resolve, without threatening the U.S. industrial base and the budget.

This book has explained how the United States can overcome the dangerous ideas represented in each of the images discussed in the Introduction. By fielding more deployable, more agile, and more versatile forces, the ground force commander can use technology to assist yet remain flexible enough to avoid the failing of the knight. Because the force is less expensive, it will become more deployable and more engaged in critical missions around the world rather than being kept hidden away like the Ferrari, or rather than hiring others, such as conscripts, to do the work. And Force 1944 accepts the reality of cost and prevents the *Star Trek* analogy. To create and field such a force requires a boldness to separate from the river of voices calling for technological advance and information-age armed forces. Our conflicts are not going to be information-age conflicts, but instead regressions toward the less technically advanced conflicts of the latter half of the twentieth century. The expense of technology could be focused on a few highly advanced, highly mobile battle forces or strike forces, and on training the existing forces to the highest level possible. The philosophy and lessons being gleaned from the U.S. military current future planning is fantastic, but it is typically being built on faulty premises of large-scale engagements. Funding and strategy must be brought to greater agreement, as stated in the National Defense Panel's review of the 1996 quadrennial defense review (QDR).[7]

The development of high-technology equipment and gadgets should not end. The potential for major conflicts with a neonationalistic Russia or an expansion-minded China in the first half of the twenty-first century is a possibility. Against such foes, high-tech equipment will be the only viable solution. The possibilities are the equivalent of a hundred-year flood. The military forces of a nation are flood insurance. Does the United States have the resources and the desire to insure itself against a hundred-year flood, or should it focus on the more likely ten-, twenty-, and fifty-year floods? The answer produced by this entire project is to field forces to fight the probable floods and continue research and development to assist in sandbagging efforts against the hundred-year flood.

Notes

Introduction

1. *Army-Navy Journal* (8 August 1959). Quoted in "Looking Back," *Armed Forces Journal International* (April 1998): 56.

2. Attrition is victory through the destruction of the enemy's combat capability. In the extreme this means the entire annihilation of every opposing soldier. The Battle of Thermopylae was a battle of attrition initiated by the Spartan defenders of the pass. Disintegration is victory through superior position. This is Sun Tzu's ideal of winning: "To subdue the enemy without fighting is the supreme excellence." Another example is the game of chess. Checkmate may be accomplished without the defeat of a single opposing player's piece, yet the game is still lost.

3. William S. Lind, et al., "The Changing Face of War: Into the Fourth Generation," *Marine Corps Gazette,* October 1989, 22–26.

4. Steven Metz, *Strategic Horizons: The Military Implications of Alternative Futures.* (Carlisle Barracks, Penn.: U.S. Army War College Press/Army After Next Project, 7 March 1997), 25–35. The ideas for the tier system came from this AAN monograph. The author suggests a trisected security system in which he leaves out the second tier. I feel strongly that the differences are going to be great enough among the United States, China, Syria, and Rwanda to warrant the four tiers instead of Dr. Metz's three.

5. Edward N. Luttwak, *Strategy: The Logic of War and Peace* (Cambridge, Mass.: The Belknap Press of Harvard University, 1987), 120.

6. Ibid. This is derived from the entire context of the book.

Chapter One

1. Earl H. Tilford, *The Revolution in Military Affairs: Prospects and Cautions* (Carlisle Barracks, Penn.: U.S. Army War College Press/Army After Next Project, 23 June 1995).

2. Frank Kendall, "Exploiting the Military Technical Revolution: A Concept for Joint Warfare," *Strategic Review,* vol. XX, no. 2 (spring 1992): 30.

3. C. Fred Bergsten, "The Primacy of Economics," *Foreign Policy,* no. 87 (summer 1992): 6.

4. Ibid., 24.

5. Robert D. Hormats, "The Roots of American Power," *Foreign Affairs* 70, no. 3 (summer 1991): 133.

6. Rick Maze, "Senate Clips Bosnia Mission's Purse Strings," *Army Times,* 19 May 1997, 11.

7. Richard L. West, "The FY 1998 Army Budget in Perspective: Prelude to Change," *Army* (May 1997): 28.

8. Editors of *Time* magazine, *Desert Storm: The War in the Persian Gulf* (New York: Time Warner Publishing, Inc., 1991), 101, 200.

9. Various cost figures used are: 1944 average for all tanks purchased, $505,714.48 (constant $) and $89,005.75 (actual $); M1A1 (1993), $2,629,757.70 (constant $) and $3.8 million (actual $); M3A2 (1993), $1,522,491.30 (constant $) and $2.2 million (actual $); M1A2 (1995), $3,608,923.80 (constant $) and $5.5 million (actual $); M1 to M1A2 conversion (1996), $1,664,596 (constant $) and $2.68 million (actual $); AGS (1997), $2,666,256.10 (constant $) and $4.33 million (actual $). These figures come primarily from the Army Green Book Internet site and the *U.S. Army in World War Two: Armament Procurement* (Washington, D.C.: Government Printing Office), Tables PR-3 and PR-7.

10. George C. Wilson, "Spinney: QDR Misses the Mark," *Army Times,* 18 August 1997, 29. Average airframe prices increase from $28 million during the Cold War to $86.7 million for the F-22 and the joint strike fighter (JSF).

11. George C. Wilson, "NATO, US Armed Forces Technology Gap Widens," *Army Times,* 13 October 1997, 34.

12. Leonard Silk, "Dangers of Slow Growth," *Foreign Affairs,* "America and the World 1992–93," vol. 72, no. 1, 180–181.

13. Hormats, 139.

14. Henry Kissinger, *Diplomacy* (New York: Simon & Schuster, 1994), 19.

15. Patrick M. Cronin, "American Global Leadership After the Cold War: From Pax Americana to Pax Consortis," *Strategic Review,* vol. XIX, no. 3 (summer 1991): 11.

16. Kissinger, 487.

17. Ibid., 480.

18. Paul H. Nitze, "Grand Strategy Then and Now: NSC-68 and Its Lessons for the Future," *Strategic Review,* vol. XXII, no. 1 (winter 1994): 12–19.

19. Ibid., 17.

20. U.S. Department of the Army, *FM 101-5-1. Operational Terms and Graphics* (September 1997): 1–43.

21.William G. Hyland, "The Case for Pragmatism," *Foreign Affairs* 71, no. 1, America and the World 1991–92, 44.

22. Ibid.

23. Editors of *Time* magazine, *Desert Storm: The War in the Persian Gulf* (New York: Time Warner Publishing, Inc., 1991), 199–201.

24. Gordon R. Sullivan and James M. Dubik, *Envisioning Future Warfare* (Fort Leavenworth, Kans.: Command and General Staff College Press, 1995), 10–11.

25. *Strategic Assessment 1996: Instruments of U.S. Power* (Washington, D.C.: National Defense University Institute for National Strategic Studies, 1996), 140.

26. Walter Goodman, "Arnett," *Columbia Journalism Review* 30 (May/June 1991): 31. Quoted in E. L. Pattullo, "War and the American Press," *Parameters* 22, no. 4 (winter 1992–93): 66.

27. Robin Wright, "No Man Is an Island," *The New Republic* (18 February 1991): 66. Quoted in E. L. Pattullo, "War and the American Press," *Parameters* 22, no. 4 (winter 1992–93): 63.

28. Sam C. Sarkesian, "Soldiers, Scholars and the Media," *Parameters* 17, no. 3 (September 1987): 83.

29. James Schlesinger, "Quest for a Post–Cold War Foreign Policy," *Foreign Affairs* 72, no. 1, America and the World 1992–93, 18.

30. Metz, 1.

31. Colin L. Powell, "U.S. Forces: Challenges Ahead," *Foreign Affairs* 72, no. 5 (winter 1992–93): 37.

32. Ibid.

33. Saad el Shazly, *The Crossing of the Suez* (San Francisco, Calif.: American Mideast Research, 1980), 82; Avraham Adan, *On the Banks of the Suez* (Novato, Calif.: Presidio Press, 1980), 82–83.

34. Congress, House of Representatives, Mr. Podell of New York speaking on A Chance for Peace, 93d Congress, 2d session, *Congressional Record* (25 October 1973), vol. 119, 35014.

35. Zachary Lum, "Region on a Roll," *Journal of Electronic Defense* 20, no. 3 (March 1997): 33–38.

36. Ian Mather, "The Bizarre Arms Bazaar," *The European,* 20–26 November 1997, 28–29.

37. *Strategic Assessment 1996: Instruments of U.S. Power,* 6.

38. These battles are described in fantastic detail in Harold G. Moore and Joseph L. Galloway, *We Were Soldiers Once . . . and Young: Ia Drang, the Battle that Changed the War in Vietnam,* paperback ed. (New York: Harper Perennial Publishers, 1993). Chapter Five is a battle analysis of the battle at LZ Albany.

39. Robert H. Scales, Jr., *Certain Victory: United States Army in the Gulf War* (Fort Leavenworth, Kans.: Command and General Staff College Press, 1994, select reprint), 220.

Chapter Two

1. The methods discussed are similar to those referred to in other articles and books as asymmetrical. Asymmetrical operations are defined in the U.S. Army *FM 3-0 Operations (2001),* paragraph 4-109, as follows: "Asymmetry concerns dissimilarities in organization, equipment, doctrine, capabilities, and values between other armed forces (formally organized or not) and U.S. forces. . . . In a larger sense, asymmetric warfare seeks to avoid enemy strengths and concentrate comparative advantages against relative weaknesses." This is one of

the oldest precepts of war—to strike where the enemy is weak, or better yet, to strike where the enemy is completely unprotected.

2. Area of influence is defined in U.S. Army *FM 3-0 Operations (2001)* as follows: "An area where a commander can directly influence operations by maneuver or fire support systems normally under his control."

3. Sean D. Naylor, "Army Takes to the Urban Streets," *Army Times,* 21 July 1997, 22.

4. Ralph Peters, "Will We Be Able to Take the Cities?" *Army Times,* 11 May 1998, 34.

5. George I. Seffers, "U.S. Arms for Urban Wars: Battles in Cities Will Require New Tactics, Technologies," *Army Times,* 9 February 1998, 26.

6. T'ao Han-chang, *Sun-Tzu's Art of War: The Modern Chinese Interpretation,* translated by Yuan Shibing (New York: Sterling Publishing Co., Inc., 1987), 94. The other factors are politics, weather, the commander, and doctrine.

7. Ibid., 118.

8. The acronym is METT-T: mission, enemy, terrain, time, troops available.

9. Gerry L. Gilmore, "Avoiding Attrition Warfare in 2020–2025," *Army Link News,* Army News Service, 28 July 1997, 1.

10. T'ao Han-chang, 97.

11. Wass de Czege, *Future (2020+) Joint Operations and Landpower Tactics,* 1997, 5.

12. David T. Twining, "Vietnam and the Six Criteria for the Use of Military Force," *Parameters* 15, no. 4 (winter 1985):12.

Chapter Three

1. S. L. A. Marshall, *The River and the Gauntlet: Defeat of the Eighth Army by the Chinese Communist Forces, November 1950, in the Battle of the Chongch'on River, Korea* (Nashville, Tenn.: The Battery Press, 1959), 16.

2. Clay Blair, *The Forgotten War: America in Korea 1950-1953* (New York: Times Books, 1987), 431.

3. Marshall, 15.

4. Ibid., 22.

5. Ibid., 14, 18.

6. Ibid., 15.

7. Ibid.

8. Max Hastings, *The Korean War* (New York: Simon & Schuster, 1987), 136.

9. Marshall, 23–26 passim.

10. Blair, 444; Marshall, 14, 18.

11. Roy E. Appleman, *South to the Naktong, North to the Yalu (June–November 1950)*, United States Army in the Korean War (Washington, D.C.: Center of Military History Press, 1956; reprint 1992), 615 (page references are to reprint edition).

12. Hastings, 135.

13. Appleman, 753.

14. Ibid., 754.

15. Blair, 434–35.

16. Ibid., 436–37.

17. Marshall, 14–30 passim. This is the most detailed account of the battle and the reference for nearly every other book on the struggles at the tactical level during this portion of the campaign.

18. Ibid.

19. Matthew B. Ridgway, *The Korean War: How We Met the Challenge; How All-Out Asian War Was Averted; Why MacArthur Was Dismissed; Why Today's War Objectives Must Be Limited* (Garden City, N.Y.: Doubleday, 1967; paperback ed., New York: Da Capo Press, 1986), 86.

20. T. R. Fehrenbach, *This Kind of War: The Classic Korean War History* (New York: Macmillan, 1963; reprint, Washington, D.C.: Brassey's, 1994), 348.

Chapter Four

1. Hereafter simply referred to as North Vietnam.

2. Charles C. Krulak, "'Not Like Yesterday'/In His Own Words, Commandant Describes His Vision of Future Warfighting," *Navy Times-Marine Corps Edition*, 19 January 1998.

3. Harold G. Moore and Joseph L. Galloway, *We Were Soldiers Once*

. . . *and Young: Ia Drang, the Battle that Changed the War in Vietnam,* paperback ed. (New York: Harper Perennial Publishers, 1993), 259.

4. Ibid., 255.

5. Moore and Galloway, *We Were Soldiers Once . . . and Young,* 261.

6. Harold G. Moore, "After Action Report of Operations in the Ia Drang Valley," November 1965.

7. Ibid., 251–58 passim.

8. Joseph L. Galloway, "Vietnam Story," *U.S. News & World Report,* 29 October 1990, 45.

9. Moore and Galloway, *We Were Soldiers Once . . . and Young,* 251.

10. Ibid., 253

11. Ibid.

12. Ibid.

13. Ibid., 288.

14. Ibid., 290.

15. Ibid., 296, 308–9.

16. The "mad minute" was a technique developed during the Vietnam War in which a unit would fire all of its weapons for one minute at a designated time. This was designed to force any unknown enemy into action. It was a direct result of the psychological fears about hidden enemy everywhere, and it produced solid tactical gains on numerous occasions.

17. Ibid., 350–70 passim.

18. Joseph L. Galloway, "Fatal Victory," *U.S. News & World Report,* 29 October 1990, 33.

19. Ibid.

20. Ibid., 32.

21. Robert S. McNamara, *In Retrospect: The Tragedy and Lessons of Vietnam,* Vintage ed. (New York: Random House Inc., 1996), 222.

22. Joseph L. Galloway, "Vietnam Story," *U.S. News & World Report,* 29 October 1990, 46.

Chapter Five

1. Gary D. Rhay, "Endurance: The British Triumph of Endurance in the Falkland Islands War," in *Combined Arms in Battle Since 1939,*

ed. Roger J. Spiller (Fort Leavenworth, Kans.: U.S. Army Command and General Staff College Press, 1992), 105–11.

2. Ibid., 111.

3. Ibid., 235–36.

4. Ibid.

5. Hastings, 235.

6. Ibid., 238.

7. Matthew S. Klimow, "Logistics: British Logistics in the Falklands," in *Combined Arms in Battle Since 1939,* ed. Roger J. Spiller (Fort Leavenworth, Kans.: U.S. Army Command and General Staff College Press, 1992), 161.

8. Hastings, 238.

9. Anthony H. Cordesman and Abraham R. Wagner, *The Lessons of Modern War, Volume III: The Afghan and Falkland Conflicts* (Boulder, Colo.: Westview Press, 1991), 283.

10. The Sunday Times of London Insight Team, 233.

11. John Laffin, *Fight for the Falklands! Why and How Britain and Argentina Went to War from Invasion to Surrender* (New York: St. Martin's Press, 1982), 106.

12. Bruce Watson and Peter M. Dunn, *Military Lessons of the Falkland Islands War: Views from the United States,* 131

Chapter Six

1. Department of Defense, *Conduct of the Persian Gulf War: Pursuant to Title V of the Persian Gulf Conflict Supplemental Authorization and Personnel Benefits Act of 1991 (Public Law 102-25)* (Washington, D.C.: U.S. Department of Defense, April 1992), 256.

2. Steve Vogel. "A Swift Kick: 2d ACR's Taming of the Guard." *Army Times,* 5 August 1991, 11. 2-1 Attack Aviation Battalion was identified as an attachment in conversation with Col. Douglas Lute, August 1999.

3. Department of Defense, *Conduct of the Persian Gulf War: Pursuant to Title V of the Persian Gulf Conflict Supplemental Authorization and Personnel Benefits Act of 1991 (Public Law 102-25)* (Washington, D.C.: U.S. Department of Defense, April 1992), 10.

4. Based on a conversation, 24 March 1992, with Jim Phipps, reg-

imental linguist for the 3d ACR. He was a reservist called to active duty to support Operation Desert Storm.

5. Based on a conversation, 22 June 1998, with Clement J. Laniewski, executive officer for C Troop, 2d ACR, during Operation Desert Storm.

6. Stephen P. Gehring, *From the Fulda Gap to Kuwait: U.S. Army, Europe and the Gulf War* (Washington, D.C.: Government Printing Office, 1998), 36.

7. The following information is taken from Bruce W. Watson, Bruce George, Peter Tsouras, and B. L. Cyr, *Military Lessons of the Gulf War* (Novato, Calif.: Presidio Press, 1991), Appendix E, I. The Egyptians supported the coalition with 40,000 ground forces, the British with 35,000 ground forces, and the French with 13,500 ground forces. This does not include contributions in the air and at sea.

8. H. Norman Schwarzkopf and Peter Petre, *General H. Norman Schwarzkopf: The Autobiography: It Doesn't Take a Hero* (New York: Bantam Books, 1992), 305. Also discussed in Bob Woodward, *The Commanders/Bob Woodward* (New York: Simon and Schuster, 1991), 271.

9. Richard M. Swain, *"Lucky War": Third Army in Desert Storm* (Fort Leavenworth, Kans.: Command and General Staff College Press, 1994), xxv.

10. Micah L. Sifrey and Christopher Cerf, *The Gulf War Reader: History, Documents, Opinions* (New York: Times Books, 1991), 351.

11. Colin Powell, *My American Journey* (New York: Ballantine Books, 1995), 495.

12. Department of Defense, *Conduct of the Persian Gulf War: Pursuant to Title V of the Persian Gulf Conflict Supplemental Authorization and Personnel Benefits Act of 1991 (Public Law 102-25)* (Washington, D.C.: U.S. Department of Defense, April 1992), 66.

13. Daniel L. Davis, "Air vs. Land Power: Both Are Vital," *Army Times,* 21 July 1997, 50.

14. During an interview (14 January 1992) by the author with a field artillery captain who served as a battery commander in the 1st Infantry Division during Desert Storm, it was revealed that some Iraqi field artillery units had the authority for chemical weapons release. This release was never realized, because the Iraqi commanders were

concerned about American retaliation. In Steve Vogel's "A Swift Kick: 2d ACR's Taming of the Guard," *Army Times,* 5 August 1991, 28, an Iraqi artillery battalion commander is quoted as saying that he did not know of any units that had chemical weapons.

15. U.S. Armor School Publication, "Mission: To Close with and Destroy Enemy Forces with Fire, Maneuver, and Shock Effect: U.S. Armor in Southwest Asia," 4.

16. Department of Defense, *Conduct of the Persian Gulf War: Pursuant to Title V of the Persian Gulf Conflict Supplemental Authorization and Personnel Benefits Act of 1991 (Public Law 102-25)* (Washington, D.C.: U.S. Department of Defense, April 1992), 76.

17. Robert H. Scales, Jr., *Certain Victory: United States Army in the Gulf War* (Fort Leavenworth, Kans.: Command and General Staff College Press, 1994, select reprint), 277.

18. James F. Dunnigan and Austin Bay, *From Shield to Storm: High-Tech Weapons, Military Strategy, and Coalition Warfare in the Persian Gulf* (New York: William Morrow and Company, Inc., 1992), 288.

19. U.S. Armor School Publication, 4.

20. Ibid., 2.

21. Steve Vogel, "A Swift Kick: 2d ACR's Taming of the Guard," *Army Times,* 5 August 1991, 10.

22. Swain, 245–46.

23. Vogel, 18.

24. Vogel, 18.

25. Swain, 260.

26. Vogel, 28.

27. Scales, 261.

28. Tom Clancy, *Armored Cav: A Guided Tour of an Armored Cavalry Regiment* (New York: Berkley Publishing Group, 1994), 257–60.

29. Scales, 262.

30. Ibid.

31. Vince Crawley, "Ghost Troop's Battle at the 73 Easting," *Armor* (May–June 1991): 8.

32. Crawley, 10.

33. Vogel, 30. This quote is from Sergeant Foltz, the Combat Observation Lasing Team sergeant for Ghost Troop.

34. Vogel, 30.

35. Scales, 262.

36. Crawley, 11.

37. Mostly derived from Steve Vogel, "A Swift Kick: 2d ACR's Taming of the Guard," *Army Times*, 5 August 1991, 10–18, 28–30, 61.

38. Rick Atkinson, *Crusade: The Untold Story of the Persian Gulf War* (Boston: Houghton Miflin Company, 1993), 448.

39. Department of Defense, *Conduct of the Persian Gulf War: Pursuant to Title V of the Persian Gulf Conflict Supplemental Authorization and Personnel Benefits Act of 1991 (Public Law 102-25)* (Washington, D.C.: U.S. Department of Defense, April 1992), xxix.

40. Joseph C. Barto III, *Task Force 2-4 Cav—"First In, Last Out": The History of the 2nd Squadron, 4th Cavalry Regiment, During Operation Desert Storm* (Fort Leavenworth, Kans.: Combat Studies Institute Press, 1993), 111.

41. Sifrey and Cerf, 449.

Chapter Seven

1. Eloise Green, "Somalia: Operations Other Than War: Newsletter No. 93-1," Updated on the Internet, 25 September 1997, A-4.

2. A brownout is when the dust cloud created by a helicopter's rotor wash is so significant that it blocks all view of the ground.

3. Charles P. Ferry, "Mogadishu, October 1993: A Personal Account of a Rifle Company XO," *Infantry* (September–October 1994), 24.

4. Mark Bowden, "Blackhawk Down: An American War Story," *Philadelphia Inquirer*, 16 November to 14 December 1997, 27.

5. Ibid., 35.

6. Ibid. These names and descriptions are found throughout the "Blackhawk Down" articles.

7. Ibid.

8. Reuven Frank, "Hitting the Beach in Mogadishu," *The New Leader* 76, no. 1 (11 January 1993): 22.

9. Vernon Loeb, "After Action Report: Spying used to mean stealing another government's secrets, but what can spies achieve in a country with no government? In Somalia with the CIA, Garrett

Jones and John Spinelli found out," *Washington Post Magazine*, 27 February 2000, 7.

10. Bowden, 27.

11. Colin L. Powell, *My American Journey*, first paperback ed. (New York: Ballantine Books, 1996), 569.

12. Bowden, 4.

13. Ibid., 16.

14. Ibid., 19.

15. Unless otherwise noted, this tactical chronology is derived from two different accounts. The first is from the *Philadelphia Inquirer* series titled "Blackhawk Down"; the second is by a company XO from the 10th Mountain Division relief column titled "Mogadishu, October 1993: A Personal Account of a Rifle Company XO."

16. Powell, 570.

17. Powell, 573.

Chapter Nine

1. Charles C. Krulak, "'Not Like Yesterday'/In His Own Words, Commandant Describes His Vision of Future Warfighting," *Navy Times-Marine Corps Edition*, 19 January 1998.

2. See the document *Knowledge and Speed. The Annual Report on the Army After Next Project to the Chief of Staff of the Army.* Fort Monroe, Va.: TRADOC Press, July 1997.

3. Ibid.

4. See the article Charles A. Jarnot, "Air Mech Strike: Revolution in Maneuver Warfare," *Military Review* 77, no. 2 (March–April 1997): 79–86.

5. This is derived from the AAN intranet Web site publication by Wass de Czege, *Future (2020+) Joint Operations and Landpower Tactics*, 1997, 5.

6. Gerry L. Gilmore, "Avoiding Attrition Warfare in 2020–2025," 4.

7. Robert Famighetti, ed., *The World Almanac and Book of Facts 1998* (Mahwah, N.J.: World Almanac Books, 1997), 958.

8. Ibid.

9. The following is a quote taken from a press release from Con-

gressman Roscoe Bartlett, 6th District of Maryland (released 19 May 1999): "A member of the Russian Duma recently told me, 'You know if we really wanted to hurt you, we would set off an atomic weapon at high altitude above your country and produce an EMP that would destroy your entire electrical power grid, computers, and telecommunications infrastructure including satellites,'" said Congressman Bartlett. "This was not a surprise to me, but it is to most Americans. In light of concerns about the proliferation of nuclear weapon and missile technology by rogue nations, I believe it's imperative that our government take steps to defend against EMP."

Damage can vary based on the height of burst and yield of the device. It is critical to understand that devices closer to the center of the blast suffer complete destruction, whereas systems in Denver would only be degraded or a few systems would be incapacitated. This is a permanent effect and allows for no regenerative capacity.

10. R. Jeffrey Smith, "Detonating Stability," *The Burlington Free Press,* 17 May 1998, 1E–2E; Steven Kormarow, "Tests Show Indian Nuke Sophistication," *The Burlington Free Press,* 17 May 1998, 2E.

11. The five declared powers are the United States, Russia, France, China, and Great Britain. Other nations are suspected of having nuclear weapons or at least having programs capable of rapidly producing weapons. These nations are India, Pakistan, Israel, Iran, Iraq, and North Korea.

12. Christine Gosden, "We've Got to Try to Do Something," *USA Weekend,* 15–17 May 1998, 14.

13. Ibid., 16.

14. Sean Naylor, "Hidden Soft Spot in Satellite Might: War Game Shows U.S. Military Systems Are Vulnerable to Enemy Attack," *Army Times,* 10 March 1997, 21.

15. Katherine M. Peters, "Space Wars," *Government Executive* 30, no. 4 (April 1998): 13.

16. Ibid.

17. Edward G. Anderson III, " The Army and Space," *Field Artillery* (May–June 1998): 8.

18. Jonathan S. Lockwood, "Growing Vulnerability in Space," *Army Times,* 20 April 1998, 54.

19. There are a variety of open sources that have also discussed these capabilities. *Popular Mechanics* and *Popular Science* are the two most prominent, with several articles in the late 1990s.

20. Katherine M. Peters, "Space Wars," 18.

21. David L. Grange and James A. Kelley, "Information Operations for the Ground Commander," *Military Review,* vol. LXXVII, no. 2 (March–April 1997): 5.

22. United States Army, *FM 100-6: Information Operations* (Washington, D.C.: Government Printing Office, 1996), 2–3. Quoted in David L. Grange and James A. Kelley, "Information Operations for the Ground Commander," *Military Review,* vol. LXXVII, no. 2 (March–April 1997): 7.

23. Montgomery C. Meigs, "Challenges for Army Leaders in an Age of Rapid Change," *Field Artillery* (May–June 1998), 5.

24. Robert L. Bateman, "Shock and the Digital Battlefield," *Armor,* vol. CVII, no. 1 (January–February 1998): 18–19.

25. Robert F. Baumann, "Historical Perspectives on Future War," *Military Review,* vol. LXXVII, no. 2 (March–April 1997): 47.

26. David L. Grange, "Information Operations for the Ground Commander," 8.

27. Several articles in the 11 May 1998 *Army Times* discussed the past views of future weapon systems: Jane McHugh, "The Future: Have We Been There Before?" *Army Times,* 11 May 1998, 12, 14. Also "The Future Wars That Never Were," "Wonder Weapons of Pulp Fiction," and "Planning Wars."

28. Brooke Tigner, "NATO Panel to Steer Nonlethal Weapon Use," *Army Times,* 13 October 1997, 33.

29. Ibid.

30. Ralph Peters, "Will We Be Able to Take the Cities?" *Army Times,* 11 May 1998, 34.

Conclusions

1. Ralph Peters, "Will We Be Able to Take the Cities?" *Army Times,* 11 May 1998, 34. Sean D. Naylor, "A Lack of City Smarts," *Army Times,* 11 May 1998, 22. Also observations of strategic planning during the Army After Next Spring Wargame at Carlisle Barracks, Pennsylvania,

20–24 April 1998. In Mr. Naylor's article there are quotes from Colonel Starry, one of the army's primary futurists, who states that sieges are a possible option. Mr. Peters refutes the idea of sieges, avoidance, and technology and states that the simple solutions of well-trained manpower provide the answer.

2. George I. Seffers, "Hyper-Speed Anti-Tank Missiles Studied for 2015," *Army Times*, 13 October 1997, 33. This describes tank-fired missiles with a five-kilometer range.

3. Michael D. Wyly, "Combat in the 21st Century: The Quality of Troops Will Matter More Than the Complexity of Weapons," *U.S. News & World Report*, 16 March 1998, 81.

4. Sean D. Naylor, "Sea Change Ahead in Leadership Training," *Army Times*, 13 October 1997, 32.

5. *Knowledge and Speed*, The Annual Report on the Army After Next Project to the Chief of Staff of the Army (Fort Monroe, Va.: TRADOC Press, July 1997), 21.

6. Donald E. Vandergriff, "Without the Proper Culture: Why Our Army Cannot Practice Maneuver Warfare," *Armor* (January–February 1998): 23. The author attacks the American army culture in general, but specifically makes reference to the use of accountability formations to regiment time management rather than being task oriented.

7. The National Defense Panel, "Assessment of the 1997 Quadrennial Defense Review," Arlington, Va.: National Defense Panel Press, 15 May 1997, 1.

Glossary

AAN: Army After Next. An organization, now disbanded, that used to run out of the U.S. Army Training and Doctrine Command (TRADOC) with the mission of looking at the future of warfare. Tasked specifically with identifying the trends and military requirements for the years 2020–25.

AANFWG: Army After Next Fall Wargame

AANSWG: Army After Next Spring Wargame

AAR: after-action review

ACR: armored cavalry regiment. Combined-arms organization that is roughly a brigade in size. It has, organic to the organization, three ground squadrons, one air squadron, and a support squadron. Within the ground squadrons are engineers and field artillery. The unit also has chemical, signal, military intelligence, and military police elements organic.

ADA: air defense artillery

ADA seam: potential gap in enemy air defense "net" that exists near unit boundaries

ADO: air defense officer

AH: attack helicopter

AK-47: Soviet-made assault rifle that fires a 7.62mm round

APC: armored personnel carrier

ARCENT: Army Central Command. Headquarters responsible for the army component of Central Command (CENTCOM). During Operation Desert Storm, this commander became the Third Army commander, in command of all U.S. Army units in theater.

ARVN: Army of the Republic of Vietnam, or South Vietnamese Army

ATACMS: army tactical missile system

ATGM: antitank guided missile

attrition: Attrition warfare is victory through the destruction of the enemy's combat capability. In the extreme, this means the entire annihilation of every opposing soldier. The Battle of Thermopylae was a battle of attrition initiated by the Spartan defenders of the pass.

AUSA: Association of the United States Army

AWACS: airborne warning and control system. Airborne platform used to control the movements of other aircraft and direct them to targets.

AWE: advanced warfighting experiment. Name given to Experimental Force (EXFOR) testing at the National Training Center (NTC) and in division-sized wargames conducted at Fort Hood, Texas.

battalion: unit consisting of one or more companies or batteries and a headquarters company. Commanded by a lieutenant colonel. The unit typically has between 500 and 800 personnel assigned.

battle lab: where concepts for near- and long-term warfare are discussed. The variety of battle labs includes dismounted, mounted, and close combat. Each battle lab is headquartered at a different installation, typically at the school for the proponent branch.

BBC: British Broadcasting Company

BDE: brigade. Unit consisting of one or more battalions and a headquarters company. Commanded by a colonel. The unit typically has between 2,000 and 5,000 personnel assigned. This is a combined-arms force that may include infantry, armor, field artillery, engineers, support units, and air defense.

BFV: Bradley fighting vehicle

BMP: boy-ye-vi-ya mah-sheen-a pee-ho-tee (Russian words spelled phonetically) fighting vehicle infantry (English translation). Infantry fighting vehicle made by the former Soviet Union and continued by Russia and other former Soviet Republics. This comes in numerous variants but is designed to carry infantry in support of a mechanized battlefield.

boresight: process of aligning the sites of a tank to the direct lay of the gun tube. Essentially the same as zeroing a rifle.

branch: (1) one of several divisions of the officer corps. Each branch denotes function of officer service. (2) Contingency plan that assumes changes in the primary plan. These changes may be caused by enemy or friendly events that, though not unexpected, are less likely than the primary plan.

C⁴ISR: command, control, communications, computers, intelligence, surveillance, reconnaissance

campaign plan: plan for a series of related military operations designed to accomplish a common objective, normally within a given time and space.

CAS: close air support, delivered by U.S. Air Force

cav: cavalry

CCF: Chinese Communist forces

CENTCOM: Central Command. Unified command (meaning that the commander can control elements from any armed service) of the United States responsible for a specific geographic area. The area includes the Middle East and Sub-Saharan Africa. Desert Storm and Operation Restore Hope were both commanded and controlled through this headquarters.

Chinook (CH-47): heavy lift helicopter used by the U.S. Army. Widely exported aircraft used by a variety of nations, including Great Britain. It can carry forty combat-loaded personnel or small tactical vehicles.

CINCCENT: Commander in Chief Central Command

CINCLANT: Commander in Chief Atlantic Command

command group: consisting of the unit commander, executive goup officer (XO), and sometimes the command sergeant major.

command sergeant major: senior noncommissioned officer (NCO) in a specific unit sergeant at the battalion level and higher. Responsible for the management of NCO careers, soldier support, and individual training as well as numerous other tasks specified and implied by the unit commander.

CONPLAN: contingency plan. Forward-looking plan based on commander's guidance to express how a unit may deal with specific branches or sequels as necessary.

CPX: command post exercise. Simulation designed to train command posts.

CW2: chief warrant officer two

disintegration: victory through superior position. This is the Sun Tzu ideal of winning: "To subdue the enemy without fighting is the supreme excellence." Another example is the game of chess. Checkmate may be accomplished without the removal of a single opposing piece, yet the game is still lost. This is a concept being strongly promoted by those who still worked in the Army After Next Project.

DOD: Department of Defense

DPICM: dual-purpose improved conventional munitions

Easting: north–south grid line designation used in the deserts of Saudi Arabia, Iraq, and Kuwait to indicate location by the use of military longitudinal structures

EMP: electromagnetic pulse. Shock wave of energy in the electromagnetic spectrum; given off by a nuclear device. This pulse effectively destroys all electrical equipment within its range.

EU: European Union

EXFOR: Experimental Force. Unit based in Fort Hood, Texas, and designated to test the equipment and doctrine for Force XXI.

FAAD: forward area air defense

FARP: forward arming and refueling point. Used by aviation units to allow forces to fuel or arm following engagements without returning to the rear assembly areas.

FEMA: Federal Emergency Management Agency

Force XXI: U.S. Army's near-term future force, named for the force designed to fight in the early years of the twenty-first century. It is a fully digitized force that began as a battalion-sized unit and expanded to the entire 4th Infantry Division at Fort Hood, Texas. Eventually, several divisions will possess Force XXI capabilities.

FRAGO: fragmentary order. This post-OPORD (operations order) is the manner in which changes to the published or issued order are given.

G-5: South African–made artillery piece. It is a 155mm towed piece with a range of approximately 40,000 meters using a base bleed system.

G-6: South African–made artillery piece. It is a 155mm self-propelled, wheeled vehicle with a range of approximately 40,000 meters using a base bleed system.

GATT: global agreement on tariffs and trade

GCT: ground cavalry troop

GHQ: general headquarters. Military headquarters in post–World War II Tokyo, headed by General of the Army Douglas MacArthur.

GPS: global positioning system. System of satellites and receivers that identifies a location through reference to latitude and longitude and/or military grid references.

Hill 219: hill in North Korea north of the Chongch'on River. The number refers to the hill's height in meters.

HIMAD: high-medium air defense

HMMWV: high-mobility multiwheeled vehicle

Huey (UH-1): one of the most ubiquitous helicopters. First truly multi-role aircraft with the ability to carry from eight to eleven combat-loaded personnel.

IO: information operations

IV line: intervisibility line

JSTARS: joint surveillance target attack radar system. Aircraft with the ability to track and direct attacks against both ground and air targets.

LNO: liaison officer. Responsible for coordinating actions between the parent unit and either higher headquarters or an adjacent unit.

LOC: lines of communication

LOGPAC: logistics package

LZ: landing zone. Site designated for the landing of helicopters.

M1A2: U.S. Army's newest main battle tank

M-16: American-made assault rifle that fires a 5.56mm round

M-79: handheld 40mm grenade launcher. The grenade canisters are loaded shotgun fashion.

MACV: Military Assistance Command–Vietnam

MH-60: Special Operations variant of the UH-60

MLRS: multiple launch rocket system

MOUT: military operations in urban terrain

MRC: major regional conflict. The term began during the Bottom-Up Review that was conducted by Les Aspin and used to identify the baseline expectation of the force—specifically that the force needed was one that could fight two major regional conflicts simultaneously and win. An MRC is similar to a Desert Storm, Korean War, Vietnam War, or Falkland Islands War.

MTOE: modified table of organization and equipment. "Master" list that identifies all the specific types of equipment and personnel that a particular unit may possess. The list is modified for each individual unit from the TOE.

MTR: military technical revolution. Technical development that when properly exploited through equipment, training, organization, and doctrine provides a decisive (although temporary) advantage.

MTW: major theater war. Term used to identify a regional conflict. It's a modification of MRC begun under the William Cohen administration of the Department of Defense (DOD).

NAFTA: North American Free Trade Agreement

NATO: North Atlantic Treaty Organization

NBC: nuclear biological chemical

NCOIC: noncommissioned officer in charge

NKPA: North Korean People's Army

NTC: National Training Center. Located at Fort Irwin, California. This is the major training ground for U.S. Army maneuver units.

NVA: North Vietnamese Army

OH: observation helicopter

OIC: officer in charge

OODA loop: observe orient decide act; a decision cycle

OOTW: operation other than war

OPCON: operational control

OPFOR: opposing force

OPORD: operations order. Either a verbal or written product that communicates the particulars of a tactical mission in five sections: situation, mission, execution, service support, and command and signal.

para: abbreviation for parachute. A British term for elements of the Parachute Regiment.

PGM: precision-guided munitions

POMCUS: pre-positioned overseas materiel configured to unit sets. Materiel stockpiled in areas deemed as potential trouble spots. The intent is that deploying units arrive, draw the equipment, and fight. This cuts down on deployment times and the need for heavy airlift to be used for the transport of tanks. The sets are configured for a standard mechanized brigade-sized unit.

PRC: People's Republic of China

PSYOP: psychological operation

QDR: quadrennial defense review. Review of the military establishment's roles, missions, and organization conducted by the Department of Defense and reviewed by Congress every four years.

QRF: quick reaction force

quad-50: antiaircraft weapon used in World War II and Korean War. The weapon featured four .50-caliber machine guns in a rotating turret mounted on the back of an armored half-track. In Korea these weapons were often used in a ground support role to provide overwhelming firepower.

REFORGER: Return of Forces to Germany

regiment: unit consisting of one or more squadrons and a headquarters troop. Commanded by a colonel. The unit typically has between 2,000 and 8,000 personnel assigned. Functions primarily in a security and reconnaissance capacity for a division or corps. This is a combined-arms force that may include scouts, infantry, armor, field artillery, engineers, support units, and air defense artillery.

retrans: retransmission. Technique used to lengthen communications ranges by a designated radio system transferring the signal from one frequency to another at the initial frequency limit.

RGFC: Republican Guards Forces Command

RISTA: reconnaissance, intelligence, surveillance, and target acquisition

RMA: Revolution in Military Affairs. Major change in the nature of warfare brought about by the innovative application of technologies, which, when combined with dramatic changes in military doctrine, and operational concepts, fundamentally alters the character and conduct of operations.

ROE: rules of engagement

ROK: Republic of Korea (South Korea)

RPG: rocket-propelled grenade

RSA: Revolution in Strategic Affairs. Acknowledgment that the context (economic, diplomatic, and military) in which future conflict will be conducted has changed dramatically since the end of World War II, influenced primarily by the end of the Cold War.

RTO: radiotelephone operator

S1: administration/personnel officer

S2: intelligence officer. Military intelligence officer who provides information about enemy capabilities, disposition, strength, and intentions as well as the effects of terrain and weather to the unit commander.

S3: operations officer

S-3: operations section of a unit staff organization. Responsible for training, planning, and other aspects of operations. If the commanding officer of the parent unit were to be a general officer, it is G-3. The senior person is designated the S3.

S4: logistics officer. Maneuver officer at the battalion level, and a logistics officer at the brigade level and higher. This officer provides information and directs the activities of the support elements of the unit. Ensures that the unit has the equipment and materiel necessary for mission success in current and future fights.

SAMS: School of Advanced Military Studies

SAS: Special Air Service. Elite commando/counterterrorist unit of the British army.

SCO: squadron commander

shamal: winter sandstorm in the Middle East

SITTEMP: situational template. Overlay prepared by the S-2 section that graphically depicts the predicted enemy activity, giving account for terrain and known weather conditions.

SOF: Special Operations Forces

squadron: cavalry unit consisting of one or more troops and a headquarters troop. Commanded by a lieutenant colonel. The unit typically has between 500 and 800 personnel assigned. Functions primarily in a security or reconnaissance capacity for a regiment or division. This is a combined-arms force that may have scouts, armor, aviation, and support assets.

SXO: squadron executive officer

T-72: Russian medium main battle tank. Designed during the late 1960s and fielded in the early 1970s to mid-1980s. It is possibly the most common tank in the world. After the fall of the Soviet Union, this (and numerous variants) became one of the most inexpensive export tanks in the world. The Chinese, Yugoslavs, and others have been licensed to make variants of the original design. It carries a 125mm smooth-bore gun as its main armament.

TAC: tactical action center. Term used at the brigade/regimental level and below to designate the command and control node that includes the unit commander and is primarily responsible for the current close battle.

terrain

unrestricted: no impediments to movement or maneuver: open plains or desert

restricted: some impediments, including vegetation, to maneuver: forests, orchards, rolling hills

severely restricted: numerous impediments, many considered impassable, to wheeled or mechanized traffic. This terrain is best characterized by steep hills with vegetation or dense jungle.

complex: urban sprawl and urban terrain: cities, built-up areas, slums, shantytowns

TF: task force. Combination of units necessary for a specific mission. Typically a battalion-sized unit or larger.

TF 160: Special Operations Aviation Regiment's designation

TOC: tactical operations center. Term used at the brigade/regimental level and below to designate the primary command and control node of the designated unit. Responsible primarily for coordinating all actions of the unit; receiving, analyzing, evaluating, and disseminating information; and conducting actions both for the current mission and planning for potential missions.

TOW: tube-launched, optically tracked, wire-guided missile

TRADOC: U.S. Army Training and Doctrine Command. An army headquarters with responsibility for the training of all U.S. Army soldiers. For example, all basic training, advanced individual training, and officer training are included under TRADOC. Additionally, the writing of all doctrinal material falls under the purview of this command. It is led by a four-star general and is considered the equivalent of a major U.S. Army command.

troop: cavalry unit consisting of one or more platoons and a headquarters section. Commanded by a captain. The unit typically has between 80 and 200 personnel assigned. Functions primarily in a security or reconnaissance capacity for a squadron or brigade. This is the lowest organic combined-arms force with scouts, armor, support forces, and mortars.

TTP: tactics, techniques, and procedures. The particular ways that tasks may be performed within the army. Some are given official sanction as part of army manuals; many are unofficial and unique to each unit.

UAV: unmanned aerial vehicle. This encompasses a large spectrum of aircraft. Virtually any unmanned aircraft is included, but typically this denotes aircraft designed to gain intelligence.

UH: utility helicopter

UH-60: utility helicopter that can carry up to eleven combat-loaded infantrymen

UN: United Nations

USMA: United States Military Academy, located in West Point, New York

VTOL: vertical takeoff and landing. Type of aircraft that can take off with little or no run-up required.

WARNO: warning order. Predecessor of the OPORD. This is designed to provide as much information as soon as possible. Typically it is not as complete or detailed as an OPORD. And unlike an

OPORD, more than one may be used to relay information during the planning of a particular mission.

XO: executive officer. Person who performs the functions of second-in-command for a unit from company to brigade size. Also responsible at the battalion and brigade level for coordinating staff functions and ensuring logistics support.

Selected Bibliography

Books

Adan, Avraham. *On the Banks of the Suez.* Novato, Calif.: Presidio Press, 1980.

Amuzegar, Jahangir. *Comparative Economics: National Priorities, Policies, and Performance.* Cambridge, Mass.: Winthrop Publishers, 1981.

Appleman, Roy E. *South to the Naktong, North to the Yalu (June–November 1950), United States Army in the Korean War.* Washington D.C.: Center of Military History Press, 1956; reprint, 1992.

Arndt, Heinz W. *The Rise and Fall of Economic Growth: A Study in Contemporary Thought.* Chicago: University of Chicago Press, 1984 (reprint of 1978 original).

Atkinson, Rick. *Crusade: The Untold Story of the Persian Gulf War.* Boston: Houghton Mifflin Company, 1993.

Barto, Joseph C., III. *Task Force 2-4 Cav—"First In, Last Out": The History of the 2nd Squadron, 4th Cavalry Regiment, During Operation Desert Storm.* Fort Leavenworth, Kans.: Combat Studies Institute Press, 1993.

Blair, Clay. *The Forgotten War: America in Korea 1950–1953.* New York: Times Books, 1987.

Bowden, Mark. *Blackhawk Down: An American War Story. Philadelphia Inquirer:* 16 November to 14 December 1997.

Builder, Carl H. *The Masks of War: American Military Styles in Strategy and Analysis.* A Rand Corporation Research Study. Baltimore: Johns Hopkins University Press, 1989.

Chapman, Anne W. *The Origins and Development of the National Training Center, 1976–1984.* Washington D.C.: Center of Military History, 1997.

Clancy, Tom. *Armored Cav: A Guided Tour of an Armored Cavalry Regiment.* New York: Berkley Publishing Group, 1994.

Clausewitz, Carl von. *On War,* edited and translated by Michael Howard and Peter Paret. Princeton, N.J.: Princeton University Press, 1976.

Cordesman, Anthony H., and Abraham R. Wagner. *The Lessons of Modern War, Volume II: The Iran-Iraq War.* Boulder, Colo.: Westview Press, 1990; reprint, 1991.

———. *The Lessons of Modern War, Volume III: The Afghan and Falkland Conflicts.* Boulder, Colo.: Westview Press, 1991.

Daily, Edward L. *Skirmish Red, White and Blue: The History of the 7th U.S. Cavalry (1945–1953).* Paducah, Ky.: Turner Publishing Company, 1992.

Dunnigan, James F., and Austin Bay. *From Shield to Storm: High-Tech Weapons, Military Strategy, and Coalition Warfare in the Persian Gulf.* New York: William Morrow and Company, Inc., 1992.

Editors of *Time* magazine. *Desert Storm: The War in the Persian Gulf.* New York: Time Warner Publishing, Inc., 1991.

Fehrenbach, T. R. *This Kind of War: The Classic Korean War History.* New York: Macmillan, 1963; reprint, Washington, D.C.: Brassey's, 1994.

Gehring, Stephen P. *From the Fulda Gap to Kuwait: U.S. Army, Europe and the Gulf War.* Washington, D.C.: Government Printing Office, 1998.

Hackworth, David H., and Julie Sherman. *About Face.* New York: Simon & Schuster Inc., 1989.

Han-chang, T'ao. *Sun-Tzu's Art of War: The Modern Chinese Interpretation.* Translated by Yuan Shibing. New York: Sterling Publishing Co., Inc., 1987.

Hastings, Max. *The Korean War.* New York: Simon & Schuster Inc., 1987.

Hastings, Max, and Simon Jenkins. *The Battle for the Falklands.* New York: W. W. Norton & Company, 1983.

Hawkins, Glen R., and James Jay Carafano. *Prelude to Army XXI: U.S. Army Division Design Initiatives and Experiments 1917–1995*. Washington, D.C.: U.S. Army Center of Military History, 1997.

Herbert, Paul H. *Leavenworth Papers Number 16: Deciding What Has to be Done: General William E. DePuy and the 1976 Edition of FM 100-5, Operations*. Fort Leavenworth, Kans.: Command and General Staff College Press, 1988.

Hunt, Michael H. *Crises in U.S. Foreign Policy: An International History Reader*. New Haven, Conn.: Yale University Press, 1996.

Kennedy, Paul M. *The Rise and Fall of the Great Powers*. New York: Random House, Inc., 1987.

Kissinger, Henry. *Diplomacy*. New York: Simon & Schuster, 1994.

Laffin, John. *Fight for the Falklands! Why and How Britain and Argentina Went to War, from Invasion to Surrender*. New York: St. Martin's Press, 1982.

Luttwak, Edward N. *Strategy: The Logic of War and Peace*. Cambridge, Mass.: The Belknap Press of Harvard University, 1987.

Macgregor, Douglas A. *Breaking the Phalanx: A New Design for Land-power in the 21st Century*. Westport, Ct.: Praeger Publishers, 1997.

Madigan, John J. III, ed. *Landpower in the 21st Century: Preparing for Conflict*. Carlisle, Penn.: U.S. Army War College Press, 1998.

Marshall, S. L. A. *The River and the Gauntlet: Defeat of the Eighth Army by the Chinese Communist Forces, November 1950, in the Battle of the Chongch'on River, Korea*. Nashville, Tenn.: The Battery Press, 1959.

Maurice, S. Charles. *Managerial Economics*. The Irwin Publications in Economics. Homewood, Ill.: R. D. Irwin, 1981.

McNamara, Robert S. *In Retrospect: The Tragedy and Lessons of Vietnam*. Vintage ed. New York: Random House Inc., 1996.

Miller, John, Jr., Owen J. Carroll, and Margaret E. Tackley. *Korea 1951–1953*. Facsimile reprint. Washington, D.C.: Center of Military History Press, 1997.

Moore, Harold G., and Joseph L. Galloway. *We Were Soldiers Once . . . and Young: Ia Drang, the Battle that Changed the War in Vietnam*. Paperback ed. New York: Harper Perennial Publishers, 1993.

Nixon, Richard M. *Beyond Peace*. 1st ed. New York: Random House, 1994.

Nuechtererlein, Donald E. *America Overcommitted: United States National Interests in the 1980s.* Lexington, Ky.: The University Press of Kentucky, 1985, 1–53.

Powell, Colin. *My American Journey.* First paperback ed. New York: Ballantine Books, 1996.

Ridgway, Matthew B. *The Korean War: How We Met the Challenge; How All-Out Asian War Was Averted; Why MacArthur Was Dismissed; Why Today's War Objectives Must Be Limited.* Garden City, N.Y.: Doubleday, 1967; paperback ed., New York: Da Capo Press, 1986.

Sarkesian, Sam C. "Presidential Leadership and the National Security Policy Process." In *Presidential Leadership and National Security: Style, Institutions, and Politics,"* Sam C. Sarkesian, ed. Boulder, Colo.: Westview Press, 1984, 255–63.

Scales, Robert H., Jr. *Certain Victory: United States Army in the Gulf War.* Fort Leavenworth, Kans.: Command and General Staff College Press, 1994 (select reprint).

Schubert, Frank N., and Theresa L. Kraus, ed. *The Whirlwind War: The United States Army in Operations Desert Shield and Desert Storm.* Washington, D.C.: Center of Military History Press, 1995.

Schwarzkopf, H. Norman, and Peter Petre. *General H. Norman Schwarzkopf: The Autobiography: It Doesn't Take a Hero.* New York: Bantam Books, 1992.

Secretary of State for Defense. *The Falklands Campaign: The Lessons.* London: Her Majesty's Stationary Office, December 1982.

Shazly, Saad el. *The Crossing of the Suez.* San Francisco: American Mideast Research, 1980.

Sifrey, Micah L., and Christopher Cerf, ed. *The Gulf War Reader: History, Documents, Opinions.* New York: Times Books, 1991.

Simpson, Howard R. *Dien Bien Phu: The Epic Battle America Forgot.* Washington, D.C.: Brassey's Inc., 1994.

Spiller, Roger J., ed. *Combined Arms in Battle Since 1939.* Fort Leavenworth, Kans.: U.S. Army Command and General Staff College Press, 1992.

Stein, Herbert. *Presidential Economics: The Making of Economic Policy from Roosevelt to Reagan and Beyond.* Revised and updated, 1st Touchstone ed. A Touchstone Book. New York: Simon & Schuster, 1985.

Stewart, Richard W. *Staff Operations: The X Corps in Korea, December 1950.* Fort Leavenworth, Kans.: Combat Studies Institute Press, 1991.

Sullivan, Gordon R., and James M. Dubik. *Envisioning Future Warfare.* Fort Leavenworth, Kans.: Command and General Staff College Press, 1995.

Summers, Harry G., Jr. *On Strategy: A Critical Analysis of the Vietnam War.* Novato, Calif.: Presidio Press, 1982.

The Sunday Times of London Insight Team. *War in the Falklands: The Full Story.* New York: Harper & Row, Publishers, 1982.

Swain, Richard M. *"Lucky War": Third Army in Desert Storm.* Fort Leavenworth, Kans.: Command and General Staff College Press, 1994.

Varner, VeLoy J., ed. *Notes for the Course in the History of the Military Art.* West Point, N.Y.: United States Military Academy Press, February 1971.

Walker, Wallace Earl. "Congressional Resurgence and the Destabilization of U.S. Foreign Policy," adapted from "Domesticating Foreign Policy: Congress and the Vietnam War." In *Democracy, Strategy and Vietnam: Implications for American Policymaking.* Lexington, Mass.: D. C. Heath and Company, 1987, 105–20.

Watson, Bruce W., and Peter M. Dunn, eds. *Military Lessons of the Falkland Islands War: Views from the United States.* Boulder, Colo.: Westview Press, 1984.

Watson, Bruce W., Bruce George, Peter Tsouras, and B. L. Cyr. *Military Lessons of the Gulf War.* Novato, Calif.: Presidio Press, 1991.

Weinberger, Caspar, and Peter Schweizer. *The Next War.* Washington, D.C.: Regnery Publishing Inc., 1996.

Westmoreland, William C. *A Soldier Reports.* Garden City, N.Y.: Doubleday & Company, Inc., 1976.

Woodward, Bob. *The Commanders/Bob Woodward.* New York: Simon and Schuster, 1991.

Army After Next Monograph Series

Johnsen, William T. *The Future Roles of U.S. Military Power and Their Implications.* Carlisle Barracks, Penn.: U.S. Army War College Press/Army After Next Project, 18 April 1997.

Metz, Steven. *Strategic Horizons: The Military Implications of Alternative*

Futures. Carlisle Barracks, Penn.: U.S. Army War College Press/Army After Next Project, 7 March 1997.

Metz, Steven, William T. Johnsen, Douglas V. Johnson II, James O. Kievit, and Douglas C. Lovelace, Jr. *The Future of American Landpower: Strategic Challenges for the 21st Century Army.* Carlisle Barracks, Penn.: U.S. Army War College Press/Army After Next Project, 12 March 1996.

Roland, Alex. *The Technological Fix: Weapons and the Cost of War.* Carlisle Barracks, Penn.: U.S. Army War College Press/Army After Next Project, 6 June 1995.

Tilford, Earl H. *The Revolution in Military Affairs: Prospects and Cautions.* Carlisle Barracks, Penn.: U.S. Army War College Press/Army After Next Project, 23 June 1995.

Government Documents and Reference Material

AAN Air-Mechanized Battle Force, January 1998, briefing slides used to explain the battle force composition.

Army After Next FY98 Tactical Wargame Final Report, April 1998, TRADOC Analysis Center presented to the TRADOC commander and used as a briefing tool for the AANSWG participants.

Army Budget Fiscal Year 1998: An Analysis. Arlington, Va.: Association of the U.S. Army Publishers, July 1997.

Cohen, William S. *Report of the Quadrennial Defense Review.* Washington D.C.: Government Printing Office, May 1997.

de Czege, Wass. *Future (2020+) Joint Operations and Landpower Tactics.* Carlisle, Penn.: U.S. Army War College Press, 1997.

Famighetti, Robert, ed. *The World Almanac and Book of Facts 1998.* Mahwah, N.J.: World Almanac Books, 1997.

Green, Eloise. "Somalia: Operations Other Than War: Newsletter No. 93-1." Updated on the Internet, 25 September 1997.

Hartzog, William W. *Force XXI: Path to the Future.* Briefing presented by the commander, U.S. Army Training and Doctrine Command, to the October 1997 AUSA Annual Meeting with updates from the November 1997 Division AWE, Washington, D.C., January 1998.

Joint Pub. 1. *Joint Warfare of the U.S. Armed Forces: "Joint Warfare Is Team Warfare."* Washington, D.C.: National Defense University Press, 1991.

Knowledge and Speed. The Annual Report on the Army After Next Project to the Chief of Staff of the Army. Fort Monroe, Va.: TRADOC Press, July 1997.

Moore, Harold G. "After Action Report of Operations in the Ia Drang Valley." November 1965.

The National Defense Panel. "Assessment of the 1997 Quadrennial Defense Review." Arlington, Va.: National Defense Panel Press, 15 May 1997.

Osborne, David L., ed. *Army 21: Domestic Trends to the Year 2015: Forecasts for the United States.* A Study Prepared for the U.S. Army, Training and Doctrine Command, Fort Monroe, Va. Washington, D.C.: Library of Congress Press, 1991.

Report on the Army After Next Project, June 1996. Report delivered to the commander, U.S. Army Training and Doctrine Command, June 1996.

Strategic Assessment 1996: Instruments of U.S. Power. Washington, D.C.: National Defense University Institute for National Strategic Studies, 1996.

Strategic Assessment 1997: Flashpoints and Force Structure. Washington, D.C.: National Defense University Institute for National Strategic Studies, 1997.

Stubbs, Mary Lee, and Stanley Russell Connor. *Armor Cavalry Part I: Regular Army and Army Reserve.* Army Lineage Series. Washington, D.C.: Center of Military History Press, 1984.

Systems: U.S. Army: AAN Systems and Weapons Common Characteristics. Carlisle, Penn.: U.S. Army War College Intranet, 1998.

U.S. Armor School Publication. "Mission: To Close with and Destroy Enemy Forces with Fire, Maneuver, and Shock Effect: U.S. Armor in Southwest Asia," 4.

U.S. Army Training and Doctrine Command. *Force XXI: Land Combat in the 21st Century.* Washington, D.C.: U.S. Department of the Army, 1996.

U.S. Congress, House of Representatives. 93d Congress, 2d Session. *Congressional Record.* 9–30 October 1973, vol. 119.

U.S. Department of the Army. *DA Pam 100-1. Operations. Force XXI Institutional Army Redesign.* 5 March 1998.

———. *FM 22-100. Military Leadership.* July 1990.

———. *FM 25-100. Training the Force: Soldiers, Units & Leaders.* November 1988.

———. *FM 25-101. Training the Force: Battle Focused Training: Battalion and Company Soldiers, Leaders & Units.* September 1990.

———. *FM 100-5. Operations.* August 1976.

———. *FM 100-5. Operations.* August 1982.

———. *FM 100-5. Operations.* August 1986.

———. *FM 100-5. Operations.* August 1993.

———. *FM 101-5. Staff Organization and Operations.* 31 May 1997.

———. *FM 101-5-1. Operational Terms and Graphics.* September 1997.

———. *MQS I: Training Support Package: Leadership.* Student handout, instructional material. MQS I S1-9001.00-0001 TSP/HO 9004. 82A. 15 April 1990.

———. *United States Army Posture Statement FY98: Soldiers Are Our Credentials: America's Army—The Force of Decision for Today, Tomorrow, and the 21st Century.* Washington, D.C.: U.S. Department of the Army, February 1997.

U.S. Department of Commerce. *Statistical Abstract of the United States.* Washington, D.C.: U.S. Department of Commerce, Economics and Statistics Administration, Bureau of the Census, Data User Services Division, October 1996.

U.S. Department of Defense. *Conduct of the Persian Gulf War: Pursuant to Title V of the Persian Gulf Conflict Supplemental Authorization and Personnel Benefits Act of 1991 (Public Law 102-25).* Washington, D.C.: U.S. Department of Defense Press, April 1992.

———. *1996 Annual Defense Report.* Washington, D.C.: U.S. Department of Defense Press, 1996.

———. *Defense '97: Almanac.* Washington, D.C.: Government Printing Office, 20 August 1997.

U.S. Department of State Dispatch. "Chronology: Background to Operation Restore Hope, January 1991–December 8, 1992," 21 December 1992, vol. 3, no. 51, 900–02.

Journal and Magazine Articles

Anderson, Edward G. III. "The Army and Space." *Field Artillery* (May–June 1998), 7–10.

Armey, Dick. "An Economic Strategy for the U.S.: Why the Market Works Best." *Strategic Review,* vol. XXII, no. 1 (winter 1994): 25–33.

Army Navy Journal, 8 August 1959. Quoted in "Looking Back." *Armed Forces Journal International* (April 1998): 56.

Arquilla, John. "The Strategic Implications of Information Dominance." *Strategic Review,* vol. XXII, no. 3 (summer 1994): 24–30.

Bartlett, Henry C., and G. Paul Holman. "Force Planning for the Post–Cold War World: What Can We Learn from Geopolitics?" *Strategic Review,* vol. XIX, no. 1 (winter 1991): 26–36.

———. "Grand Strategy and the Structure of U.S. Military Forces." *Strategic Review,* vol. XX, no. 2 (spring 1992): 39–51.

Basso, John. "M1A2: One Year Later." *Armor* (January–February 1998): 31–34.

Bateman, Robert L. "Shock and the Digital Battlefield." *Armor* (January–February 1998): 14–19.

Baumann, Robert F. "Historical Perspectives on Future War." *Military Review,* vol. LXXVII, no. 2 (March–April 1997): 40–48.

Bautz, Edward. "Forest or Trees, Principles or Process?" *Armor* (May–June 1997): 18–21, 43.

Bergsten, C. Fred. "The Primacy of Economics," *Foreign Policy,* no. 87 (summer 1992): 3–24.

Bhagwati, Jagdish. "The Diminished Giant Syndrome: How Declinism Drives Trade Policy." *Foreign Affairs,* vol. 72, no. 1 (spring 1993): 22–26.

Bingham, Price T. "Air Interdiction and the Need for Doctrinal Change." *Strategic Review,* vol. XX, no. 4 (fall 1992): 24–33.

Black, Frederick H. "The Military and Today's Congress." *Parameters* 17, no. 4 (December 1987): 37–48.

Blaker, James R. "Understanding the Revolution in Military Affairs." *ROA National Security Report* (May 1997): 23–34.

Blumenson, Martin. "The Korean War." *Army* (May 1997): 53–59.

Breemer, Jan S. "The End of Naval Strategy: Revolutionary Change and the Future of American Naval Power." *Strategic Review,* vol. XXII, no. 2 (spring 1994): 40–53.

Brinkerhoff, John R. "The American Strategy of Unpreparedness." *Strategic Review,* vol. XXII, no. 1 (winter 1994): 34–42.

Clinton, William J. "American Security in a Changing World." Prepared remarks for an address at George Washington University, Washington, D.C., 5 August 1996.

"Controversy over the War Powers Act." *Congressional Digest* 62 (November 1983): 259–62, 288.

Cowhey, Peter F., and Jonathan D. Aronson. "A New Trade Order." *Foreign Affairs.* "America and the World 1992–93," vol. 72, no. 1 (spring 1993): 183–95.

Crawley, Vince. "Ghost Troop's Battle at the 73 Easting." *Armor* (May–June 1991): 7–12.

Cronin, Patrick M. "American Global Leadership After the Cold War: From Pax Americana to Pax Consortis." *Strategic Review,* vol. XIX, no. 3 (summer 1991): 9–21.

Drew, Dennis M. "The Airpower Imperative: Hard Truths for an Uncertain World." *Strategic Review,* vol. XIX, no. 2 (spring 1991): 24–31.

Drucker, Peter F. "The End of Japan, Inc.?: An Economic Monolith Fractures." *Foreign Affairs* 72, no. 2 (spring 1993): 10–15.

Dubois, Thomas R. "The Weinberger Doctrine and the Liberation of Kuwait." *Parameters* 21, no. 4 (winter 1991–92): 24–38.

The Editors. "U.S. in a New World: What Goals? What Priorities?" *Great Decisions* (1993 ed.): 3–11.

Eikenberry, Karl W. "Take No Casualties." Taken from the 1998 AANSWG Intranet.

Etzold, Thomas H. "The Strategic Environment of the Twenty-First Century: Alternative Futures for Strategic Planners." *Strategic Review,* vol. XVIII, no. 2 (spring 1990): 23–31.

Faith, John C. "The Overcontrolling Leader: The Issue Is Trust." *Army* 47 (June 1997): 7–12.

Fastabend, David A. "FM 100-5, 1998: Endless Evolution." *Army* 46 (May 1997): 45–50.

Ferry, Charles P. "Mogadishu, October 1993: A Personal Account of a Rifle Company XO." *Infantry* (September–October 1994): 22–31.

Frank, Reuven. "Hitting the Beach in Mogadishu." *The New Leader* 76, no. 1 (11 January 1993): 20–24.

Galloway, Joseph L. "Fatal Victory." *U.S. News & World Report,* 29 October 1990, 32–35.

———. "Vietnam Story." *U.S. News & World Report,* 29 October 1990, 36–46.

———. "Where Have All the Young Men Gone?" *U.S. News & World Report*, 29 October 1990, 50–52.

———. "Once More, Into the Valley of Death: American and Vietnamese Soldiers Meet Again." *U.S. News & World Report*, 6 December 1993, 32–34.

Gilmore, Gerry L. "Avoiding Attrition Warfare in 2020–2025." *Army Link News*, Army News Service (28 July 1997).

Goldstein, Walter. "Europe After Maastricht." *Foreign Affairs* 71, no. 5 (winter 1992–93): 117–32.

Goodman, Glen W., Jr. "Nowhere to Hide: New Smart Munitions Rain Certain Destruction from the Sky." *Armed Forces Journal International* (October 1997): 58–64.

Goshko, John M. "Haggling Over U.N. Reform: The Third World Has Its Own Agenda, but Jesse Helms Holds Virtual Veto Power." *The Washington Post National Weekly Edition*, 17 March 1997, 14.

Grange, David L., and James A. Kelley. "Information Operations for the Ground Commander." *Military Review*, vol. LXXVII, no. 2 (March–April 1997): 5–12.

Grau, Lester W. "Desert Defense and Surviving PGMs: The New Russian View." *Parameters* (July 1996).

Gray, Alfred M. "Planning for the Future: A Policy of Stability." *Strategic Review*, vol. XIX, no. 1 (winter 1991): 9–16.

Gray, Colin S. "Off the Map: Defense Planning After the Soviet Threat." *Strategic Review*, vol. XXII, no. 2 (spring 1994): 26–35.

Guertner, Gary L. "The Armed Forces in a New Political Environment." *Strategic Review*, vol. XXI, no. 3 (summer 1993): 79–83.

Hammes, Thomas X. "The Evolution of War: The Fourth Generation." *Marine Corps Gazette* (September 1994).

Hillen, John F. III. "Policing the New World Order: The Operational Utility of a Permanent UN Army." *Strategic Review*, vol. XXII, no. 2 (spring 1994): 54–62.

———. "Military Blues: America's Shrinking Armed Forces Face Even Larger Challenges in the Post–Cold War Era," 26 April 1998.

Holland, John R. "Crusader Update." *Field Artillery* (May–June 1997): 12.

Hormats, Robert D. "The Roots of American Power." *Foreign Affairs* 70, no. 3 (summer 1991): 132–49.

Hyland, William G. "The Case for Pragmatism." *Foreign Affairs* 71, no. 1 (America and the World 1991–92): 38–52.

Jarnot, Charles A. "Air Mech Strike: Revolution in Maneuver Warfare," *Military Review,* vol. LXXVII, no. 2 (March–April 1997): 79–86.

Kendall, Frank. "Exploiting the Military Technical Revolution: A Concept for Joint Warfare." *Strategic Review,* vol. XX, no. 2 (spring 1992): 23–30.

Krepinevich, Andrew F., Jr. "The Clinton Defense Program: Assessing the Bottom-Up Review." *Strategic Review,* vol. XXII, no. 2 (spring 1994): 15–25.

Krugman, Paul. "Executive Summary." *The Age of Diminished Expectations: U.S. Economic Policy in the 1990s.* The Washington Post Company, Washington, D.C. (1990): 5–8.

Larson, Charles R. "Forward Presence: It Shapes Our Future." *Strategic Review,* vol. XXI, no. 3 (summer 1993): 74–77.

Libicki, Martin C. "The Next Enemy." *Parameters* (July 1995).

Lind, William S., Joseph Nightengale, John F. Schmitt, Joseph W. Sutton, and Gary I. Wilson. "The Changing Face of War: Into the Fourth Generation." *Marine Corps Gazette* (October 1989): 22–26.

Linn, Thomas C. "Naval Forces in the Post–Cold War Era." *Strategic Review,* vol. XX, no. 4 (fall 1992): 18–23.

Loeb, Vernon. "After Action Report: Spying used to mean stealing another government's secrets, but what can spies achieve in a country with no government? In Somalia with the CIA, Garrett Jones and John Spinelli found out." *Washington Post* magazine, 27 February 2000, 7.

Loh, John M. "Adapting U.S. Military Organizations to the New Security Environment." *Strategic Review,* vol. XXII, no. 2 (spring 1994): 7–14.

Loughlin, Don. "Remaining Relevant: Army's Future Combat System Must Shake Off a Case of Bad Genes." *Armed Forces Journal International* (October 1997): 52–56.

Lum, Zachary. "Region on a Roll." *Journal of Electronic Defense* 20, no. 3 (March 1997): 33–38.

Mahnken, Thomas G. "Planning U.S. Forces for the Twenty-First Century." *Strategic Review,* vol. XX, no. 4 (fall 1992): 9–17.

Manz, Charles C., and Henry P. Sims, Jr. "SuperLeadership: Beyond the Myth of Heroic Leadership" (1991).

Mattingly, Richard Thomas, Jr., and Wallace Earl Walker. "The Military Professional as Successful Politician." *Parameters* 18, no. 1 (March 1988): 37–51.

Mazza, Jacqueline. "Trade and the Global Economy: Projecting U.S. Interests." Great Decisions 1993, 47–55.

Meigs, Montgomery C. "Challenges for Army Leaders in an Age of Rapid Change." *Field Artillery* (May–June 1998): 3–6.

Metcalf, Arthur G. B. "Strategic Airpower in Conventional Warfare: Some Considerations." *Strategic Review,* vol. XIX, no. 2 (spring 1991): 16–23.

Milton, T. Ross. "Strategic Airpower: Retrospect and Prospect." *Strategic Review,* vol. XIX, no. 2 (spring 1991): 7–15.

Miskel, James. "Thin Ice: Single Sources in the Domestic Industrial Base." *Strategic Review,* vol. XIX, no. 1 (winter 1991): 46–53.

Moore, Harold G., and Joseph L. Galloway. "Death in the Tall Grass." *U.S. News & World Report,* 12 October 1992, 50–59.

Morningstar, James K. "Points of Attack: Lessons from the Breach." *Armor* (January–February 1998): 7–13.

Murray, Alan. "The Global Economy Bungled." *Foreign Affairs* 72, no. 1 (America and the World 1992–93): 158–66.

Nannini, Vance J. "Universal Observers: Punching Our FIST into the 21st Century." *Field Artillery* (May–June 1997): 13–16.

Nitze, Paul H. "Grand Strategy Then and Now: NSC-68 and Its Lessons for the Future." *Strategic Review,* vol. XXII, no. 1 (winter 1994): 12–19.

Nye, Joseph S., Jr. "What New World Order." *Foreign Affairs* 71, no. 2 (spring 1992): 83–96.

Olinger, Mark A. "Too Late for the War: The US Industrial Base and Tank Production 1950–1953." *Armor* (May–June 1997): 15–17.

Ott, David E. "Range, Range, Range." *Army* (May 1997): 13.

Owens, Mackubin T. "Force Planning in an Era of Uncertainty." *Strategic Review,* vol. XVIII, no. 2 (spring 1990): 9–22.

———. "Desert Storm and the Renaissance in Military Doctrine." Editorial. *Strategic Review,* vol. XIX, no. 2 (spring 1991): 5–6.

Palmer, Peter J. "Decision Point Tactics and the Meeting Battle:

Fighting the Enemy, Not the Plan." *Infantry* (January–February 1997): 28–35.

Parshall, Gerald. "The Strategists of War." *U.S. News & World Report,* 16 March 1998, 50–79.

Pattullo, E. L. "War and the American Press." *Parameters* 22, no. 4 (winter 1992–93): 61–69.

Pendley, William T. "Mortgaging the Future to the Present in Defense Policy: A Commentary on the Bottom-Up Review." *Strategic Review,* vol. XXII, no. 2 (spring 1994): 36–39.

"The Pentagon's Quadrennial Defense Review." *ROA National Security Report* (May 1997): 21–22.

Perry, William J. "Fulfilling the Role of Preventive Defense." Prepared remarks for address to John F. Kennedy School of Government, Harvard University, Cambridge, Mass., 13 May 1996.

Peters, Katherine M. "Space Wars." *Government Executive* 30, no. 4 (April 1998): 12–20.

Peters, Ralph. "The New Warrior Class." *Parameters* (summer 1994): 16–26.

Powell, Colin L. "U.S. Forces: Challenges Ahead." *Foreign Affairs* 72, no. 5 (winter 1992–93): 32–45.

"Quadrennial Defense Review Requires Strategy-Based Approach." *Army* (May 1997): 6.

Rathbun, Robin E. "Strategic Mobility for the 1990s: The Mobility Requirements Study." *Strategic Review,* vol. XX, no. 3 (summer 1992): 48–56.

Reich, Robert B. "The Real Economy." *The Atlantic* 267, no. 2 (February 1991): 35–37, 40–44, 46–47, 50–52.

Richburg, Keith B. "Spreading the Wealth: How 'Globalization' Is Helping Shift Cash from Rich Nations to Poor Ones." *The Washington Post National Weekly Edition,* 17 March 1997, 6–8.

Romm, Joseph J., and Amory B. Lovins. "Fueling a Competitive Economy." *Foreign Affairs* 71, no. 5 (winter 1992–93): 46–62.

Roos, John G. "Honing a Digitized Force: Army's Top Trainer Draws Lessons from Service's Advanced Warfighting Experiment." *Armed Forces Journal International* (October 1997): 40–48.

Sarkesian, Sam C. "Soldiers, Scholars and the Media." *Parameters* 17 (3 September 1987): 77–87.

Scales, Robert H., and John A. Parmentola. "The Army After Next: Intertwining Military Art, Science and Technology out to the Year 2025." *Army RD&A* (May–June 1998): 2–5.

Schlesinger, James. "Quest for a Post-Cold War Foreign Policy." *Foreign Affairs* 72, no. 1 (America and the World 1992–93): 17–28.

"Service Manpower Drawdown: After Korean and Vietnam Wars." Department of Defense Selected Manpower Statistics, fiscal year 1992. Taken off the Internet.

Sherman, Jason. "Digitization Decisions." *Armed Forces Journal International* (October 1997): 14, 16.

———. "The Little Plane That Could: Army Recce Bird Finds New Missions in the Post–Cold War World." *Armed Forces Journal International* (October 1997): 37–38.

Silk, Leonard. "Dangers of Slow Growth." *Foreign Affairs* 72, no. 1 (America and the World 1992–93): 167–82.

Spulak, Robert G., Jr. "Strategic Sufficiency and Long-Range Precision Weapons." *Strategic Review,* vol. XXII, no. 3 (summer 1994): 31–39.

Stedman, Stephen John. "The New Interventionists." *Foreign Affairs* 72, no. 1 (America and the World 1992–93): 1–16.

Steele, Dennis. "Testing EXFOR: Task Force XXI Advanced Warfighting Experiment at NTC." *Army* (May 1997): 14–23.

———. "AWE: Testing Soldiers and Equipment." *Army* (June 1997): 26–38.

Summers, Harry G., Jr. "Military Doctrine: Blueprint for Force Planning." *Strategic Review,* vol. XX, no. 2 (spring 1992): 9–22.

Swardson, Anne, and Sandra Sugawara. "After Nike's Foot in the Door, a Stampede." *The Washington Post National Weekly Edition,* 17 March 1997, 8–9.

Twining, David T. "Vietnam and the Six Criteria for the Use of Military Force." *Parameters* 15, no. 4 (winter 1985): 10–18.

Vandergriff, Donald E. "Without the Proper Culture: Why Our Army Cannot Practice Maneuver Warfare." *Armor* (January–February 1998): 20–24.

———. "Before There Was Digitization: How MG J.S. Wood's 4th Armored Division Stormed Across France Without Written Orders." *Armor* (September–October 2000): 20–27.

Walker, Jim. "Vietnam: Tanker's War?" *Armor* (May–June 1997): 24–30.

West, Richard L. "The FY 1998 Army Budget in Perspective: Prelude to Change." *Army* (May 1997): 24–31.

Wilson, Johnnie E. "The Necessity of Advanced Technology: The Information Age Army." *Army* (June 1997): 14–22.

Wyly, Michael D. "Combat in the 21st Century: The Quality of Troops Will Matter More Than the Complexity of Weapons." *U.S. News & World Report,* 16 March 1998, 80–81.

Newspaper Articles

Army News Service, "1/5 Infantry Ready for NTC Action," *Inside the Turret* (Fort Knox post newspaper), 27 March 1997, 3A, 18A.

Davis, Daniel L., "Air vs. Land Power: Both are Vital," *Army Times,* 21 July 1997, 50.

Erlich, Jeff, "No Place in U.S. for Arrow II," *Army Times,* 31 March 1997, 30.

Ferster, Warren, "Congress Backs Anti-Satellite Weapon," *Army Times,* 31 March 1997, 30.

Gosden, Christine, "We've Got to Try to Do Something," *USA Weekend,* 15–17 May 1998, 14–16.

Holzer, Robert, "QDR's High-Tech Focus Bothers Officials: Worries Concentration on Weapons May Leave Troops Ill-Equipped for Combat," *Army Times,* 7 April 1997, 26, 28.

———. "Reimer Pushes Elite Joint Force," *Army Times,* 16 June 1997, 26.

———. "Systems Let Bosnia Troops Stay Ready While Keeping Pace," *Army Times,* 16 June 1997, 27.

Keener, Dennis E., "A Voice from the OPFOR," *Army Times,* 21 July 1997, 50.

Kormarow, Steven, "Tests Show Indian Nuke Sophistication," *The Burlington Free Press,* 17 May 1998, 2E.

Krulak, Charles C., "'Not Like Yesterday'/In His Own Words, Commandant Describes His Vision of Future Warfighting," *Navy Times–Marine Corps Edition,* 19 January 1998.

Lockwood, Jonathan S., "Growing Vulnerability in Space," *Army Times,* 20 April 1998, 54.

Mather, Ian, "The Bizarre Arms Bazaar," *The European,* 20–26 November 1997, 28–29.

Maze, Rick, "Stretched to the Breaking Point: House Report: Shrinking Budgets and Force Structure, Plus More Peacekeeping Missions Force Army to 'Do More with Less,'" *Army Times,* 21 April 1997, 3.

———. "Senate Clips Bosnia Mission's Purse Strings," *Army Times,* 19 May 1997, 11.

———. "Budget Agreement Nets Pentagon $17 Billion," *Army Times,* 26 May 1997, 30.

———. "Task Force: 'No Military Bearing in Military,'" *Army Times,* 26 May 1997, 8.

———. "House Sets Its Own Military Agenda," *Army Times,* 14 July 1997, 4.

Maze, Rick, and Jack Weible, "Skelton: Personnel Cuts Would Force Fewer to Do More," *Army Times,* 26 May 1997, 4.

Maze, Rick, and George Wilson, "Bases vs. People: Pentagon Looks for Ways to Pay for Much-Needed Weapons Modernization," *Army Times,* 19 May 1997, 10.

McHugh, Jane, "The Future: Have We Been There Before?" *Army Times,* 11 May 1998, 12, 14.

———. "The Future Wars That Never Were," *Army Times,* 11 May 1998, 13.

———. "Wonder Weapons of Pulp Fiction," *Army Times,* 11 May 1998, 14.

———. "Planning Wars," *Army Times,* 11 May 1998, 15.

Mirelson, Robert N., "Template for a New Army," *Army Times,* 19 May 1997, 54.

Naylor, Sean D., "Digital Revolution Shows Promise, but Needs Proof: Spring Experiments Will Test Prowess of Communications," *Army Times,* 13 January 1997, 45.

———. "Digitized Brigade Struts Its Stuff in First Action," *Army Times,* 13 January 1997, 45–46.

———. "Sheehan: Technology Poor Substitute for Troops," *Army Times,* 24 February 1997, 16.

———. "Hidden Soft Spot in Satellite Might: War Game Shows U.S. Military Systems Are Vulnerable to Enemy Attack," *Army Times,* 10 March 1997, 20–21.

———. "What the Future Holds . . . War Game Shows That Faster Deployments May Require All Army Units to Own Planes," *Army Times*, 17 March 1997, 20, 22.

———. "Mission: Accomplished: Army Fires First Round in Battle for the Future," *Army Times*, 28 April 1997, 12–14, 18, 20.

———. "The Javelin Missile: A Lethal Ace up the Sleeve," *Army Times*, 28 April 1997, 14.

———. "Experiment Sharpens Debate on Logistics Redesign," *Army Times*, 28 April 1997, 18.

———. "Army Takes to the Urban Streets," *Army Times*, 21 July 1997, 22.

———. "Tough Choices," *Army Times*, 6 October 1997, 32.

———. "Sea Change Ahead in Leadership Training," *Army Times*, 13 October 1997, 32.

———. "The Future Army Debate Rages On: What Stays, What Goes?" *Army Times*, 20 April 1998, 13.

———. "Strike Force Concept Could Spread," *Army Times*, 11 May 1998, 23.

———. "A Lack of City Smarts?" *Army Times*, 11 May 1998, 22.

Patterson, Kristin, "EXFOR Puts Dismounted System to Test," *Army Times*, 13 January 1997, 46.

———. "History in the Making: Army Takes to the Sea: New Combat Support Strategy Responds to Need to Get Forward Bases Quickly," *Army Times*, 3 March 1997, 19.

———. "Guard May Bear Brunt of QDR Restructuring," *Army Times*, 12 May 1997, 26.

Peters, Ralph, "Ruinous Generals: Heroes Gone Astray," *Army Times*, 16 February 1998, 31.

———. "Will We Be Able to Take the Cities?" *Army Times*, 11 May 1998, 34.

Peterson, Donna M., "Strategy or Numbers," *Army Times*, 12 May 1997, 29.

Richter, Paul, "Newest Computer Technology Is Tested for a New Age of Warfare," *Inside the Turret* (Fort Knox post newspaper), 27 March 1997, 3A.

Ricks, Thomas E., "Charmed Forces: Army's Baby Generals Take a

Crash Course in Sensitivity Training," *Wall Street Journal*, February 1998.

Seffers, George I, "Budget Numbers Hinder Army's Modernization Push," *Army Times*, 3 March 1997, 16.

———. "Analysts Fear Base Closings from QDR," *Army Times*, 31 March 1997, 30.

———. "Experiment: Two Revolutions in One: Advanced Warfighting Test Exhibits New Technologies, Acquisition Methods," *Army Times*, 7 April 1997, 26.

———. "A Century of Cleanup," *Army Times*, 16 June 1997, 26.

———. "Nations Turn Away from Ground Combat," *Army Times*, 16 June 1997, 50.

———. "Hyper-Speed Anti-Tank Missiles Studied for 2015," *Army Times*, 13 October 1997, 33.

———. "U.S. Arms for Urban Wars: Battles in Cities Will Require New Tactics, Technologies," *Army Times*, 9 February 1998, 26.

Smith, R. Jeffrey, "Detonating Stability," *The Burlington Free Press*, 17 May 1998, 1E–2E.

Spence, Floyd R., "How Ready Are We?" *Army Times*, 26 May 1997, 54.

Spring, Baker, "Calling the Pentagon's Bluff," *Army Times*, 14 July 1997, 54.

Tigner, Brooke, "NATO Panel to Steer Nonlethal Weapon Use," *Army Times*, 13 October 1997, 33.

Vogel, Steve, "A Swift Kick: 2d ACR's Taming of the Guard," *Army Times*, 5 August 1991, 10–18, 28–30, 61.

Weible, Jack, "CBO: Taking to the Sea Could Mean Big Savings," *Army Times*, 24 March 1997, 16.

———. "Wealth of Information Proved Good, Bad for Bosnia Troops," *Army Times*, 21 April 1997, 29.

———. "Vulnerable to Attack: Subcommittees Get an Earful on Threats to Information Systems," *Army Times*, 21 April 1997, 29.

———. "Shali: QDR Is Peaceful Compared to Past Reviews," *Army Times*, 12 May 1997, 28.

Wilson, George C., "Sheehan Would Break Mold as New Joint Chiefs Chairman," *Army Times*, 13 January 1997, 48.

———. "Report: Military Caught Between Past, Present: What's

Best: Holding on Too Long to Cold War Strategy or Rushing into New Force Structure," *Army Times,* 3 March 1997, 3.

———. "CBO: Aircraft Budget Will Come up Short," *Army Times,* 3 March 1997, 19.

———. "Secy. Cohen Sets the Ground Rules: Tells Defense Chiefs What He Expects of Quadrennial Defense Review," *Army Times,* 17 March 1997, 3.

———. "Cohen Likes What He Sees at NTC: Defense Secretary Pledges 'Very Strong Support' for Army's High-Tech Venture," *Army Times,* 31 March 1997, 3, 27.

———. "Sheehan: The Military as He Sees It: What Does the Army After Next Really Look Like? Atlantic Command's Controversial Leader Would Like to Know," *Army Times,* 7 April 1997, 10–11.

———. "QDR Panel Grows . . . Again," *Army Times,* 21 April 1997, 27.

———. "High Level of Fratricide Could Raise Some Eyebrows," *Army Times,* 28 April 1997, 13.

———. "Aircraft Buyers in a Tailspin," *Army Times,* 28 April 1997, 54.

———. "The QDR Attempts to Redirect Funds into Procurement: 55,000 Active Duty May Be Cut," *Army Times,* 12 May 1997, 10.

———. "The Ideal State of the Military," *Army Times,* 12 May 1997, 54.

———. "Rating the Experimental Force at the NTC: EXFOR Performance Comes Under Scrutiny," *Army Times,* 26 May 1997, 3.

———. "Cohen's Game Plan: Two Wars at Once," *Army Times,* 26 May 1997, 4.

———. "Spinney: QDR Misses the Mark," *Army Times,* 18 August 1997, 28–29.

———. "Army Leaders 'Surprised' by Number of Friendly Fire 'Killings,'" *Army Times,* 13 October 1997, 3.

———. "Report Blames Land Mines for Fratricide at NTC," *Army Times,* 13 October 1997, 3.

———. "NATO, U.S. Armed Forces Technology Gap Widens," *Army Times,* 13 October 1997, 34.

Wood, David, "Fewer Troops, More Money," *Army Times,* 13 January 1997, 70.

Interviews, Conversations, Speeches, and Electronic Mail
Abrams tank team chief, DCSOPS. Phone conversation with author, 12 November 1997, Northfield, Vt. Handwritten notes.

Bartlett, Roscoe. Press release. "Electro-Magnetic Pulse (EMP) Makes Y2K Worries Seem Like Chicken Feed," 19 May 1999.

Battery commander, 1st Infantry Division, during Operation Desert Storm. Conversation with author, 14 January 1992.

Clinton, William J. Remarks by the president at National Defense University, Fort McNair, Va. Given in late January or early February 1998.

Laniewski, Clement J. Executive officer for C Troop, 2d ACR, during Operation Desert Storm. Conversation, 22 June 1998.

Lute, Douglas. Regimental operations officer, 2d ACR, during Operation Desert Storm. Interview, August 1999.

McMaster, H. R. Commander for E Troop, 2d ACR, during Operation Desert Storm. Conversations, March–June 1999.

Nuclear, Biological, Chemical Warfare Experts at the Army After Next Spring Wargame 1998. Conversations reference the use of NBC.

Phipps, Jim. Regimental linguist for the 3d ACR. Conversation, 24 March 1992.

Salas, Mark, to Cliff Wheeler, 12 February 1998. Subject: read and comment, forwarded by Cliff Wheeler to Brian Steed.

Index